DATE DUE

OCT 4 1997	
JAN - 6 1999	
MAR 1 6 2001	
FEB 2 7 2002	

BRODART   Cat. No. 23-221

Brute New World

The Rediscovery of Latin America
in the Early Nineteenth Century

Desmond Gregory was born in 1916 and educated at Uppingham School and Balliol College, Oxford. He taught history for over thirty years at Bristol Grammar School and then Downside School. He is the author of *The Ungovernable Rock: a history of the Anglo-Corsican Kingdom and its role in Britain's Mediterranean strategy during the Revolutionary War, 1793–7*, *Sicily the Insecure Base: a history of the British occupation of Sicily, 1806–15*, *The Beneficent Usurpers: a history of the British in Madeira* and *Minorca the Illusory Prize: a history of the British occupations of Minorca between 1708 and 1802*.

Brute New World

The Rediscovery of Latin America in the Early Nineteenth Century

DESMOND GREGORY

British Academic Press
London · New York

Published in 1992 by
British Academic Press
45 Bloomsbury Square
London WC1A 2HY

An imprint of I.B. Tauris & Co Ltd

175 Fifth Avenue
New York
NY 10010

In the United States of America
and Canada distributed by
St Martin's Press
175 Fifth Avenue
New York
NY 10010

A CIP record for this book is available from the British Library

Library of Congress catalog card number: available
A full CIP record is available from the Library of Congress

ISBN 1-85043-567-7

Printed and bound in Great Britain by WBC Limited,
Bridgend, Mid Glamorgan

Contents

List of maps and illustrations   vii

Preface   ix

Acknowledgements   xiii

Introduction   1

Chapter 1   The United Provinces of the River Plate   5

Chapter 2   Chile   31

Chapter 3   Peru and Bolivia   59

Chapter 4   Gran Colombia   89

Chapter 5   Mexico   133

Chapter 6   Brazil   155

Chapter 7   Conclusion   175

Abbreviations   185

Notes and references   187

Bibliography   209

Index   217

List of Maps

1 La Plata Provinces and Paraguay   4
2 Chile   30
3 Peru   58
4 Gran Colombia   88
5 Mexico   132
6 Brazil   154

List of Illustrations

Plates section between pages 114 and 115
(All reproduced by permission of The British Library, London)

1 Buenos Aires (Landing Place and Alameida)
2 Plaza de la Independencia, Santiago, Chile
3 An early view of Valparaiso, Chile
4 View of Callao and distant view of Lima
5 Angostura
6 View of the city and valley of Mexico from Tacubaya
7 Rio de Janeiro (1809)

Preface

There are two matters that should be made clear for the benefit of readers of this book who are unfamiliar with the history of Latin America in the early nineteenth century. The first is that of nomenclature when applied to the countries of Latin America.

Colonial Spanish America by the end of the eighteenth century was made up of three viceroyalties – New Spain, New Granada and Rio de la Plata, together with the captaincies general of Chile and of Guatemala. New Spain consisted of Mexico (which in those days comprised modern Mexico, Texas, New Mexico and California). The Captaincy General of Guatemala included what today are known as the Central American Republics, save only for Panama. The viceroyalty of New Granada consisted of modern Venezuela, Colombia, Ecuador and Panama. The viceroyalty of Peru corresponded roughly to modern Peru. The viceroyalty of Rio de la Plata included not only modern Argentina but also the modern states of Paraguay, Uruguay and Bolivia. The captaincy general of Chile consisted of modern Chile approximately, though without its Patagonian province.

When Spanish colonists in New Granada revolted first in 1810, they erected the state of Venezuela. In 1819 these colonists declared at a congress at Angostura that all the states of New Granada were federated into Gran Colombia (or plain 'Colombia', as it was called – 'Gran Colombia' is a historian's term), though this did not become a reality until after two more years of fighting. In 1830 Venezuela and Ecuador both seceded from Gran Colombia and what then remained became known as the Republic of New Granada. It did not change its name to Colombia until 1861. Panama remained part of Colombia till it gained independence in 1903.

In the former viceroyalty of La Plata, Paraguay became an independent state in 1814, Bolivia in 1825 and Uruguay in 1828, after its territory had been disputed in a war Buenos Aires fought with Brazil and which was only brought to an end as a consequence of British mediation. The United Provinces of the Rio de la Plata, proclaimed independent in 1816, changed their name to the United Provinces of the Argentine in 1853. The other matter needing clarification is the policy of Britain towards Latin America in the first three decades of the nineteenth century. Initially Britain was the foe of Spain, allied as Spain was from 1804 to the empire of Napoleon; and for that reason Spanish America was fair prey for the British navy. However, in 1809, after Spain had revolted against the rule of King Joseph Bonaparte, Britain became the ally of Spain and stayed so for the rest of the war. After 1814, Britain remained on friendly terms with the Spanish government, though popular opinion in Great Britain greatly favoured the Spanish colonists in their struggle to obtain their independence.

Britain's attempt to maintain neutrality was put under considerable strain when in 1817 British volunteers went to fight in the army of Simón Bolívar and two years later the government was forced to pass the Foreign Enlistment Act in order to remain on good terms with Spain. When in 1820 Spain acquired a constitutional regime that lasted till 1823, Spain's relations with Britain were somewhat eased but this was to be a temporary respite while the problem of the revolted colonies in South America remained unresolved. What Britain wanted in that area was trade and political stability and preferably some accommodation between Spain's government and its colonists. Britain however could not wait too long. If the Spanish government could not reach a settlement with its rebellious colonies, whose armies were winning the military struggle, then Britain must take unilateral action, if only to end the depredations of pirates in Latin American waters.

The policy of George Canning, who became foreign secretary in 1822, was to favour recognition of the rebel colonies as soon as they were seen to be viable states. Canning was not a republican, but he was a liberal-minded Tory whose natural sympathies were with those who were struggling to achieve some degree of autonomy. He was also under very strong pressure from commercial interests in Great Britain that had benefited enormously from the opening of Spain's colonial markets and did not wish to see the colonists crushed by royalist armies sent over from Europe and their markets closed once again to foreigners. But what really guided Canning's policy was determination to prevent the French from getting a hold on Latin America and the USA from capturing its markets. In 1822 the USA had recognized the republics of La Plata, Chile, Peru, Colombia and Mexico, while France had, despite British protests, marched her armies into Spain at the invitation of the Spanish king, and in 1823 crushed the constitutionalists and restored despotic rule to the country.

The threat of a Spanish army being ferried across the Atlantic under French naval escort was one that Canning felt bound to prevent. He did prevent it by forceful diplomacy – a veiled threat of war was quite sufficient – and in 1826, addressing parliament, he referred to this in words that were soon to become familiar to every schoolboy: 'I was resolved that if France had Spain, it would not be Spain with the Indies. I called in the New World to redress the balance of the Old.' Recognition of three South American republics followed in 1824, and of the remainder some years later.

So far as Brazil was concerned, the alliance of Portugal with Britain dated back over 400 years. It was a British naval squadron that escorted the regent and the Portuguese court to Rio de Janeiro in 1807, in order to escape the clutches of Napoleon, and in 1810 a treaty was signed that opened up to British merchants the lucrative markets of Brazil.

In 1821 the Portuguese king returned to Lisbon, leaving behind as regent of Brazil his son Dom Pedro who, in 1822, proclaimed himself emperor of an independent country. The Portuguese king disputed this claim but, two years later and through British mediation, he accepted the fact of Brazilian independence.

Acknowledgements

I should like to express my gratitude to the following who have helped me in various ways in the completion of this book: Professors John Lynch, D. A. G. Waddell and Roy Foster, Dr Malcolm Deas, Sir Edgar Vaughan, Dr Anthony Seymour, Dr Marianne Elliott, Dr Kevin Whelan and Mr George Bartle, archivist. (Professor Waddell, Dr Deas and Sir Edgar Vaughan all lent me important books, published in Caracas, that are not available in this country.)

All transcripts of Crown copyright records appear by permission of the Controller of Her Majesty's Stationery Office.

For permission to quote from the Swinburne (Capheaton) MSS deposited in the Northumberland Record Office I am indebted to Mr J. Browne-Swinburne.

Introduction

In the first flush of their independence, the states of Latin America seemed to hold out to Europeans (more particularly denizens of the United Kingdom of Great Britain and Ireland), and to United States citizens, wonderful opportunities to acquire wealth, cheap and fertile land, glory, honour on the field of battle, fighting for liberty against the forces of oppression, even possibly gratitude for rendering assistance of whatever kind (money, technology, the provision of goods, valour, leadership and organization) in the struggle to create a brave new world.

These men were, it seems, the helpless victims of an almost invincible ignorance about conditions in Latin America, where the Spanish had for centuries endeavoured to keep out the foreigner and, if they were informed to any degree, relied on the writings of Alexander Humboldt. The latter at the end of the eighteenth century had travelled widely in Latin America and had painted a very rosy picture of the prospects for future development in lands at that time under the rule of comparatively enlightened Spanish viceroys.

The continental blockade of Napoleon, together with the US Embargo Act, had effectively closed their usual markets to British manufacturers. It was to respond to a serious crisis confronting the British economy that merchants went to Latin America, or dispatched their agents to sell goods that had become unsaleable elsewhere. Golden opportunities seemed to beckon them with the opening up of potential markets in the newly proclaimed independent republics. Brazil, with the Portuguese royal family now living in Rio de Janeiro and offering favourable commercial terms by a treaty signed in 1810, also seemed to beckon with open arms. Not unnaturally US merchants were also very interested in exploiting the South American markets, and the US government was quick to recognize the independence of the new states and give them consular representation.

There were high hopes of exploiting mineral wealth in the almost legendary mining areas of Peru, Bolivia and Mexico, as well as the famed pearl fisheries in the Caribbean and the Gulf of California. Mining companies were formed in London, attracting capital from imprudent investors who were led to believe that spectacular profits would soon accrue from the renting or purchase of numerous gold and silver mines that the governments in Latin America seemed only too anxious to lease or sell. Their agents were dispatched across the Atlantic to reconnoitre and sign contracts, while engineers who had made their name in the field of steam haulage and locomotion (for example Trevithick and Robert Stephenson) were lured to Peru and Colombia to develop the mines with their new machinery.

British banks were also interested in lending money to the new republics who found themselves financially embarrassed by the dislocation of local finances caused by the struggle for independence, and by the need to find ready cash to meet all their military expenses. The banks therefore sent their agents out to the capital cities of Latin America to negotiate or renegotiate loans, and report on conditions prevailing there.

The vast spaces of empty land, fertile and enjoying an equable climate, extending throughout much of South America, seemed to hold out the brightest prospects for prospective emigrants from Europe, particularly to the impoverished victims of unemployment and low living standards in the Britain and Ireland of the 1820s. Latin American governments seemed to want to encourage immigration, conscious of the sparseness of their populations and the need to increase them if their economies were ever to progress beyond stagnation. Agencies were formed both in England and Scotland to promote schemes for emigration to Buenos Aires, Brazil and Venezuela and their promoters or their agents, together with batches of emigrants, travelled to South America (the emigrants naturally intending to stay) in the third decade of the nineteenth century.

Latin America also presented a curious and novel spectacle for the well-to-do and audacious traveller, whether specifically interested in geology, botany or social customs, or not. Several such travellers found their way to various parts of Latin America, once the area was opened to foreigners in a way it had never been before. Some stopped for only brief periods of time, but if they were often repelled or dismayed, they were still fascinated by what they discovered.

There were also a few religious evangelists, inevitably of the

Protestant faith: emissaries of the Bible Society, educational missionaries, who combined the desire to disseminate literacy among foreign
peoples with an introduction to the writings of Scripture; and a
Quaker like Joseph Lancaster, a world-famous educationalist, who
snatched at the opportunity to resuscitate his faded reputation. There
were also diplomats sent from the United States, fired with enthusiasm
for the cause of free thought and free expression, religious toleration
and democratic rule. These men, sent on missions to Latin America,
hoped to find there fellow republicans of the type they were used to in
North America, who could be made into useful allies and ready
providers of lucrative markets.

Finally, there were the naval officers, at a time before the British
government was driven to recognize the new republics. Throughout
this period Britain maintained in the waters of the South Atlantic, and
in the Caribbean sea, naval squadrons whose task was to protect
British shipping and British merchants established on shore. These
officers had to fulfil the role later filled by British consuls. Their
dispatches make interesting and enlightening reading.

From about 1810 to 1830, numerous accounts (diaries, journals,
memoirs and narratives) were written in English by a motley collection
of men and some women, of their experiences in Latin America. They
included army and naval officers, consuls from Britain and the USA,
mining engineers, merchants, travellers, and wives of diplomats or
naval officers. Their accounts, when they appeared in print, sold well
and most of them remain very readable. In all, they convey a lively
impression of the South American continent as it appeared to an
educated European or a citizen of the United States.

This book sets out to summarize and assess these various literary
contributions with a view to increasing understanding of the problems
posed by the opening up of Latin America to the outside world.

Potosi

Tarija

Salta

Asuncion

Tucuman

Corrientes

Famatima

PARAGUAY

Cordoba

R. Parana

R. Uruguay

△ Mt. Aconagua
Mendoza

BANDA

San Luis

ORIENTAL

San Pedro

BUENOS AIRES

CHILE

LA PLATA
PROVINCES
&
PARAGUAY

LA
PLATA

R. Plata

0   100   200 mls

1 · The United Provinces of the River Plate

No country in South America seemed to hold out more promise and brighter hopes to British merchants and to British speculators in the early decades of the nineteenth century than what is now known as Argentina. Captain Sir Home Popham, notorious for his expedition in 1806 to take possession of Buenos Aires, described it to the Admiralty as the best commercial site in South America, within sixty to seventy days' sail of all countries that were Britain's most important customers. The population of the area, incorrectly reckoned at 6–7 million, would provide a new market for British manufacturers, while it could in exchange yield important commodities such as bullion, hides, tallow, meat, cocoa, coffee, wool and hemp.[1] Lord Melville, giving evidence at the subsequent court-martial of Admiral Popham, stated that he 'always considered the Rio de la Plata as the most important position for the interests of Great Britain upon that side of South America'.[2] After the British government, on learning of the capture of Buenos Aires, declared it annexed and open to trade, *The Times* forecast that the government's action would result in there being in the River Plate area a 'never-failing market for our commodities'.[3] This euphoria over the River Plate continued during the next twenty years. To British soldiers, sent to serve in the campaign to secure the Plate estuary, the country seemed to offer an easy life and General Whitelocke, before he surrendered Buenos Aires in 1807, wrote home of the lively incentive it presented to potential deserters from the British army: 'The more the soldiers become acquainted with the plenty the country affords, and the easy means of acquiring it, the greater will be the evil, as the temptation is irresistible to the common mind, beyond the calculation of those unacquainted with the locality.'[4]

Alexander Gillespie, a British officer who was taken prisoner at this time and did not return to his home country until ten years after his release, wrote in glowing terms of Buenos Aires – 'No city in the

globe has such a glorious future.'[5] This paean of praise was still being
sung as late as 1826, a decade after the independence of the United
Provinces of the Plate was declared. Woodbine Parish, the first consul-
general appointed by Britain to Buenos Aires, wrote to Canning in
1824: 'Nature has done her utmost in climate and situation, and it
only remains for civilized Man in these regions to make the most of
these inestimable blessings which Providence on the one hand has
bestowed upon them and a paternal government on the other, is
anxious by all possible means to improve.'[6] While two years later Lord
Ponsonby, the first British minister to serve in Buenos Aires (though
he personally disliked the Argentine), wrote in glowing terms of the
opportunities the republic offered to enterprising Britons: 'The settler
finds here an abundance of horses and cattle, a rich soil, and a
constant and easy communication with England; Religion not only
tolerated but respected; and person and property as well protected as
the persons and property of the native inhabitants, and a prospect,
almost a certainty, that by industry and skill a considerable fortune
may be rapidly accumulated', even if he did add the important proviso
that the estuary of the Plate must be safe for navigation.[7]

In May 1810 the Spanish viceroyalty of Buenos Aires had been
replaced by a revolutionary junta and the ex-viceroyalty then came to
be known as the United Provinces of the Rio de la Plata. Between
1811 and 1813 the new government introduced a series of radical
reforms, and in 1816 a constituent assembly formally declared its
independence in a congress assembled at Tucumán. The congress
chose a Supreme Director, Juan Martin de Pueyrredón who finally
resigned in 1819, having failed to persuade the provinces to accept a
centralized government. A year of anarchy and civil war followed.
Finally the government at Buenos Aires, under the leadership of
Martin Rodriguez, threw up a minister of vision – Bernardino
Rivadavia.

Between 1820 and 1827 Rivadavia tried to encourage the economic
growth of the republic by trying to attract foreign investment, foreign
trade and immigration but he was unable for very long to command
support for his policies. Elected president in 1826 he was forced to
resign after sixteen months by his opponents, the federalists. The
latter represented the landed classes and it was they who completely
dominated the local administration and the militia. Moreover throughout the whole of the period from the setting up of a creole junta to the
final downfall of Rivadavia, the government of Buenos Aires was never

able to assert its authority over Upper Peru (soon known as Bolivia), Paraguay or the eastern shore of the estuary of the River Plate, the so-called Banda Oriental, later to become the state of Uruguay.

The area of the La Plata provinces, though vast, was sparsely populated. Popham's figure of 6–7 million must have been intended to refer to the whole of the population of Spanish America, for the population of the future Argentina was in 1820 only one third of the population of contemporary London, and even in 1825 still only a little over half a million and the population of Buenos Aires, the only city of any size, was in 1822 only 56,000. The pampas or vast plains that stretched to the Andes were populated by tribes of Indians, herds of wild cattle and gauchos (or cowboys). The term 'gaucho', when loosely used, seems to have included the sedentary peasant who worked the land for himself or his landlord, but the true gaucho lived on his horse, led the life of a nomad and was quite independent,[8] and it was the latter who succeeded in grasping the imagination of British travellers.

How far, one may ask, is the picture painted by Popham, Gillespie, Parish and Ponsonby borne out by the various accounts given by a variety of travellers, British merchants and mining engineers or agents for British associations designed to promote mining, commerce, emigration and agriculture, during the era of independence and the years immediately following it?

George Love, who wrote as 'An Englishman' *Five Years' Residence in Buenos Aires* (between 1820 and 1825) and was later editor of *The British Packet*, a Buenos Aires newspaper, described the trade of the River Plate as being mostly in the hands of the British, the large proportion of them being Scotsmen (a subject perhaps for no surprise). They were not only holders of land and stock but also directors of local banks. Apart from the merchants there were many British shop-keepers; fifty-six of them subscribed to the Buenos Aires Commercial Rooms, established in the city in 1810. British merchants had resided there for a number of years before that date, though of course entirely illegally, but since 1810 the trade of the city had been thrown open to British merchants. Love's book was published in 1825 and according to a consular report there were living in the city in 1824 1355 British subjects. Seven years later the number was given as 4072 who were registered, though the consul-general thought there were many more who had never troubled to inscribe their names. Those registered included 466 merchants, 193 shopkeepers and 1245 artisans. The partiality to British goods caused the Americans, according to Love, to pass off their own home products as British and he himself had bought American soap that bore the stamp of the British crown. A knowledge of English was much in demand – parents were eager for their children to learn it and Love thought that 'the next generation will become completely anglicised'. Already at the time he was writing he noticed the anti-British prejudice fading: the British were no longer regarded as heretics, renegades and 'God-abandoned', in marked contrast to the attitudes prevailing twenty years earlier when England and Englishmen were as little known and understood as the interior of China was to the remainder of the world. Indeed there were now several Argentine youths being educated at Stonyhurst, the Jesuit college in Lancashire.[9]

When a treaty of commerce was eventually signed between Buenos Aires and the British government, as it was in 1825, there was wild excitement in the capital. Parish wrote home to the Foreign Office that 'on the occasion of Public Dinner and Entertainments, the people [here] are perfectly mad. There is an entertainment preparing in celebration of our treaty towards which the first subscriber has put down £400, and 10 more have subscribed £200 each or 1000 dollars. A shopkeeper thinks nothing of laying out 200 or 300 dollars in fireworks'.[10]

During the preceding fifteen years British merchants' interests had had to be looked after by naval officers who were commanding the British South American squadron. In Love's opinion they were not the most suitable type of men for that work and, in the words of an English MP, rather more ready 'to fight than to write'.[11] This view has not been shared, however, by recent British historians. Graham and Humphreys in their book *The Navy in South America* pay glowing tribute to the dexterity and political judgement of these naval officers. In the officers' proven ability to resolve several hundreds of disputes without bloodshed they were, in Graham's and Humphreys' opinion, entitled to rank with experienced diplomats. The fighting between Buenos Aires province and the other provinces of the federation, a struggle that involved both Portugal and Brazil for control of the Banda Oriental or eastern bank of the River Plate, caused foreign merchants in Buenos Aires to be threatened with having to make forced loans, with military service and even death. Captain Bowles RN in 1818 intervened on behalf of the British who were faced with a demand upon them for $150,000, reduced later to $30,000 when

Staples, a leading Irish merchant, made representations on behalf of his colleagues. However, when $26,000 were paid, the original sum was redemanded and if not paid within twelve days the British were threatened with banishment and sale of all their property. Bowles had to intervene again (much to the anger of the head of the government, Juan Martin de Pueyrredón, who wanted to deal with civilians only and was hoping a consul would be appointed). Bowles told the British Admiralty he thought the government of Buenos Aires was only restrained from violence by the presence of the British naval squadron. Fortunately (Bowles continued), poverty prevented the Buenos Aireans from having a navy of their own, since such a force would be officered and commanded by foreign adventurers who would be tempted to resort to violence. The government's actions, he thought, were due to its ignorance of the way commerce functioned and of the terms of international law, not to mention the absurd belief that all the English were extremely rich and (like other foreigners) a sponge to be squeezed.[12] Few English merchants, wrote Henry M. Brackenridge, secretary to the US commission sent by Congress in 1817 to make a report on South America and the progress of revolution there, had a good word to say for the local people and doubted their ability to form a government. Brackenridge himself, though often enthusing about the republican spirit prevailing in the capital city of Buenos Aires (he felt himself 'in a land of freedom' where all was plainness and simplicity and even the Supreme Director lived without pomp or ceremony) had to admit at the end of his book *A Voyage to South America* that though his impressions of it were favourable in a very large number of respects, he had no desire to settle in the country. Buenos Aires, he was forced to concede, 'is very far removed from the civilized world' and the lack of security prevailing and the instability of its governments were factors that weighed most heavily with him. To which he added the plainsmen's savagery, the 'gloominess' of the Catholic faith, neglect of literature and the arts, the feverish state of the public mind, with mutual distrust, warring interests, jealousies, hatreds and bitter envies.[13]

The lack of order and political stability remained a feature of the new-found republic throughout the period covered by this book, despite the confidence inspired by the liberal regime of Rivadavia. Francis Bond Head, a former army officer and general manager of a British mining company, who travelled across the breadth of the republic, reported in 1825 that most of the so-called united provinces were incapable of self-government. They consisted of small communities possessing virtually no education, riven by local jealousies, unequal to the responsibility of electing their own governor and junta and sending a delegate to Buenos Aires. The result was an endless series of disputes and the overthrow of each governor in turn. Some of the governors were tyrants, the public funds at their disposal were often quite inadequate for the tasks they were called upon to perform and they were faced by the envy and spite of adjoining provinces and of Buenos Aires. The latter was anti-clerical, its material interests bound up with the port, while the provinces were bastions of clerical influence and for their economic survival they looked to the land and not the sea.[14]

John Parish Robertson, whose activities in Paraguay will be dealt with later in this chapter, thought that all South American despots, with the sole exception of Dr Francia, the egregious dictator of Paraguay, cloaked their intentions under the names of Liberty and Democracy. Elections were always characterized by bribery and intimidation and every newly-elected congress, having proclaimed the freedom of the person and of private property, proceeded to violate its pledges. Some people were imprisoned, others banished, editors were forced to change their tune, heavy taxes were imposed and forced loans levied, while the great men at the head of government were replaced by greater with more troops at their command. Robertson found the attempt to define the nature of executive power in South America to be impossible. 'One day you find the governor shooting a man upon his own responsibility and the next applying to congress for leave to celebrate high mass or increase the salary of a clerk in the government offices. A few days after he dissolves congress altogether.'[15]

Barber Beaumont, who tried to effect a farming settlement in the Plata provinces in the third decade of the century, wrote with disillusion in 1828, when reflecting on disunion in the Plata provinces: 'They are ... scattered settlements in the vast wilderness of South America, in which the wants of the scanty inhabitants are so few and so easily supplied among themselves, that they are independent of each other. Most of the provinces consist of little more than one town in each, with a number of cattle walks around it, leaving extensive wastes between them and other provinces ... occupied only by wild animals or wandering Indians.' Spain, he went on, had united them by force and war against Spain had kept them united. Now the need for union was gone. All of them disliked the *porteños* (the name they gave to the Buenos Aireans), seeing the latter growing rich at their expense by exacting heavy duties on the River Plate and giving no protection in return. Beaumont recorded his disbelief that any joint-stock association could succeed in the country for many years – standards of public conduct were too loose and the inducements to local agents to deceive and to rob remained too strong. There was no legal restraint on fraud; the laws were too vague and badly administered and the governments were feeble and prey to intrigue.[16]

The most colourful accounts of attempts to defeat prejudice, tyranny and obstruction come from the pens of the Scottish brothers John and William Parish Robertson. They, in their *Letters on Paraguay* and their *Letters on South America* graphically describe their attempts to establish a thriving trading concern in Paraguay and in the provinces of Corrientes and Entre Rios on the River Paraná. When John, at the early age of nineteen, first arrived in Asunción, as he did in the year 1811, he found he was met by a chilly reception. It was said he intended to monopolize trade, he carried munitions of war on his ship, he had been making a map of the country and indulging in other suspicious activities. When his ship did eventually arrive, bearing the goods he intended to sell, the cargo was placed in a government store. John was only allowed to withdraw a limited amount at any one time, forbidden to export any bullion or to import any more goods; every package was carefully examined and double guards were placed on the vessel. However, within the space of three months, he had succeeded in convincing the junta of the harmlessness of his enterprise and was starting to trade on a very large scale.[17]

In 1814 Dr José Francia became the dictator of Paraguay. Francia was a difficult man to deal with, though John succeeded, for a time, in being able to humour him. Francia, in the manner of enlightened despots of Europe in the eighteenth century, intervened in affairs of the smallest detail. He examined lengths of imported cloth and if he found gaps in between the thread that the manufacturer had filled with starch, he allowed the vendor only half the cost price. And he once berated an English merchant for trying to dispose of shoddy goods: 'This is the way you hucksters of rags vend your unsound and deceitful manufactures over the world. The Jews are cheats but the English are downright swindlers ... you are the veriest mountebanks and pedlars ... for filthy lucre, filthily gotten is the rotting disease of your heart's core ... go about your business, and the next time you come to Paraguay with linens, bring them from honest Germany.'[18]

In 1814 John was joined by his brother William Parish Robertson, who, like John, very soon established a *modus vivendi* with the dictator, though he found him both arbitrary and vindictive, suddenly ordering the closure of a port and as suddenly decreeing its reopening and reclosure, while produce for export rotted in warehouses.[19]

Francia who, on principle, never allowed a foreigner to leave Paraguay once he had taken up residence there, made an exception in favour of John, having entrusted him with a mission to gain recognition from the British government. John was given the impossible task of trying to bribe the House of Commons to vote in favour of concluding with Francia a political and commercial treaty. The bribe consisted of a bale of maté (Paraguay tea), 200 hundredweight of tobacco, a demijohn of the local spirits, a large loaf of sugar, bundles of cigars and a specimen of embroidered cloth. Francia also commissioned John to bring him back an ornamental sword and pistols and some musical instruments. John felt unable to refuse the commission but never got further than Buenos Aires before deciding to return to Paraguay. He went back bearing a sealed letter from General Alvear, the Supreme Director, asking Francia to provide recruits for the struggle being waged against José Artigas, then leader of the anti-porteño federalists, in return for some arms and ammunition. On the journey up the Paraná John's vessel was seized and its cargo plundered by soldiers loyal to José Artigas and John had to appeal to Captain Percy, in command of the British naval squadron operating in the River Plate, to request Artigas to set John free and to release his property. The business of getting his boat released entailed John visiting Artigas personally, bearing the letter from Captain Percy which was to have the desired effect. John gives a memorable description of the scene he encountered at the headquarters of the highly successful federalist leader whom John with dry irony refers to as 'the all-powerful Protector of half the world'. He found Artigas 'seated on a bullock's skull, on the mud floor of his hut, eating beef off a spit, and drinking gin out of a cow horn! He was surrounded by a dozen officers in weather-beaten attire, in similar positions and similarly occupied ... All were smoking, all gabbling. The Protector was dictating to two secretaries, who occupied, at one deal table, the only two dilapidated rush-bottom chairs in his hovel.' In another room occupied by the staff, the floor was strewn with envelopes addressed to 'His Excellency the Protector', and at the door were the horses of couriers who were arriving every half-hour and leaving at similar intervals. Artigas received him courteously and took him on a tour of his camp before allowing him to leave, armed with the authority he had been seeking. When Francia learned of what had happened he vented his anger on the Robertsons. He had expected that *his* letter, and not Captain Percy's addressed to Artigas, would suffice to procure the release of John and the cargo in which he had a personal interest. Furious because the British seemed not to have the necessary authority to ensure the free passage of arms and ammunition up the river to Paraguay, he refused to allow the Robertsons to stay any longer in his country. William wrote to his brother John, at that time staying at Corrientes, that he should not return to Asunción. Francia was apparently saying: 'England shall know that unless she will protect a trade in arms, she shall have none to Paraguay in manufactures. We do not want her rags unless we can have muskets too, and so you may write to your naval commander, or to your prime minister, if you please.' John did in fact go back to Asunción but was ordered to leave within 48 hours and got little of his property out. All Francia allowed him to take was $10 in silver, a pair of small spurs, a silver *bombilla* worth £4 and $200 to pay the crew.[20]

Eventually in 1817 William Robertson, who had gone south to Corrientes, and there ran a most successful business under licence from José Artigas trading on a very large scale in hides, sold his property and returned to Buenos Aires.[21] There, in his words, 'a more civilized policy, a British frigate, the vicinity of a large naval force at Rio de Janeiro, and a fast-increasing community of our own country-men rendered a residence more agreeable and secure.' There he founded a new business on a far greater scale than in the interior, entered into commercial correspondence and into business dealings with leading English bankers and merchants as well as European ones, and engaged in vastly more complex matters than those arising from the sale of goods and the purchase of *yerba* (*maté*) in Paraguay, or of the barter of manufactures and doubloons for hides and wool at Corrientes. John did send two more vessels to Asunción with cargoes for sale to Francia's subjects and both seem to have been well received, one with mathematical and scientific instruments, the other with salt, but after that (1819) Francia refused to grant any more trading licences.[22]

Six years later Woodbine Parish, Britain's newly-appointed consul-general, was successful in persuading the dictator Francia to release British subjects detained in Paraguay from between four and fourteen years – a carpenter, shoemaker and a cabinet maker, five merchants and three sailors. The quid pro quo was an offer to Francia to enter into diplomatic relations. Francia wanted to get Parish to force the government of Buenos Aires to allow free transit on the river to Paraguay but this was to ask the impossible, since Buenos Aires was likely to remain a far more valued customer of Britain than Paraguay could ever be.[23]

The value of British exports to the Plate fluctuated in the 1820s and was totally disrupted by the three-year war between Buenos Aires and Brazil that ended only in 1828. Even so, by 1837 Parish reckoned that it was greater than the total value of all the exports of all other countries in Europe put together. 'The manufactures of Great Britain [he wrote in 1839] are become articles of primary necessity. The gaucho is everywhere clothed in them. Take his whole equipment . . . and what is there not of raw hide that is not British? If his wife has a gown, ten to one it is made at Manchester; the camp kettle in which he cooks his food, the earthenware he eats from, the knife, his poncho, spurs, bit, are all imported from England.'[24]

British goods found their way into the interior despite all the difficulties of travel that were constantly remarked on by all British observers. John Robertson commented on the disgraceful state of all the roads in the vicinity of Buenos Aires: 'As far out as three leagues from the city, they present, during six months of the year, the most frightful barriers which the imagination can conceive to any safe intercourse between town and country.'[25] And when rain fell the difficulties were compounded; there was no attempt made at draining or camber and the water stagnated in the deep ruts made by the wheels of the bullock carts. But though the overland journey to Chile from Buenos Aires was exhausting and dangerous, travellers from Britain preferred its hardships to continuing the comfortless voyage by sea – it took less time than the trip round the Horn and passages to the Pacific were irregular and uncertain.[26]

Samuel Haigh, a young Scottish merchant asked by a rich relation and his partners to manage a cargo dispatched to Chile, made the long journey in 1817 across the pampas from Buenos Aires to Mendoza – a distance of 900 miles. He described his experience of travel in much the same terms as Francis Bond Head who made the same journey some eight years later. Head became famous as 'Galloping Head' for

he covered the whole of the huge distance on the backs of horses and
at the gallop (the normal pace of the Argentine gaucho). There were
no roads across the flat plain and the latter was intersected by streams,
bridgeless rivers and numerous marshes, with the horses changed at
staging posts from 12 to 36 miles apart. Haigh travelled in a *galera*, a
springless carriage slung on traces of bullock hide that he described
as a miniature ark – a closed van with seats at the sides, and a rear
door, drawn by four or six horses. Its wheels, each of which had an
immense circumference to allow it to wade through the marshes and
streams, were wound around with strips of hide to withstand the
numerous shocks of the journey. It travelled at a speed of 12 miles an
hour and the change of horses at every stage was effected in a matter
of minutes, so the distance covered in any one day was between 60
and 75 miles.

Desperate poverty was encountered at every stage of the long
journey. Haigh described the village people as 'squalid, filthy, the
picture of indolence', while the posthouses were bare huts, flea-ridden
and often unable to provide anything but beef to eat.[27] Head enjoyed
his pampas journey rather more than did Samuel Haigh; he found
excitement in the rapid progress, always riding at the gallop, though
admitting the cruelty shown to the horses. On arrival at the staging
post, 'the spurs, heels and legs of the peons are literally bathed in
blood, and from the sides of the horses the blood is constantly flowing
rather than dropping'. Head got accustomed to the hard riding, after
enduring it for three or four months, living off only beef and water,
the staple diet of the gauchos and their families. He found, he wrote,
no exertions could kill him, 'though constantly arriving so exhausted I
could not speak – yet after a few hours sleep on saddle and ground, I
was so recovered I could be on horseback before sunrise and could
ride till two to three hours after sunset, having tired ten to twelve
horses a day'. Head loved the solitude of the pampas that he found
'placid beyond description', with no one in sight save the occasional
gaucho, 'his scarlet poncho streaming horizontally behind him', his
bolas flying around his head, ready to hurl at some fleeing ostrich.[28]
This was the romantic view of the pampas, later immortalized by
W. H. Hudson, but not one shared by other British travellers who
have left their accounts of Argentine travel.

Robert Proctor who in 1822 went out to South America, as agent
for a British concern negotiating a loan to Peru, was a rather more
sensitive traveller than Head. He was deeply shocked by the huge iron

spurs with which the peons goaded their horses, causing such terrible suffering to their mounts. He had seen these come in with their flanks swollen and perforated and resembling a sponge, and he had even been able to track a carriage by the blood flowing from the wounds of the horses. The pampas he considered 'most dreary, savage country', constantly under threat from the Indians. He witnessed the evidence of a reprisal for a recent raid that the Indians had made – a body of an Indian that had been left hanging by his wrists from a tree. Proctor's sensitivity apparently did not extend to the corpse of a savage and he recounts cutting off one arm from it (it was by then dry and odourless) and keeping it as a curiosity.[29]

Alexander Caldecleugh, another Scotsman, who crossed the pampas in 1819, found himself constantly threatened by Indians. The unsettled state of the country had made them much bolder than they had been before. 'In these plains,' he wrote, 'where a gallop is the only pace, it is quite impossible to say where the Indians are not. They may be in one place today and 150 miles off tomorrow.' On one occasion he and his party had been compelled to flee for their lives, riding in the heat of the afternoon for 42 miles to effect their escape.[30] Conditions gradually improved, but Head on his journeys in 1825 was at pains to stress the necessity of always carrying arms when one travelled.[31]

The food and accommodation provided where Proctor stopped were as Haigh described them. One of his party almost lost his teeth in endeavouring to chew the meat that was served him and Haigh preferred to drink a soup of onion, pumpkin, maize and lean beef, though he was lucky to have found any vegetables. Every posthouse was vermin-infested, and at one he was forced to carry out of doors the mattress and bedding on which he was lying, 'and sweep off the disgusting insects with a broom, the fowls flocking round us and picking them up greedily'.[32] Other travellers told the same story. 'The filth of the posthouses [wrote Parish] is beyond description, dirt and vermin of every kind in them, and no accommodation of any kind for the traveller; even our peons preferred sleeping in the open air.' The country was, in Parish's view, 'more uninteresting than any I ever travelled over, in any quarter of the globe. I should divide it into five regions; first that of thistles, inhabited by owls and *biscachas* [a burrowing rodent of South America, a cross between a rat and a rabbit]; secondly that of grass, where you meet with deer and ostriches and the screaming horned plover; thirdly the region of swamps and bogs, only fit for frogs; fourthly that of stones and ravines, where I expected every moment to be upset; and lastly that of ashes and thorny bushes, the refuge of the tarantula and binchuco or giant bug.'[33]

Journeying to Paraguay in 1811 was even more uncomfortable. When William Robertson travelled to Asunción, in order to join his brother John, he had to make the journey up-river in a filthy and uncomfortable brig averaging 2½ leagues a day. Once arrived at Corrientes he took the shorter route overland, through marshes infested with mosquitoes and 'tigers', not undressing once in four days. He had to subsist on hard maize, normally only fed to horses, and dry, unsavoury local nuts, finding en route the village people living in filth and the direst poverty.[34]

Head admired the gaucho way of life – hard, primitive but dignified. He compared the gaucho huts to the Scottish crofters' – one room, infested with bugs, a door consisting of bullock's hide, lit by a lamp of bullock tallow and heated by a fire of charcoal; the ground outside strewn with the carcases and bones of the animals that had been slaughtered, and in both its smell and its appearance resembled 'an ill-kept dog-kennel in England'. Children learnt to ride at the age of four and later to gallop and use the lasso and the *bolas* in pursuit of cattle or game. The gaucho was tough, despised civilized life, lived on a diet of beef and water and never dreamt of walking anywhere. Yet, despite the uncouthness of his manner of life, the gaucho (Head found) was very polite and always extremely hospitable.[35]

Alexander Caldecleugh, like Head, was indulgent towards the gaucho's shortcomings. 'Most of their faults [he wrote] may be deduced from their way of life.' The transitory nature of their employment led to their wandering and predatory habits and on the pampas law enforcement was difficult. In temperament he found the gaucho little different from the town dweller, the citizen of Buenos Aires – 'free from deceit – would be most obliging were it not for his indolence – and most amiable if he had the slightest command of his passions'.[36]

Edward Temple, whom Tom B. Jones describes (perhaps a little unfairly) as merely 'a young rich idler' – he wangled a job as secretary to a company hoping to mine at Potosí – travelled across the pampas to Bolivia at the end of the year 1825. His facetious and unattractive style when recounting his impressions of the countryside unfortunately tell one more about the author than the people and places he is describing. Compared to the English farm-worker he knew, the gaucho seemed to Temple to be little better than 'a species of carnivorous baboon'. He thought the gaucho's monotonous diet was due to his reluctance to grow vegetables or grain – indifferent to what was beyond his reach and in consequence easily satisfied. He did concede that among the gauchos he had never witnessed 'that degrading misery which is so general among the peasantry of Erin',[37] but he might have remarked in that connection that the gaucho was not burdened by an absentee landlord, had no tithe to pay to an alien church and lived in a climate that was certainly drier and perhaps more healthy than that of Ireland.

John Miers, an entrepreneur and British mining engineer who travelled across the pampas to Chile not long after Robert Proctor had done so, found the inhabitants he met at the posthouses 'filthy, ignorant and debased'[38] (much the same words that were used by Haigh). Ignorant they certainly were, as Charles Darwin remarked in 1832, for like many South Americans they had little knowledge of the outside world – Spanish rule had been careful to see to that. 'Most [wrote Darwin mockingly] had an indistinct idea that England, London and North America were different names for the same place, but the better informed well knew that London and North America were separate countries close together, and that England was a large town in London.'

Yet Darwin, unlike the conceited Temple, was neither cursory nor dismissive in his estimate of the South American gaucho. He described him as being tall and handsome, proud and dissolute in appearance and, while greeting you with a graceful bow, seemed perfectly ready to cut your throat, if the circumstances seemed to require it. He commented, like other British travellers, on the gaucho's passion for gambling, his excessive drinking in the numerous *pulperias*, the robberies that resulted from his dissipation and his ineradicable indolence. The gaucho, Darwin went on to point out, had little real incentive to work, with horses abundant, no lack of food (if a meat diet was deemed sufficient) and so many feast days to celebrate.[39]

In contrast the life that was lived in the city, that is the city of Buenos Aires, was very different, though not necessarily more agreeable to the minds of most of the British observers. Accounts of their impressions are very similar. Parish in 1824 described how, as he first entered the roadstead, he was greeted by the masts of several wrecks, testimony to the dangerous passage. Three English vessels, he recounted, had gone down in that part of the river with cargoes worth over £100,000. The River Plate, as George Love remarked, was 'considered the hell of navigators' and a shortage of labour, not only skilled, made it difficult to build moles and docks. Ships drawing 15 feet or more of water had to anchor 7 or 8 miles out and, except in settled weather, the landing was hazardous, especially during the winter fogs. When 40–50 yards from the shore he was transferred to a horse-drawn cart, made of cane and open at the bottom (the same that Haigh had found himself soaked in). John Miers recalls that he found 'the sight of this first specimen of South American handicraft' to be 'both ominous and depressing'.[40]

To Haigh the city at a distance presented 'a gloomy and monastic appearance, on account of its numerous domes and steeples', an impression that was later strengthened by the sight of so many priests and friars in the streets. He found it had 'a wild and unfinished look', the effect of which was 'anything but pleasing'. Save in a few streets near the Plaza all the houses were low and dirty, one storey high, built of brick and whitewashed in the Spanish style. The windows were without glass for the most part and their iron grills gave to the buildings the depressing appearance of a prison. The churches were large and gloomy outside, few of the streets had any paving and the footpaths were narrow and 'disagreeable'. Haigh was however much impressed by the beauty of Buenos Aires women and the elegant clothes of the better-to-do. The young men dressed as well as their class in London or Paris were wont to do, but without affectation or foppery. Haigh thought the fashions of Buenos Aires to be much in advance of those of old Spain 'with regard to modern style and improvement'.[41]

When it came to the insides of the houses, Head thought them comfortless and damp, with floors cracked and full of holes, no ceilings and only charcoal fires. Even the houses of the principal families seemed to him furnished without any taste. A Brussels carpet, a chandelier that was suspended from open rafters, a number of tawdry North American chairs placed against a whitewashed wall, an English piano and some marble vases.[42] Love found many of the larger houses, formerly occupied by leading Spanish families, were now tenanted by British merchants and their drawing-rooms used as storehouses. 'The city of Buenos Aires [he wrote] when viewed from the outer roads at a distance of eight miles, has an imposing appearance. The domes of the numerous churches, the public buildings etc give it an air of grandeur which a nearer approach diminishes.

On landing, the dilapidated mole [destroyed by the storm of 21 August 1820] and the mean streets near the beach do not augur well; it requires an inspection rightly to appreciate it, for there are edifices worthy of attention.'

Love who lived for many years in Buenos Aires thought that the climate was more congenial to British habits than most places abroad, but considered its healthiness overrated. He looked in vain for Italian skies and 'a soul-breathing softness in the air'. Dust, fleas and flies made the summer objectionable and the surrounding country had a dreary sameness. He did not expect villas and parks and nicely cultivated grounds, 'but I thought it would be more diversified'. Though the *quintas* with their orchards were pleasant enough, he missed the roots and plants of England and found the hedges and trees so dwarfish they seemed an apology for the real thing.

The *Alameida* on the beach near the mole was 'totally unworthy of such a city, and in the neighbourhood of all the rabble of the town' – clearly no place for the genteel to stroll in. The beach well deserved its title of *Wapping*, crowded as it was with the sailors of all nations, frequenting the grog shops and adjoining stores. Love thought that the number of English sailors idling on the beach would crew a man-of-war and 'a stranger, seeing so many English faces, might suppose it an English colony'. Beaumont also wrote disparagingly of the *Alameida* as an illustration of the general lack of public amenities in Buenos Aires: a miserable walk along the beach, with a few stunted trees and brick seats on one side, and numerous drinking shops on the way sending out parties of drunken sailors – not to mention the appalling stench from dead fish and the carcases of horses that were strewn along the beach.[43] Most English travellers with money used to stay at Faunch's hotel, not always an elegant establishment but by the time that Love was writing he thought it very superior, 'hardly to be exceeded in London'.[44]

Woodbine Parish's first experience of Buenos Aires was very far from agreeable, though one would never guess it from the account (quoted earlier) he had given to Canning. Writing to Planta at the Foreign Office in November 1825, he told the latter he 'would willingly exchange £3000 a year in Buenos Aires for £1500 in England. The rent of the only house suitable for us is over £500 a year, and it will be necessary to spend another £500 on it before it becomes habitable for an Englishman. The most ordinary servant, who will not do half the work of an Englishman, is paid £36 a year. My seven servants cost me £340 in wages alone. The keep of horses is 25 per cent more than in England . . . beef and mutton are the only cheap articles. Bread is very dear and so is water.' Four years later he still found the city 'a disagreeable and disheartening place'.[45]

Lord Ponsonby, despite his eulogy of the country in his official dispatch to London, heartily detested the La Plata region. 'No eye ever saw so odious a country . . . I will not trust myself to speak of it', he confided to a friend, Sir Charles Bagot. 'I do not recollect [he went on] having ever before disliked any place so much' and thoughts of Italy increase 'my disgust at this land of mud and putrid carcases . . . no roads, no houses . . . no books, no theatre that can be endured . . . nothing good but beef.' And when writing to Canning in 1827, describing the inhabitants of the future Uruguay as being both wild and savage, he added 'but no more so than here and, I believe, everywhere else on this continent'. 'Let nothing induce you [he told another friend, Lord Howard de Walden, in 1826] to visit this depraved country. It is the vilest place I ever saw, and I certainly should hang myself if I could find a tree tall enough to swing on. The climate is detestable, the thermometer varies sometimes 20 degrees in a day, but there is *always* either mud or dust enough to smother or choke one. Then we have republican conceit in all its vigour. It is a beastly place!'[46]

The Robertsons, it seems, thought differently, their expectations being rather lower than those of the English upper class. Tough young Scotsmen, they clearly relished the society of Buenos Aires after their rougher experiences in Asunción and Corrientes. William Robertson described the period 1810–1830 as a golden age in Buenos Aires – 'for the first twenty years that the English knew it . . . [it] might really be called a delightful place', in marked contrast to the next decade. John and William both liked getting back there, away from the suspicions of Francia and Artigas. There were (wrote William) few places where there was such ready intercourse between foreigners, and especially Britons, and the indigenous population. The English were invariably well treated, partly because they were wealthy people but also because of the creoles' good manners.[47] Captain Bowles in 1819, when handing over to his successor as senior British naval officer, told the latter that he would find the British were popular in Buenos Aires and more respected than most other foreigners, because they avoided political intrigue and interference in local affairs, in marked contrast to the behaviour of the North Americans and the French.[48]

Apart from bringing trade to the republic, the British through the work of James Thomson also brought a measure of public education. The triumvirate governing Buenos Aires in the early days of independence had in 1811 passed laws permitting secular schools to be set up as well as the freedom of the printed word. Thomson was the South American agent of the British and Foreign Bible Society and in 1818 was commissioned by the government to start a school for boys in the city. By 1820 he was able to report that no fewer than 1004 pupils were now regularly attending his school and that no hindrance had been placed in his way in distributing copies of the New Testament (400 in a Spanish translation). By the time Thomson left for Chile in May 1821, two of his schools were open in the city and he had left them in the charge of a local priest he had found most helpful. He had been informed that through lack of funds the government was unable to pay his salary but it made him an honorary citizen as some recognition of his services. In a report he made five years later to the British and Foreign Schools Society (the society sponsoring Lancasterian schools) it seems there were then eight schools operating in Buenos Aires supported by the local authorities and as many more in surrounding villages, Thomson having received the support of Rivadavia, the Supreme Director, as well as the Catholic hierarchy.[49] Brackenridge had already commented on the progress being made in the spread of literacy during his visit in 1818. Three printing offices had been set up and all seemed to be doing good business. Books were imported free of duty and Voltaire's works were selling well, as were translations into Spanish of Paine's *Common Sense* and his *Rights of Man*, Washington's farewell address as president and an abridged history of the USA. There was, he wrote, an almost extravagant admiration for the USA, though the volume of North American trade was not to be compared to that with Britain.[50]

Trade by the British with the Plata republic remained until 1826, when the war with Brazil closed down traffic on the river, a source of very considerable profit. Not so the attempt to mine precious metals. Mining companies were formed in England as a result of encouragement by the Buenos Aires government, desperately anxious for foreign investment. Rivadavia wrote to Hullett & Co, who were acting as his agents in London, a letter designed to publicize the opportunities that existed for investment in Argentinian mining. 'An immense mineral deposit is situated in the midst of fertile plains in a climate healthful and temperate, provided with all kinds of fuel, water and the means of obtaining cattle and all kinds of vegetables, and, it should be added, located only twenty easy miles from the city of Mendoza.'[51]

Francis Bond Head, the 'Galloper', a former officer in the Royal Engineers, was employed by the Rio Plata Mining Association to supervise its mining operations. Arriving in July 1825, accompanied by his family, a French assayer, two Cornish mining 'captains' and three miners also from Cornwall, he set about reconnoitring the mines to which his company was claiming title. These were gold mines to the north of San Luis and silver mines at Uspallata, lying to the north-west of Mendoza. All these mines, Head soon discovered, had already been sold to rival companies, landowners or other individuals and title had been granted the Association by a government that could not perform.

Head made clear in his report to the company, and in his book describing his journeys, the various obstacles that existed to exploiting the mines with a hope of profit. First, there were the vast distances that separated the sites of the mines from the sources of supply of men, tools and provisions. The roads were appalling, there were torrents and ravines and the mines were situated in high barren mountains. There was no water to work the machinery or to wash the ores when they were extracted, and even very little water to drink. The machinery sent out was inapplicable to the requirements of the Andean mines; the temperature was not conducive to work and the lodes, once located, were of poor quality when compared with those that were to be found in Mexico, Bolivia and Peru.

The local people were not easy to deal with, being narrow-minded and lacking education. The rich were unaccustomed to business and the poor to doing any hard work. There was no conception of the meaning of a contract or of punctuality. It was impossible to get free competition and almost no respect for the law. The Cornish experience of mining had little relevance to South America and the Europeans who came out to the country were corrupted by the climate, the wine and the women. The mines needed frequent inspection, yet the huge distances precluded this and Head thought it dangerous to rely on the honesty of individuals.

The political conditions of the area also presented a serious obstacle. Governments were unstable and always liable to be over-thrown by a sudden revolution. The provinces were jealous of Buenos

Aires and had little regard for what was decreed there. Local governments levied heavy taxes on any wealth that was leaving the country or that was merely passing through it, and contracts signed by a governor were nullified if he was overthrown. When he first arrived in Buenos Aires with his little party of Cornish miners (whose wages were costing £15,000 a year), Head discovered that no law had been passed to authorize his Association. Moreover, by another law, passed only in January of that year, the right to issue mining concessions had been devolved on provincial governments. Clearly private interests had triumphed and Rivadavia seemed unwilling to help. Head then found out that the governments of Rioxa, Catamarca, Cordoba and San Luis had disposed of exclusive mining rights to Buenos Aires companies, which meant that his Association had lost any claims they might have had to mines at Famatima and at San Luis. Only the governors of the provinces of Mendoza and San Juan expressed any willingness to receive him.

Though told that the mines at Uspallata (the other area in which his Association had shown an interest) were covered by snow and so inaccessible, Head discovered this was not so. But he did, on inspection, decide that the mines were certainly not rich in ore, were without water to work machinery and without pasture to feed cattle, if the latter were used instead of water. It was obvious the mines would never pay. He then had an interview with the ex-governor of San Juan, recently displaced by a revolution, who told him that he hoped to return and that the revolution was temporary, but in the meantime it was inadvisable for Head to try to go to San Juan. Head then decided to return to Mendoza only to find the governor was now rather less co-operative and merely concerned to know by how much his province would profit by granting a lease: on learning that the profit would be only a fifth of the silver the company managed to extract, he informed Head that the deal was off.

It now appeared that the eagerness shown by Head's company to purchase mines had led to speculation in Buenos Aires resulting in every piece of land that might hold minerals being bought up. The situation was seemingly hopeless, so Head decided to go on to Chile where the Association also had interests. His experiences there will be recounted in another chapter of this book, but suffice it to say he had no more success there than he had in the provinces of La Plata.

On eventually returning to Buenos Aires and finding there some German miners his company had brought over from Europe, Head decided he had no alternative but to pay them off and send them home. Having then sold the stores of the company at a considerable profit (prices locally being much inflated because of the blockade of the Plate by Brazil), he returned to England only to be blamed by the angry directors for the loss of their investments. The directors behaved very shabbily and at first refused to pay Head anything for his expenses, let alone his salary, though he had on their behalf travelled 6000 miles, endured considerable hardships, shown great energy and enterprise and saved the shareholders a good deal of money by winding up the enterprise when he did. In the end the company's directors were forced to submit to arbitration, but even when the arbitrators' award was made and Head properly compensated, the directors continued to blame Head for the failure of their speculation. In fact everyone had been deceived and, as Head wrote in his report, the great mistake they had all made was to imagine that gold and silver could be mined with any hope of profit in a land whose products consisted only of beef-cattle, horses and thistles.[52]

The Famatima Mining Company, organized by the Robertson brothers, also found it had purchased mines that had been sold already to other people. The mines they did attempt to work never succeeded in making a profit and in 1827 its shares, which when they were first issued had been priced at £50 a share, now realized only £2 a share. The failure of this company was partly responsible for the Robertsons' eventual bankruptcy.[53]

Captain Andrews who arrived like Head at Buenos Aires in 1825, though interested primarily in mining concessions in Bolivia (the former Upper Peru) and Chile, on behalf of a London-based mining company, made enquiries about the possibility of mining in the La Plata provinces of Cordoba, Salta and Tucumán. Though given encouragement by the authorities, he discovered that Buenos Aires speculators had in almost every case forestalled him. He did not share Head's pessimism about the future of mining projects in any of the areas he visited (his book was published in 1827), but rather deplored the publicity that the writings of Head had received in England so soon after the stockmarket crash of mining shares in 1826. One of the great mistakes that had been made by mining companies such as Head's was (in Andrews's view) to think that English miners could usefully be employed in South American mines. He conceded that a few miners recruited in Europe could help in the mines, even though the latter must be worked in the first place by native Indians, capable of coping with primitive conditions and costing far less to pay and feed. But to his mind the German miners were far superior to the English – 'more hardy, patient and enduring, and far less nice and punctilious about trifles. Cornishmen are intractable if put the least out of their way' and did not mingle easily with strangers, particularly South Americans.[54]

Mining was not the only field that had seemed to promise great rewards and yet succeeded in yielding none in the early years of the La Plata republic. Gillespie in 1817 had drawn attention to the vast extent of uncultivated land in the provinces and the huge profit he thought could be made by improving the quality of the grain grown and the feed that was offered to the cattle. In his opinion a good farmer could hope to raise three crops in a season and find a prompt sale for all his produce.[55] Edward Temple, ten years later, described how for a sum in England that would barely keep its owner alive a man could buy an extensive estate in the great plains of the Argentine that could support fifty head of cattle, as well as horses, sheep and goats, or a similar one that could grow anything. The climate was good, the hunting was excellent and a mere £5–6000 could 'purchase ease, comfort and independence' in the provinces of Salta, Cordoba or Tucumán. 'An intelligent priest' had told Temple that for only $25,000 he could buy an estate in that area and double its value in a very few years, enjoying on it a standard of living to equal that which was then enjoyed by the Cardinal Archbishop of Toledo.[56] Temple was somewhat credulous. Even so, individuals did manage to prosper. What did not prosper were organized attempts to settle emigrants on the land. Barber Beaumont in 1825, with the agreement of the Buenos Aires government, bought an estate at a place called San Pedro, in the province of Buenos Aires, and proposed to make grants of part of the land to British emigrant families. In exchange for a plot of 50 acres the emigrants were to pay £1 quit-rent and the government of Rivadavia agreed to find the passage money required for 200 emigrant families. Two hundred and fifty families in fact left England that year for Buenos Aires under the sponsorship of Beaumont, but before awaiting the success of this project, Beaumont was persuaded to join in floating the Rio de la Plata Agricultural Association in which various Englishmen took shares and became directors of the company. The Association purchased land situated in the province of Entre Rios and the Buenos Aires government, by the terms of the treaty signed with Britain that year, offered the emigrants powerful incentives – exemption from taxes for ten years, no liability for military service and no need to pay customs duties on necessities imported or on produce exported. Yet all these land grants proved to be worthless. It was soon clear there was no intention to allow the settlements to be made and when the emigrants arrived at San Pedro they found no land to which they had title. Most of them then returned to Buenos Aires and some took service in the government's fleet that was then engaged in fighting Brazil.

Beaumont's son, who has left an account of these doings and himself went out to Buenos Aires to try to sort out the company's affairs and recoup some of the sums invested, met, it appears, with little understanding or with any sort of sympathy: 'From the government I could obtain [he wrote] neither aid, assistance or gratitude, nor even a single shilling on account of between twenty and thirty thousand pounds, which, on the whole, we had advanced for the passage money, sustenance and stores of six hundred and twenty emigrants whom we had conveyed to Buenos Aires, and who were fighting the battles of Buenos Aires, or adding to the population or productiveness of their province.' A personal interview with Rivadavia left Beaumont no further forward – he found the director pompous and distant – and a further interview with another minister gave him no better satisfaction.

Beaumont junior, while in Buenos Aires, was able to learn from some of the emigrants just what had happened in Entre Rios. They had been forbidden to work by the governor and their stores had been pillaged and their cattle rustled. Having first sent a man to Entre Rios with $1000 to relieve the wants of those emigrants remaining there, he was so disturbed when the man returned with tales of lack of government assistance and the fraud and extortion practised on the settlers that he felt he must go himself to Entre Rios and try to persuade the latter to return. On arrival he found that the few still there were very reluctant to leave the place, the country appearing so fertile and attractive, but eventually he got them away.

On his return he visited San Pedro to see the other detachment of emigrants. He found a small town in a healthy position on the north bank of the River Paraná containing four British and Irish families. One man was cultivating 4 acres, two were working in a local store and two had adopted the gaucho way of life. All of them said they were happy to remain.[57]

Beaumont tried unsuccessfully to enlist the help of the British Foreign Office in his claims against the Buenos Aires government.

Fox, the British minister in Buenos Aires, told Palmerston in 1832 that the immigration projects were the work 'of vile speculators and company-mongers who ... brought ruin upon so many industrious families and disgrace upon the British name in South America'. The Beaumonts had been foolish and shown lack of foresight, according to opinion in Buenos Aires, and Ponsonby in 1827 said so to Canning in a dispatch.[58] It had been the South American agents of the Agricultural Association who had behaved criminally in selling its stores for little more than half their value, and the government that followed Rivadavia refused to hold itself responsible for the actions of its predecessor.

The Robertsons also burnt their fingers in trying to establish a Scottish settlement near Buenos Aires in 1825. Six thousand pounds was invested by them in constructing houses, farm buildings and a church on an estate of 16,000 acres, 1000 of which were turned over to orchards and 2500 cultivated. The project was not a financial success, all involved blaming one another, and the whole settlement was abandoned when it was plundered by the military in the civil war of 1829.[59] This was presumably the enterprise to which Head referred when he wrote of a scheme to send out Scottish milkmaids to make butter. The butter would not keep fresh in the climate and the local people preferred oil in their cooking.[60] The historian Henry Ferns comments that the immigration projects 'were the victims of the optimism concerning human affairs and the simple-minded theories of human nature which characterized the utilitarian idealists so numerous among the enterprising classes of Great Britain'. But he adds that individual emigrants did prosper materially, whether with skills or without, labour being as scarce as it was and the wages paid being as high as they were:[61] Brackenridge reckoned in 1818 that a day labourer from England or from the United States could earn higher wages in Buenos Aires than in any other part of the world ($1500 to $2000 a year was, it seems, a common salary).

Head however did not advise the English poor to emigrate if they could help themselves in England. He admitted that pay in Buenos Aires was good and that coarse beef was cheap enough, but the lodgings available were filthy, the high wages people were able to earn were eaten up by the high cost of living, and beef was sold in so mangled a state that the Cornish miners refused to buy it. Common necessities such as salt and pepper, even bread and water were terribly dear and clothes were also very expensive, costing far more than they did in England. All the Cornishmen that accompanied him said 'they had rather work their fingers to the stumps in England than be gentlemen in Buenos Aires'.[62] Nevertheless emigration continued and Beaumont noted that all the emigrants who wanted work did well for themselves, one telling him he expected to receive in prize money $2000 from his share in a privateer, though of course privateering was brought to an end by the peace with Brazil in 1828. It was, as Beaumont went on to say, only the capitalists who were disappointed.[63]

A number of North Americans and English took service in the armed forces, either the navy or the army, of the Buenos Aires government. The only written record of their experiences is contained in the memoirs of Anthony King, a subject of the United States, who enlisted at the age of fourteen in the armed forces of the United Provinces. He served with them for twenty-four years and clearly enjoyed the experience, reaching eventually the rank of colonel. He records how in 1817 he met an Englishman called Chapman who held a commission in the same corps and who strongly advised him to leave the service, advice that King was unwilling to take. Apparently Chapman had had three brothers who had all died in the Argentine service, 'perished [Chapman bitterly exclaimed] like brutes, without thanks, gratitude or blessing':[64] clearly a risk all mercenaries face.

The civil war that continued between Buenos Aires and the inland provinces, the struggle waged for the eastern shore of the River Plate with the Portuguese, José Artigas and finally Brazil, the refusal of the dictator Francia to open his trade to the outside world and his bitter hostility to Buenos Aires, and finally the fall of the apparently stable and ordered regime of Rivadavia, all combined to frustrate British hopes of a vast expansion of trade and profits in the La Plata provinces. Even the peace of 1828 failed to herald the promised era of wealth and exploitation earlier forecast by Popham, Gillespie and Woodbine Parish. Instead (in the words of Henry Ferns), it only managed to usher in 'commercial stagnation, debt repudiation, political tension and blighted hopes'.

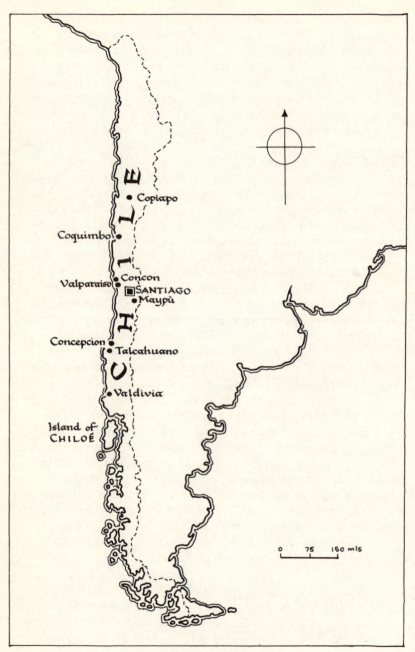

Copiapo

Coquimbo

CHILE

Concon
Valparaiso
☐ SANTIAGO
Maypù

Concepcion
Talcahuano

Valdivia

Island of
CHILOÉ

0   75   150 mls

2 · Chile

Chile in the era of independence was another South American country that seemed to promise British merchants and British mining companies rich rewards, though it was (in the words of Professor David Bushnell) 'sparsely populated, isolated and characterised by a static agrarian society in which a few aristocratic families wielded near absolute influence'.[1] The Chilean port of Valparaiso was to become in the 1820s almost a British colony, sailors and British naval officers took service in the Chilean navy and tales of untapped mineral wealth lured British investors (encouraged in any case by a government eager as was that of Buenos Aires to bring in foreign currency) to squander money in enterprises that had no hope of showing a profit.

The influence of events in Spain and other parts of Latin America had resulted in Chile in 1810 establishing its own ruling junta and in the spring of the following year opening its ports to the trade of the world. A populist dictatorship followed, under the creole José Miguel Carrera, to be replaced in 1813 by that of the better-known Bernardo O'Higgins. O'Higgins and other patriot leaders were forced to flee in 1814 when a royalist army from Peru defeated their forces and restored Spanish rule, but three years later Chile was freed, this time by an army from Argentina under command of San Martín who brought back O'Higgins to rule the country. However the southern part of Chile continued to be wracked by civil war till the fortified port of Valdívia was taken by a squadron of the Chilean navy. Even so it was not till 1826 that the island of Chiloé agreed to surrender and royalist resistance came to an end.

The dictatorship of Bernardo O'Higgins lasted until 1823 when the unpopularity of his style of rule and his social and economic programme resulted in his being replaced as director by the 'well-intentioned liberal' Ramón Freire. Freire however proved unable to provide an honest and stable government and his liberal experiment came to an end when in 1830 he was defeated by a coalition of conservative elements.[2] Such was Chile's political instability that, although Canning in 1824 sent a consul-general to its capital Santiago, it was not until 1839 that it finally received recognition of its independence by a British government.

The trade of Chile was thrown open to foreigners on 20 February 1811 and from that date on, with the exception of the period of restored royalist rule between 1815 and 1817, the small fishing village of Valparaiso grew to become an important port, the hub of international trade, but more especially British trade, on the western coast of South America. Captain Basil Hall, a naval officer in command of the frigate *Conway* (who had been sent by Admiral Hardy to protect British commercial interests at ports along the Pacific coast) visited Valparaiso in 1820. He described the port as 'filled with shipping, its customs-house wharfs piled high with goods, too numerous and bulky for the old warehouses [and] the road between the port and the capital . . . always crowded with convoys of mules, loaded with every kind of foreign manufacture'. Numerous ships were taking on board wine, corn and other country produce, but more especially precious metal, with which to pay for imported manufactures.[3]

Haigh, who had come to Chile via the Andes (and who has been mentioned in the previous chapter) noted how in 1818 prices had risen as a result of the rapid influx of foreigners that followed the patriot victory at Maypú, won by the army of San Martín. Once the English appeared prices always rose since, as Haigh observed, Englishmen never haggled (a characteristic they still display) and in consequence were always defrauded without being considered generous or gaining the respect of those they bought from. Haigh who had been sent to manage a cargo recently arrived at Valparaiso and to test 'the colour of the market' found difficulty in selling the goods, as there no longer existed in Chile rich Spanish merchants with capital – the recent war had seen to that – so he had to dispose of it in small packets. Part he sold in his first week there, but it took him all of a further twelve months in which to dispose of the remainder. His experience was not unique, and other vessels arriving that year found the same sort of market that Haigh had found.[4]

So many ships were now arriving from Britain and the United States that the Valparaiso market was glutted. As the author Peter Schmidtmeyer, whose moralizing book about his travels, written in a most inflated style, was published in 1824, observed of Valparaiso in

1820, the sale for British manufactures was strictly limited in a country like Chile, its spending power being far too small and also far too concentrated to allow the consumption of foreign goods in any significant quantity. Schmidtmeyer noted how English vessels sold what they could in Valparaiso and then continued to Peruvian ports to try to find buyers for the bulk of their cargo.[5] John Miers, an entrepreneur, who wrote a rather sour but most readable book about his experiences in Chile between 1819 and 1826, also remarked on the exiguity of the Chilean market for British goods and laid the blame for commercial losses on the lack of adequate market research. Goods were sent in small consignments by English merchant adventurers, and manufacturers unknown to each other, to agents resident in Chile, and it was these agents who reaped the profits and the venturers in England who lost their money.[6]

Valparaiso was an entrepôt for the trade of the South Pacific coast and not in itself a significant market. Charles Nugent, newly appointed as consul-general in Santiago sent home to Canning in 1826 a petition signed by ten British firms then established in Valparaiso, requesting the protection of a British warship, in view of the great volume of trade that was then being transacted in that port. Valparaiso, they contended, far exceeded all other ports on that side of the South American continent in the size and importance of its foreign trade and scarcely a vessel doubled the Horn without touching there for refreshments and orders.[7] It was clear that the British had come to dominate such trade as there was to be had in Chile. When Captain Beechey of the British navy, commissioned to explore the Northwest Passage, called at Talcahuana (Concepción's port) in October 1825, he was driven to remark that an Englishman could see with pride the inferior manufactures of his own country more highly prized than all the costly textiles of Spain or the gold and silver tissue stuffs, treasured and entailed in families even to the third and fourth generation. Even guitars had been replaced by pianofortes imported from England.[8]

Valparaiso in 1818 was described by Lieutenant William Bowers (a British ex-naval officer now trading on his own account) as a town having a population of somewhere around 8000 heads, made up largely of vagabonds, rogues and various adventurers.[9] John Miers, writing of the early 1820s, thought estimates of the town's population, such as that made by Bowers, had been much exaggerated, though Stevenson, in 1822, revisiting the place after twenty years, thought its population must be 15,000. Miers was sure that Valparaiso could not contain more than 6000 at most and certainly not more than 400 English, including the masters of foreign vessels, supercargoes and naval officers. Most of the people who were not sailors he described as being very low class. The place's atmosphere he found depraved and there were only six English families whom respectable people in Santiago were willing to associate with. The situation and lay-out of the town Miers considered most disappointing and ridiculed the absurdity of its title Valparaiso, 'The Vale of Paradise'. There were no fine trees, no rich foliage, no almonds grew in its *Almendral*, there were no buildings worthy of note, no inviting walks or rides, but only 'a few miserable houses' built irregularly on a steep hollow that rose above the shore to 1200 feet. There was no society, no public amusement, no theatre, no reading rooms, and nowhere to walk save up steep hills or along the narrow, dirty streets, choked by the clouds of dust and sand.[10]

Farquhar Mathison, a travelling Scotsman who had introductions to prominent merchants, saw Valparaiso in 1821 and confirms its general impression of squalor. What however seems to have impressed him most was the town's remarkable Englishness – 'but for [its] mean and dirty appearance . . . a stranger might almost fancy himself arrived at a British settlement'.[11] Maria Graham, that intelligent, perceptive but also slightly snobbish observer, widow of a British naval officer, who spent some time in both Brazil and Chile and saw Valparaiso in 1822, was also struck by its English character: 'English tailors, shoemakers, saddlers and inn-keepers hang out their signs in every street; and the preponderance of the English language over every other spoken in the chief streets would make one fancy Valparaiso a coast town in Britain.' The English society, however, was no more to her liking than it was to that of Miers. 'There is a sad proportion . . . here of trash,' she wrote, though she did concede that vulgarity, ignorance and coarseness often disguise a kind heart. The local English ladies reminded her of Mrs Elton in Jane Austen's novel *Emma* (a rich but distinctly ill-bred young person). It was mostly the wives of merchants' clerks who gave the society 'a very low tone'.[12]

It was however not English women but the prosperity of Valparaiso that impressed the sailor Stevenson, who had known it twenty years before. The bay, which formerly had stayed empty of shipping for more than half the year, now (in 1823/4) contained on an average fifty foreign vessels, no matter what the time of year. Stevenson who had spent many years in Chile, Peru and Ecuador and became Admiral

Cochrane's naval secretary, was enthusiastic in his description of the rise in general living standards that had taken place since 1803. Then the peasant 'if possessed of a dollar, would bore a hole through it and hang it to his rosary – the same peasant can now jingle his doubloons in his pocket'. Those who twenty years before could afford to wear only the coarsest clothing, that had been locally spun and woven, were now dressed in European linens, or European cotton and woollen clothes.[13] He did not, needless to add, reflect that the abundance of cheap English goods was ruining the local textile industry. A few years later (1829) the place was visited by the Reverend Charles Stewart, chaplain on board an American warship. 'A less appropriate name than Valparaiso . . . could scarce have been chosen for such a spot' was Stewart's considered comment on the site, but he had a better opinion of the town. By then it had, it seems, well-paved streets, many good houses with glazed windows, handsome shops well provided with goods. He thought the Chileans a handsome people and praised the quality of the horses, carts, waggons and oxen he saw on the roads. What he deplored naturally were the sights familiar in all sea-port towns: the prominence of grog-shops and drinking-dens, drunken sailors lying around and the presence of numerous prostitutes.[14]

Santiago, as opposed to Valparaiso, seems to have made a generally favourable impression on most of the British who visited it. Haigh in 1818 found it not as large as Buenos Aires but rather pleasanter to look at and its streets cleaner because of the channels of water that ran along their length. He discovered an abundance of social life and attended parties enlivened by the presence of visiting British naval officers who taught the Chileños the quadrille. The friars too, Haigh found, were very hospitable and he remarked on the welcome disappearance of the former religious prejudice – people no longer believed the story that every Protestant was born with a tail. He was able to visit several convents, no doubt hoping to catch a glimpse of beautiful young novices forced by their families and social convention to enter some religious order, but came away bitterly disappointed. Forty of the nuns seemed to have 'the appearance of wizened pineapples', the majority were no longer young and he did not see one on whose behalf he would willingly 'scale a wall or break a bolt'; and as for their choral singing in chapel, 'it was such wild and discordant screaming that it vibrated through every nerve'. What impressed him most in Santiago was the quality of the patriot troops – not, as people believed in Europe (fed by stories of British officers who had served for a time in Venezuela) a thoroughly wild and undisciplined lot, but well clothed and orderly. On parade days he saw regiments so well turned out that he thought they would not have disgraced a parade in Hyde Park or the Tuileries.[15]

Though the patriot troops in Santiago may have been models of discipline and decorum, the Anglican chaplain on board HMS *Cambridge*, the Reverend Hugh Silvin, also an author, had a rather different story to tell when his ship made a call at Talcahuana. After a parade at Concepción and a show of military manoeuvres, the Indian troops got very drunk and then began to fight each other, much to the alarm of the local citizens; while three of their officers, invited to dine in the wardroom of the *Cambridge*, complained of not being allowed to join the company in the captain's cabin and ended by committing the social gaffe of asking to be given some money.[16]

Richard Vowell, the Irish soldier of fortune who having served in Bolívar's army commanded marines in the Chilean navy, had a similar story to tell of indiscipline encountered on board the frigate *Lautaro*. In the ship's gunroom the creole officers, for the most part illiterate and ill-bred, crowded the tables when meals were served to the exclusion of the ship's officers and spent their time gambling, dicing and quarrelling. More seriously, their total lack of control over the troops under their command nearly caused the ship to blow up. As it was impossible for all the rations to be cooked on the galley fire at once, some of the troops, too impatient to wait, lit a fire on their own that ignited the planks and nearly reached the powder magazine. The alarm so caused resulted in the troops becoming almost ungovernable – some endeavoured to lower the boats that would have been swamped by the heavy seas, some tried to shout to other vessels that were too far off to hear their cries, and some, even the officers, made ready to jump overboard. Admittedly these troops were recent recruits, unwilling conscripts who were often jail-birds, vagabonds and the usual detritus with which contemporary armies were filled, but clearly the patriot army in Chile was not always the perfect picture of well-drilled soldiery depicted by Haigh.[17]

John Miers who first arrived in Santiago in 1819 was not as easily impressed by it as Haigh. He did admit that the streets were clean but contrasted them with what he termed 'the disgusting filthiness of the people' and their dirty habits in public places, by which he meant presumably their urinating and defecating. The buildings, apart from religious structures, he found dull and unimaginative; the mint, the largest of the public buildings, seemed to him ugly and badly proportioned, yet Chileños thought it magnificent – a reflection on their lack of education and aesthetic sensibility. 'A foreigner [he wrote] who visits South America, if he wish to keep on good terms with the natives, must forget all he has left behind him in Europe, and bring his taste to a level of that of the creoles.'[18] Unlike the testy John Miers, Basil Hall liked Santiago when he visited it in 1820. He thought its streets and houses neat in appearance and the people he met better educated and wealthier than in Valparaiso and more conversant with world affairs, their manners were more polished, they were better dressed, though they were equally kind and hospitable and showed an agreeable indulgence to those whose knowledge of Spanish was minimal.[19]

Schmidtmeyer also liked the city when he stayed at the only British hotel. By that time (1822) there were resident in Santiago 130 foreigners, of whom 100 were British nationals, though five years earlier Haigh had found only 11 British residents, the majority of whom understandably were merchants. Schmidtmeyer was favourably impressed by the public works undertaken linking the city with Valparaiso.[20] Head, however, in 1825, was much less willing to enthuse about the place – perhaps his hard riding across the Andes had left him feeling tired and short-tempered. Surprisingly, he thought the streets were dirty and generally he considered the town had only a very mean appearance, with most of its houses cracked by earthquakes. What seems however to have galled him most was the sight of so many Catholic clergy; the streets were crowded with what he termed 'lazy, indolent, bloated monks and priests' to whose dire influence he attributed the general ignorance and immorality, even though the state had enacted laws to remove the power of the Catholic church.[21]

Mathison, like the younger Haigh, enjoyed the society of Santiago, though agreeing with Miers that it was useless to look for taste, refinement, manners, conversation or any cultivation of the intellect. Most of the people were ignorant and social intercourse was confined to dancing, music and of course flirtation. No one ever read a book and few spoke a language other than Spanish.[22] Isaac Coffin, a young North American, who was interned in southern Chile (Concepción and the area round it) when his ship was seized by the royalists, confided to his diary that in more than six months he had never found a Spanish grammar or dictionary nor succeeded in discovering where he could locate one. He could swear there was not a Chileño in the province in whose library were to be found more than a dozen elementary works, books of devotion, collections of sermons or volumes on surgery and medicine. Chileños, he wrote, never travel, save those women who married Spanish officials, and their only contact with the outside world was with the crews of whaling ships from England or the United States, a contact that scarcely added much to intellectual advancement or knowledge.[23]

Schmidtmeyer records that there was in Santiago a college teaching 100 pupils drawn from the principal families, as well as a so-called university. The last housed the government printing-press as well as a public library though, if Mathison is to be believed, few if any availed themselves of it.[24] Miers certainly corroborates this. He tried to gain admission to the library, obtaining a special permit from O'Higgins, only to find that its door was locked and there was no one to open it. Miers mentions that Maria Graham had presented the library with a number of books on the fine arts and history but she never received an acknowledgement of them. Miers was also scathing about the college designed for the sons of the rich, where he found no useful knowledge being taught. Boys left the college at twelve or fourteen to train to become lawyers or priests or returned to the family hacienda 'to reassume the habits and ignorance of the *guasos* [peasants]'. Such indeed was the lack of education of most of the men holding senior office that the president of the senate boasted to Miers that he had not even opened a book over the space of the past thirty years. In this respect he was no different from every other high-placed official.[25]

There were Lancasterian schools in the capital and the government paid the cost of them, schools started by the worthy James Thomson, a Scottish Baptist, 'free lance evangelist' and unofficial correspondent of the British and Foreign Bible Society and the British and Foreign Schools Society. He was also the author of a book bearing the somewhat forbidding title of *Letters on the Moral and Religious State of South America* (published in 1827). Thomson was asked by O'Higgins's government to set up schools throughout the country and in Santiago, where he made a start, it put at his disposal a large room in the so-called university. By October 1821 he was running a school for 200 boys and was preparing to open another, the demand apparently being so great. O'Higgins showed a personal interest, visited the school every afternoon and in December 1821 allowed Thomson to institute a Schools Society with himself as patron and the first minister as president. Its object was to establish and inspect primary schools throughout the country and to print elementary texts for the children to read at home and in the school. The result was, according to Thomson, the establishment of three schools in Santiago, one in Valparaiso and one in Coquimbo, though after he left and went to Peru, as he did in 1822, and his deputy became a sick man, the schools apparently declined (writing in 1826, he was not sure they had not been abandoned). Yet even when the schools were functioning, the instruction they imparted was of course elementary (given the Lancasterian system of older pupils teaching the younger).[26] Schmidt-meyer was not impressed by the way the children repeated their lessons 'by bawling out as loud as their lungs will allow. The noise of the school is therefore stunning and heard at a great distance'.[27]

A principal reason for the schools' decline had been the opposition of the clergy to educational establishments inspired and directed by a Protestant. O'Higgins, in the battle for religious toleration, had been well in advance of most people in Chile. Thomson had, through O'Higgins's influence, been permitted to import New Testaments, and texts from these were frequently used in the newly-opened Lancasterian schools; but as O'Higgins told Maria Graham, he knew he was fighting an uphill battle. It had not been possible, he confided to Graham, to grant very much religious freedom without disturbing the public peace, and he was inclined to censure Protestants who pressed for further and more generous concessions, such as the right to build a chapel or have Protestant worship recognized. People, he continued, forgot how recently liberty of conscience and a private cemetery had been allowed to exist in Chile, and that it was only twelve years ago that the Inquisition held sway in the country. O'Higgins had encouraged the import of books, but Ramón Freire brought back clerical censorship and the veto on all imported books, until examined in Santiago by the agents of the Catholic bishop. This, Miers commented acidly, could hardly have affected most Chileños since they never read in any case, but he firmly believed that religious intolerance was worse in the Chile of 1826 than it was in any part of South America that he had ever visited. Graham was shocked by the Catholic observances she came across in southern America and in her journal makes reference to what she considered absurd superstitions 'naked in their ugliness [and] not glossed over with the pomp and elegance' she had encountered in Italy.[28]

Apart from Santiago and Valparaiso, the only other towns of size

were Concepción, with its port of Talcahuano, and Coquimbo in the
north of the country. Concepción, the capital of southern Chile, had
suffered the ravages of civil war in a way the other main towns had
not. Miers described it in 1819 as poverty-stricken and desolate. Its
population of 20,000 had been reduced to a mere 5000 and those of
the very lowest class, the more prosperous having long since fled. The
public buildings had all been destroyed, the principal houses were in
ruins, the streets filthy and evil-smelling. The trade of the place was
at a standstill and robbery and all kinds of crime were the main
occupation of the inhabitants. Six years later, when Talcahuana was
visited by Captain Beechey, it appeared to him 'much dilapidated',
dirty and in places overgrown with grass. However trade was beginning
to recover, there were several vessels in the port and Concepción was
coming to life after the appalling depredations it had suffered at the
hands of the brigand Benavides.[29]

As for the Chileños generally, those English who have recorded an
opinion appear to have found them likeable. Lieutenant Bowers
considered the Chileños 'a well-made, brave and lively race, with a
peculiar frankness and vivacity of manner'.[30] Miers, perhaps predict-
ably, was more restrained in his admiration. Willing to concede that
the Chileños had fewer vices than other creoles, that they were patient
in the face of privation and endured hardship with stoicism, he un-
generously likened their passivity to that of the llama, camel or alpaca.
In business he deplored their lack of honesty, their lack of regard for
punctuality when it came to paying for goods received and their bland
disregard for verbal commitments. He thought they resembled the
Chinese in their cunning, egotism and propensity for thieving and as
an example of the last cited the case of one Chileña, of the utmost
respectability, who had stooped to stealing a diamond brooch from
Admiral Cochrane's wife at a ball. Only when the lady confessed her
sin and was told by her confessor to make restitution did Lady
Cochrane recover her brooch. Herman Allen, the United States
minister to Chile, shared the gloomy view expressed by Miers about
the character of the Chileños. Writing in February 1825, when he had
then been ten months in the country, he described them as being
'unaccustomed to obligations of honour or contract, or to any constitutional, moral or legal restraint . . . skilled in all the arts of deception,
and are literally the avengers of their own wrongs'. They were also
very opinionated and he found it difficult to give them advice.[31]

Probably they resented his interference and their Spanish pride made them unsusceptible to the counselling of a foreigner.

Charles Darwin, in his *Voyage of the Beagle*, drew an interesting comparison between the *guaso* that he met in Chile and the gaucho of the La Plata pampas. He thought the former more civilized but, in acquiring a more polished veneer, the *guaso* lost much of his individuality. In Chile there was an aristocracy of wealth and gradations of rank were much more marked than he had found in the provinces of La Plata. There was none of the friendly hospitality he had experienced among the gauchos – in Chile everything had to be paid for and even the rich were willing to accept an offer of a mere two or three shillings in return for a meal or a bed for the night. The gaucho was always a gentleman, even if willing to cut your throat, but the *guaso*, though more respectable, was nothing but an ordinary, vulgar fellow. The *guaso* even worked in the fields, while the gaucho always seemed part of his horse and was never content to be parted from it.[32]

As for the Araucanian Indians who lived south of Concepción and had never been subdued by the armies of Spain, Stevenson in his *Narrative* expressed an interest in their condition and their relations with the patriot rulers once the era of independence dawned, having himself spent some time among them as a young man at the start of the century. Remarking on their abstention from pork-eating, he recounts that this was 'a prejudice that has supplied some fanatical priests with a reason for considering [them] of Jewish extraction'. The Indians yielded some proselytes to Spanish missionaries in their territories, since few demands were made on the converts in the shape of religious conformity, but when Valdívia fell to the patriots, the Indians accused the missionaries of being the enemies of independence and proceeded to massacre many of them. Even so, most Araucanians took sides with the Spanish against the creoles, presumably because the latter made no attempt to conciliate them, even though these Araucanians despised the Spanish for being defeated.[33]

As for the patriot leaders of Chile, British observers were generally agreed that O'Higgins was an honest man, though weak. Mathison recorded in 1821 that the general opinion in Santiago was that O'Higgins was well-intentioned but not an effective ruler of the state. Stevenson, who actually met him, described him as brave and resolute in carrying out a decision once made, but slow to come to that decision. In endeavouring to make up his mind, he seemed always to think that the best advice was that which he had been offered last – as a result he fell under the sway of the other members of the ruling junta. A kindly man, he seemed (Stevenson thought) 'more at home at his evening tertullias than under the canopy of the supreme dictatorship'. Richard Cleveland, the New England sea captain and trader on the Pacific coast who met O'Higgins in 1818, thought his appearance plain and simple, as befitted a good republican, and nearer to that of an honest farmer than to a gentleman of refinement. Proctor saw him later in Valparaiso living under a sort of house arrest, after Freire had assumed the supreme directorship. He described him as being short and fat, with a face that reminded him of Oliver Cromwell, but considered that, though brave and a competent general, he (O'Higgins) had 'a character too open and undesigning for these times of intrigue and revolution'. Admiral Cochrane subscribed to this view – O'Higgins he thought was generous and honest but had, unfortunately, surrendered power to what Cochrane called 'an unscrupulous clique'.[34]

San Martín who so much impressed Commodore Bowles when the two met in 1818 – 'the only man in whose integrity and disinterestedness reliance may be placed' – left a different impression on the shrewd Maria Graham who found him 'hateful though plausible'. She thought him polite and graceful in his movements, with an impressive personality (he dominated the conversation), but his views she deemed 'narrow, and I think, selfish'. He seemed to her to have talent without genius, no learning and little general knowledge, very pleasant to spend half an hour with but lacking compassion and genuine candour, so forbidding intimacy, still less friendship.[35]

The other prominent patriot in Chile about whom strong views were expressed was Zenteno, minister of war and marine as well as governor of Valparaiso. Cochrane described him as his sworn enemy and he, undoubtedly, as will be shown later, made life difficult for the admiral. In referring to him in his *Narrative*, Cochrane thought it sufficient to use the words of Maria Graham to sum him up: 'Like San Martín he dignifies scepticism in religion, laxity of morals and coldness of heart, if not cruelty, with the name of philosophy; and while he could show creditable sensibility for the fate of a worm, would think the death or torture of a political opponent matter for congratulation.'[36]

About the nature of the patriot government, the British were unanimous in finding it deplorable. Lieutenant Bowers, after his experiences in the five years following the victory of Maypó, deplored the caucus of corruption and venality that stood in the way of economic improvement. Chile to his mind had great advantages in its fine climate, fertile soil and a coastline eminently suited to trade – 'under a wise government it cannot but thrive'. If only it could clean the Augean stables of Customs and Excise, the country would have sufficient revenue and the people would be relieved of taxes.[37] Miers, writing of the same period, despaired of the Chilean government ever conducting its finances properly. Under Freire it seemed things had got worse, with a small clique of powerful men defrauding the public and plundering its revenue. Yet men were prepared to put up with Freire for fear of meeting something worse. San Martín, people told Miers, had started to take away from them, the ministry of O'Higgins had then fleeced them and the present administration had stripped them – any other government would do the same.[38] When Cochrane in 1823 declined Freire's offer to reemploy him as commander-in-chief of the Chilean navy, Cochrane wrote: 'I admire the middle and lower classes in Chili [sic] but I have ever found the Senate, the Ministers and the Convention, actuated by the narrowest policy, which led them to adopt the worst measures.' These views were not unique to the British. Herman Allen, the United States minister, wrote to the US secretary of state that he despaired of the Chilean government as he found it in February 1825: 'without money, credit or capacity, and the constitutional apathy, so peculiar to all classes of people, seems rather to incline them to indolence and sleep, than to any exertion, either of body or mind, particularly the latter;' though to this he added a pious hope that time and experience would produce a remedy.[39]

John Miers, wealthy entrepreneur, who was given the chance, as he recounts in his *Travels*, to set up copper mines in Chile, found the experience utterly frustrating, due to the way the government behaved to him and the tortuousness of the judicial process. He describes his enterprise as being one 'of considerable magnitude' and one in which he and a friend had invested considerable sums of money. The inducements to do so had been 'powerful and alluring', for he was assured the finest copper was to be found in abundance in Chile where it could be bought for half the price it was realizing in English markets. Coal was available for almost nothing, labour cost half what it did in England and demand for sheet copper locally, particularly by manufacturers of sugar was (Miers was told) considerable. Two deputies from Chile in London then enlarged on the possibilities such an undertaking opened up and Miers was assured by the Chilean ambassador of help and protection from the Chilean government. As a result, in 1818, Miers had dispatched to Valparaiso 100 tons of machinery and he himself followed shortly in another boat, together with his pregnant wife, 70 further tons of machinery, tools, baggage, skilled workmen, engineers, millwrights and metal refiners. On arrival he was officially welcomed, first by San Martín and then by O'Higgins, and all seemed set for a successful undertaking. Yet five years later Miers decided it was useless to continue to work in Chile, left the country and went to Buenos Aires (where he was able to set up a mint), having lost the whole of his investment of $40,000 in machinery and tools and $40,000 in building factories. His failure he attributed entirely to the obstruction of government ministers and to powerful individuals who had influence in high places.

Having chosen Concon, near Valparaiso, as the site for building his factory because there was water available there, no danger from marauding Indians and the sea close by on which he hoped to be able to transport the heavy machinery, he had already been assured that his title to the land was secure and therefore, without further delay, set about the task of building his factory. Only after he had constructed a mole, roads, workshops, warehouses, and dwellings for the workpeople and had begun hydraulic works, was he informed that his title was questioned and that he must start an expensive lawsuit. The lawsuit lasted for two years, during which time he put up a flour mill (the first of its kind in South America) and suspended work on his copper refinery. Meanwhile the minister for war interposed in the litigation, supposedly as a friendly mediator but in fact to ruin Miers's case. The reason for this, Miers surmised, was because Miers was a foreigner and the friend of Lord Cochrane, whom the minister detested.

When eventually a verdict was pronounced, it seemed to Miers to be totally absurd, for though it established his right to the land, it did not do so to the machinery on it. An appeal from Miers to O'Higgins resulted in the latter giving an order that the judges ought to revise their verdict; even so, it needed another two years, during which an earthquake caused further delays, to clear up the legal formalities. Miers by that time had reached the conclusion that the wisest course was to cut his losses and abandon his enterprise altogether.[40]

In the account he gives in his *Travels* of his experiences in Chile, there are further examples of the way the Chilean government treated foreigners who were trying to set up factories. There was the case of Henderson and Wooster, one English, the other North American, who had invested $60,000 in a sperm-oil factory at Coquimbo, after receiving government assurances that they would be helped in their enterprise, that they would not have to pay import duties on materials required for their factory nor export duties on the oil they produced. When, however, in 1820 the government found it had not sufficient watercasks to supply its forces being sent to liberate Peru, it ordered the seizure of all the barrels and barrel staves from the sperm-oil factory. When Henderson and Wooster, having lost their casks, sank a reservoir to store the oil blubber, they were stopped by an order from the government on the grounds that the location would endanger public health, even though this reservoir was sited several miles from the town of Coquimbo. The whole speculation was therefore abandoned and Henderson and Wooster lost a lot of money.

Miers also cites the case of an Englishman whom he describes as very intelligent, with scientific and mechanical knowledge, who tried to set up a brewery in Chile. The government had encouraged the project, but as soon as the beer was put up for sale, it decreed that the brew was foreign spirits and so liable to excise duty. Though the rate of tax was not exorbitant, it seemed likely it would soon be raised and the English brewer therefore decided, probably wisely, to abandon the project. The only successful foreign manufacturer whom Miers ever discovered in Chile was a German in Santiago who used machinery to make hemp bags.

Miers also drew attention to the lack of security for private property in Chile, citing the case of Admiral Cochrane who was able to purchase an estate at Quintero. This purchase led the government to suspect that he wanted the land for smuggling and, without any evidence to support this, it claimed the property in the name of the state, having reserved the right to preempt any prospective purchaser if the land were needed for public services. Cochrane was eventually successful in getting the government order rescinded, but the Chilean law remained unchanged and Miers advised no Englishman to try to buy real estate in Chile.[41]

So obsessed was the Chilean government (as its royalist predecessor had been) with the possibilities for smuggling and the danger this posed to the national revenue, that it failed to encourage the coastal trade, though, given the mountainous nature of Chile, transport by sea was by far the cheapest and most practical way of conveying goods. Miers pointed out that along a coastline stretching for over 1000 miles, with innumerable little bays and inlets, it was absurd for the government to license only seven ports from which a vessel was permitted to sail. Cochrane apparently had done his best to have this irrational system changed, but 'like every other useful suggestion, it was received with a professed acquiescence in its utility, but with a silent resolve to afford no relaxation in the old established principles of the Spaniards'. Miers suffered personally from this restriction, since he had to see all his machinery landed at the port of Valparaiso, though his factory was on the coast and only ten miles by sea from Valparaiso. O'Higgins had issued Miers with permits to land his machinery near Concon, but once the director had fallen from power the difficulties multiplied and Miers was forced to witness consignments stranded on the Valparaiso docks and left to rust there for as much as two years. Again the obsession with smuggling also inhibited the development of any prosperous fishing industry. Though, as Miers points out, good fishing grounds existed 50 miles from the coast, the fishermen were not encouraged to use them and laws restricted the use of coast land. As a result the fishermen became lazy and profligate and preferred to live by stealing cattle instead of pursuing their true avocation.[42]

As to mining gold, silver and copper, British experiences were not encouraging. Captain Basil Hall in 1821 visited the northern part of Chile, partly in order to enquire into the commercial resources of the coast. He made an inspection of several mines, saw smelting 'in the rude manner of the country', went down silver mines near Copiapó and remarked on the total lack of machinery and the great cost (he thought) of working such mines, some at depths of nearly 300 feet. Even so, he wrote optimistically about the prospects for British investors, there being 'no saying what British capital and enterprise, aided by machinery, may effect'.[43] The adventures however of Francis Bond Head in inspecting and evaluating the chances of profitable mining in Chile were enough to deter any future prospector.

On arriving in Chile from the Plata provinces Head discovered his company's agent was a trickster who refused to give him a list of the names and the descriptions of those mines in respect of which his company had obtained concessions. The agent told Head that snow and bandits made a visit to the mines impossible but Head was not easily put off. He first visited the gold mine at Caren, 160 miles north of Santiago, described by the agent in glowing terms, only to find that all the ore the agent had extracted 'would scarcely fill a wheelbarrow' and, when assayed, yielded no gold at all. The rest of the lode, when it was assayed, yielded some gold but of very poor quality. The sheer physical difficulties Head had encountered in getting to the site are graphically described in his *Rough Notes*. The path he ascended was so steep that he was in constant apprehension of falling backwards over the tail of his mule. Finally he was told they could ride no further, so they dismounted and scrambled upwards till they reached a hut on the edge of a precipice. It then became clear that the mine in question had not been worked for 100 years.

Head went on to inspect a silver mine at a site near a place called San Pedro Nolasco, 75 miles north-west of Santiago. It had been described to him by the company's agent as being 'the best silver mine in the country', worth at the least $5000 and capable of employing up to 2000 miners. The journey to the mine was even more arduous than the one Head had made to the Caren mine, the ascent the steepest he had made in the Andes and for five hours he had to hold on to the ears or neck of his mule to stay seated. The mine he found was situated on one of the highest peaks of the Andes and all that was visible above ground was a little hut around which were gathered two or three worn-looking and exhausted miners. Though it was midsummer the scene was stark and Head could hardly contemplate what it was like in the depth of winter, with the snow 120 feet deep. Though the mine was inaccessible for seven out of twelve months in the year, the miners lived there all the year round and many had died in the violent storms – numerous crosses by the wayside bore silent testimony to their fate.

In order to penetrate into the mine, Head had to climb down and up notched sticks which were all that served the miners as ladders, and found the activity so tiring he could not imagine what the miners felt when having to carry a heavy load. He tried to lift a near-normal load and could scarcely walk with it on the flat and several of the Cornish miners who accompanied him tried to do the same but found the task as daunting as he had. The bottom of the mine was filled with water. When Head later saw the owner of the mine, she told him the agent had only got a lease on it for a five year period, after which the lease must be renegotiated; and as to paying for the lease, the agent, she said, had given her nothing.

Nearer Santiago and more accessible was a silver mine at Aconagua, again glowingly described by the agent, who wanted to arrange for its sale. Head, inspecting it, discovered it consisted of a solitary hole eight fathoms deep whose lode contained no silver at all. He also inspected a tiny copper mine for which the agent asked $5000. It was 600 miles north of Santiago, situated in a remote position only approachable on hands and knees. The mineral deposit proved of little value. One further mine containing gold was also described by the company's agent as being extremely profitable, this time at El Bronce de Pitorca. What the agent failed to disclose to Head was that an earthquake, three years before, had completely destroyed the establishment and in consequence the mine in question could not be worked nor even inspected. The agent had for his services drawn on the company for $27,000, yet it was clear he had never once visited one of the mines he was sponsoring.

Head, perhaps understandably, declined the offer to visit more mines. He had, as he wrote in his report, travelled for five weeks, almost day and night, often under the most adverse conditions, and his party was exhausted, disappointed and incapable of making any further exertion. It was obvious to him that mining in Chile would never repay the expense involved. Indeed he had seen two other companies, despite the protection of ministers, fail in the end to show a profit; hence his return to Buenos Aires and decision to wind up the mining project.[44]

Captain Andrews who visited Chile in 1826, with a view to making a purchase of mines, was rather more optimistic than Head, though like Head he encountered an agent who was thoroughly dishonest and told him lies. He visited the Coquimbo area, which he thought the most thriving region in the country, wanted to buy the lease of a copper mine, though his colleague refused to sign the contract for as long a term as twenty years; built a lime kiln and laid the foundations of the first British smelting furnace in Chile. But Andrews came to the conclusion that the only way to profit by mining, at any rate in this area of Chile, was to combine it with agriculture or with extensive breeding of cattle. This was what the Spanish had always done, owning and farming a tract of land in the vicinity of their mines.[45]

John Miers had some scathing comments to make on the foolishness of British people who invested their money in Chilean mines. Though (he wrote) it was well known in London that mining in Chile on any large scale was not a practical proposition, mining companies had still been formed: the Chilean Mining Company, the Anglo-Chilean Mining Association, the Chilean and Peruvian Mining Association, all with a nominal capital of one million or one and a half million pounds and fraudulent prospectuses, backed by great names, held out the

prospect of mining gold, silver, tin, copper and lead. Many of the
mining districts were described in the prospectuses as being located
near the coast, enjoying an abundance of cheap labour as well as of
water, wood and coal (in the south). The numerous rivers of the
country, it was alleged, could be used to transport tools, machinery
and eventually the precious ore. Copper ore, they made out, was
plentiful, often only just below the surface, and the coal for smelting
was virtually inexhaustible and could be mined at trifling expense.
The reality, Miers wrote, was very different. If a mining district meant
extensive beds that could be worked on a massive scale, 'there is not
one mining district of gold and silver in all Chile'. Copper could only
be found in the north, at Coquimbo and Copiapó, and the insignificant
establishments there could scarcely be called a mining district. In any
case in that area there was not a single navigable stream, nor coal nor
fuel of any kind, save what could be used by the smallest concern. He
saw no chance of the manufacture of copper there being much
increased. Any attempt to mine by a foreigner would so drive up
wages as to wipe out the profit; and even if sufficient labour were
found, the cost of supervision, tools and buildings and transporting
coal from Concepción would in themselves be prohibitive. If mineral
wealth had existed in these places, Spain would have mined it long
ago, preferring the mild climate and rich soil of Chile to the high,
bleak and inhospitable mountains to be found in Bolivia and Peru.
'The fact is that no single great mine has ever been known [to exist]
in Chile.'[46]

All this makes strange reading today, when the state of Chile has
become the world's largest producer of copper, and mineral ores
(most of which is copper) and responsible for the production of one
half of Chile's total export revenue. Miers was unable to foresee how
modern technical improvements would make possible extensive
mining, nor was he to know that in 1832 a huge silver mountain would
be discovered at Chanarcillo, south of Copiapó. Miers's comments
are therefore illuminating only because they explain the degree of
disillusion felt by Britons, active and industrious like himself, when
faced with the unfamiliar conditions of investment in this Latin
American country.

Another figure, better known than Miers, who left Chile an
embittered man was Thomas Cochrane, commanding admiral of the
newly created Chilean navy. Cochrane had served as an officer in the
British navy until 1814, though by 1810 it was clear that he had

forfeited any chance of further promotion by making enemies of too
many admirals. 'He was [a modern historian has written] a seaman
not far inferior to Nelson in skill, in insight and dash; but his qualities
as a commander were marred by an impracticable violence of temper
and an intrusion of personal aims which produced constant quarrels
and undignified recriminations.' His unfortunate involvement in a
stock exchange fraud earned him a year's imprisonment, his expulsion
from the House of Commons, of which he had been for eight years a
member, and from the order of Knights of the Bath. Re-elected as
member for Westminster, a genuinely democratic constituency in a
sea of pocket and rotten boroughs, he spent his time, once out of
prison, attacking Lord Liverpool's government and residing in France
in comparative poverty. Then in 1817 he received the offer to come
to Chile to organize, train and command the Chilean squadron that
had only recently been formed.[47] Cochrane, in the words of Donald
Worcester, was to bring to the nascent navy of Chile 'a knowledge of
maritime law and custom, a talent for organization and discipline, and
a prestige which itself was an exceptionally valuable asset'. At that
time Chile's situation as a new republic seemed fairly desperate.
Spanish warships were blockading Valparaiso, and Madrid was making
strenuous efforts to reinforce its Pacific fleet, while the Chilean navy
opposed to it was untrained, unorganized and lacking equipment. It
consisted only of seven vessels including a former Spanish frigate (the
O'Higgins armed with fifty guns), two former East India vessels (the
San Martín and the Lautaro, armed with fifty-six and forty-four guns);
a brigantine bought from the British navy (the Hecate of eighteen guns,
now renamed the Galvarino) and three other sloops (the Chacabuco,
the Araucano and the Pueyrredón). The squadron, which suffered from
lack of funds, personal rivalries among its officers, lack of crews, lack
of standard rules of service and of signalling and any coherent plan of
battle, was under the command of the Chilean admiral Manuel Blanco
Encañada, a former Spanish artillery officer who had served as
midshipman in the Spanish navy and who very generously gave up his
post when Cochrane arrived in 1818. Cochrane, accompanied by his
wife and two children, was personally welcomed by O'Higgins and the
feastings and celebrations that followed went on for so long and were
so overwhelming that Cochrane had in the end to protest he had come
to work, not make holiday.[48]

Many of the officers of the Chilean squadron were men who had
served in the British navy. Maria Graham met a number of them and

took an instant liking to them. Captain Crosbie, Cochrane's flag-captain, she described as 'a pleasant gentlemanlike Irishman' whom she thought to be brave and intelligent, and Captain Cobbett who was the nephew of the more famous William Cobbett and had, she thought, 'a great deal of the hard-headedness of his uncle', was polite, intelligent and communicative.[49] By 1821 the Chilean navy was employing eleven British officers, ten of whom held command of a ship. The orders were given in the English language, since the officers could speak no Spanish, and the uniform worn was very similar to that which was worn in the British navy.

Commodore Bowles initially voiced his deepest suspicions of Cochrane's motives, believing him intent on plunder and piracy, and expressed himself anxious to leave Valparaiso to avoid the danger of quarrelling with him. Bowles was also afraid that Cochrane's intention to blockade the Peruvian port of Callao would disrupt British trade very seriously. These fears were however laid to rest after Cochrane had had an interview with the senior British naval officer, then stationed in Peruvian waters. Bowles was able to tell the Admiralty that Cochrane was willing to work with the British and anxious to emphasize that he still considered himself to be loyally English (he was of course not English but Scots) and that England's commercial interests were ones that were still extremely dear to him. He also promised that he would hand over any deserters from the British navy or from any British merchant ships who tried to enlist in the Chilean squadron.[50]

Farquhar Mathison in 1821 met some of the mercenaries at Santiago, most of whom were serving in the Chilean navy. According to him, the Englishmen he talked to all expressed unqualified regret at having left home for service in Chile; their health they said had suffered and their hopes were unfulfilled – hopes presumably of plentiful prize-money. Some praised Cochrane but others abused him.[51]

The great achievement of Cochrane's squadron off the coast of Chile had been the capture in 1820 of Valdívia, the royalists' principal depot in the south. An astonishingly bold assault with inferior numbers on the fifteen forts and batteries that commanded the harbour of Valdívia, at the point of the bayonet and at night, had resulted in the surrender of the town with the loss of only seven men killed together with a further nine wounded. Huge quantities of military stores were captured, including 1000 hundredweight of powder, 10,000 cannon, shot, 17,000 cartridges, many small arms and 128 guns. The surrender of the place to the patriots was of immense importance to their cause – Chile no longer needed to keep a naval and military force in the south, as a check on the Spanish and the hostile Indians, and its hands were now free to assist Peru. But the news of Cochrane's dramatic success had a mixed reception in government quarters. O'Higgins was delighted but ministers were not, their noses being sadly put out of joint by the fact that Cochrane had acted without orders. The congress decided to vote him their thanks and an estate near Concepción (an offer he refused to accept) but as to prize-money or reward in cash, these Cochrane discovered were not forthcoming. The government said, according to Stevenson then acting as Cochrane's secretary, that it could not understand how prize-money could possibly be due to a naval expedition for services rendered on shore, not at sea. It ordered the Spanish royalist ship, taken by Cochrane at Valdívia and carrying many valuable warstores, to be unloaded at Valparaiso arsenal, refusing to compensate the captors for its value, on the grounds that the ship was state property.[52]

Little wonder that the English mercenaries, interviewed by Mathison in 1821, were discontented with their lot, though it was not just prize money but normal pay that was unfortunately unforthcoming. Cochrane had the greatest difficulty in getting the government to pay his crews and then only as a result of the intervention of San Martín. Cochrane became exasperated not only by the lack of pecuniary reward for his undoubtedly valuable services but also by the suspicious way he was treated by Chilean ministers, more particularly the minister for war, Zenteno. He became furious when he found that his officers (Chilean, not European) were encouraged to disobey his orders in regard to not shooting prisoners of war whose safety he had personally assured. Worse still, the officers in question were not disciplined but actually promoted. Twice Cochrane offered his resignation but each time was persuaded by O'Higgins to withdraw it. He believed that ministers suspected him of trying to set himself up as a ruler, backed by popular support, because he had accepted an estate at Rio Clara and had bought another at Herradura. This is ironic since Cochrane refused to get mixed up in local politics and would have nothing to do with the attempt of Ramón Freire to displace O'Higgins. What finally decided him to throw in his hand was the discovery that orders were being given to ships in his squadron without his being first consulted, and on receiving an offer from Brazil to take command of that country's navy, he resigned and left Chile never to return.

When in April 1823 (two months after his resignation) the new administration of Freire asked Cochrane to come back to Chile in order to resume command of the squadron (Chile once more being threatened by the Spanish), he replied that it was impossible, in view of the treatment he had received. To organize crews, to navigate ships destitute of sails, cordage, stores and provisions, to secure them in port without anchors and cables was, Cochrane wrote, difficult enough, but to have to live among officers and men who were discontented and mutinous because they had not received arrears of pay and because of suffering various other privations and then, to crown all, to be accused of fraud (following an incident in Peru that will be recounted in another chapter) was more than any man could endure; this without the enmity of the governor of Valparaiso and of San Martín, with whom Cochrane had quarrelled in Peru.[53]

Cochrane, as he shows in his *Narrative*, remained very bitter about the treatment meted out to him by the governments of both Chile and Peru. The only reward he had received for his services was an estate that was confiscated when he left Chile in 1823. Once back in England, he became involved in a series of expensive legal actions brought by the owners of neutral ships he had seized on behalf of the Chilean government. He was forced to sell his property in Britain to cover the costs of the litigation amounting to £25,000, which was double the amount he had received in pay while in command of the Chilean navy. Thirty years later the Chilean government did pay Cochrane £6000 (a sum he described as 'absurdly inadequate') but only after pressure from Palmerston and the British minister in Santiago.[54] Cochrane thus joined the ranks of those who were soured by their experiences in the new republics of South America.

If it is asked why he was not prosecuted under the Foreign Enlistment Act that became law in 1819 when he finally returned to England, the reply Cochrane gave was that he had accepted his initial foreign commission from Chile before the act had come into force. The Attorney General accepted this plea for the act was specifically non-retrospective, but in any case the British government must have decided it was inadvisable to prosecute a man who would without doubt have turned his trial into a show one, and would have appealed to the British public to exonerate him for his services in having thrown open to British trade what he described as 'the largest field of enterprise of modern times'.[55]

The other mercenary officers who have left accounts of their activities in the service of the Chilean government wrote without any of the bitterness that informs and deforms Admiral Cochrane's *Narrative*. Thomas Sutcliffe, who in 1841 published *Sixteen Years in Chile and Peru*, was clearly more interested in fighting and adventure than in receiving a monetary reward. He had served first in 1817 as an officer in the Colombian army and was taken prisoner by the Spaniards. Released in 1821, he went in the following year to Chile, hoping to serve under Admiral Cochrane, but found Cochrane had already resigned. Given a commission by Bernardo O'Higgins in the army sent to free Peru, he later returned and was given command of a squadron of *Granaderos Lanceros*. After that he was posted south and took part in the campaign being waged against the brigands round Concepción. As a fairly experienced campaigner (he had been awarded the Waterloo medal), he found that fighting in South America was more exacting than in the Peninsula or in the blood-sodden plains of Flanders, quite apart from knowing that, if captured, he could expect no quarter to be shown him. Later he obtained a staff appointment first as aide to General Borgoño and then as adjutant to the chief-of-staff; after that he became chief instructor to the Chilean national militia and was thankful that his duties in Santiago spared him the risks involved in the fighting between the rival patriot groups (two English captains in the service of Freire had both been murdered in cold blood). On the access to power of General Prieto, Sutcliffe resigned his army commission and found it prudent to leave Santiago, such was the outcry against all foreigners. Sheltered by friends in the countryside, he was some years later able to emerge and ended up by holding the appointment of the governor of San Fernandez.[56]

Richard Vowell was another mercenary (the probable author of *Campaigns and Cruises*) who seems to have found the life of adventure offered in Chile a reward in itself. Having served with distinction in the army of Bolívar in Venezuela, Colombia and Ecuador, he obtained a post as marine officer in Cochrane's squadron when it lay off Guayaquil. He later served under General Freire and took part in the assault on Chiloé. His experiences on board the *Lautaro* have been described earlier in this chapter. He returned to Europe in 1829 on an extended leave of absence, without apparently bearing any grudge against the Chilean administration, though he did admit he found it difficult to discover to whom to apply for leave among the two or three rival contenders for the control of the government.[57]

The other and better known mercenary officer who served in both Chile and Peru with great distinction was William Miller, whose *Memoirs* were published by his brother John. Miller had been an artillery officer in the army of Wellington in the Peninsula and he later served in North America in the war against the United States. In search of adventure after the peace, he chose Buenos Aires not Venezuela, the latter being in his opinion 'already overrun with adventurers'. Given a commission as a captain, he set off across the pampas, crossed the Andes and joined the army of San Martín at Valparaiso. There, with a company of infantry, he was put on board the patriot frigate *Lautaro*, a ship commanded by a Captain O'Brien and officered almost entirely by Englishmen. Most of the crew were Chileños who had never been to sea in their lives, the Europeans in the crew were drunk, having just received their bounty money, and hardly one of the officers could utter a word in the Spanish language. Nevertheless the ship succeeded within ten hours of weighing anchor in driving off a Spanish frigate and brig engaged in trying to blockade Valparaiso. Promoted to major and given command of all troops on board four of the ships that made up part of the Chilean squadron, he was soon engaged in a naval action to intercept a royalist convoy bringing troops from Europe to subdue the rebellion. Taken prisoner and then released, he soon returned to Santiago to witness the arrival there of Admiral Cochrane. Miller recounts how at a dinner given by Cochrane on St Andrew's Day, in return for a banquet he had enjoyed given by the governor of Valparaiso, Cochrane presided at the banqueting table in the full regalia of a Scottish chieftain, he being the head of the clan Dundonald, and doubtless suitably impressed his guests.

Miller was then put in command of all the marines on Cochrane's ships and played a crucial part in the capture by Cochrane's squadron of Valdívia. Badly wounded in an assult on Chiloé, he went on to serve with distinction in the final campaign to free Peru. Miller was a dedicated soldier who made South America his home and no evidence of recrimination against his South American masters is to be found in the book of his memoirs.[58]

Whatever the views of the disillusioned men who wrote and had published their accounts of their dealings with the Chilean government, one thing emerges from the various recollections – the

admiration felt by Chileños for everything associated with England
and fulsome compliments were constantly paid to English politicians,
more especially Canning. Richard Vowell recounts how he found the
people of Santiago most Anglophile, always speaking with the greatest
respect and gratitude of 'el gran Canning'. The more educated men
in Chile were full of praise for the English constitution, British civic
virtues and the British press. When the chaplain of the battleship
Cambridge first met the bishop of Santiago, the latter pronounced with
great emphasis, 'I'm a great friend of the English', and when Maria
Graham paid a social visit to the governor's wife in Valparaiso, she
found not only an English carpet, an English grate and even English
coal, but 'even a little affectation' in the governor's great admiration
for things English.[59]

58

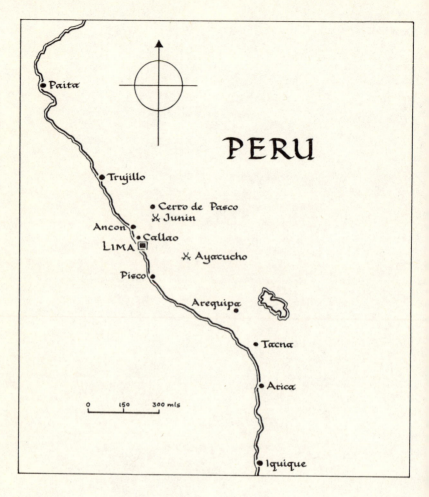

3 • Peru and Bolivia

Peru was the one area in Spanish South America that Spain continued to control effectively until the last months of 1820. It contained many discontented creoles but opposition did not become manifest until San Martín landed at Pisco in September with the army of liberation from Chile. Then the coastal cities in the north of the country declared in favour of independence, though Lima itself remained staunchly loyalist. San Martín refrained from assaulting the capital, hoping for a negotiated peace, and only in July 1821, when the Spanish army withdrew from the city did the patriot forces enter it. The independence of Peru was proclaimed on 28 July of that year and San Martín, without political rival, was proclaimed 'Protector' or temporary ruler.

The situation in Lima now, with its population of 50,000, part military part civilian, was not an enviable one. The royalists held the fertile uplands and the problem of feeding the city was serious. Drastic measures had to be adopted to cope with the economic crisis and these included compulsory levies and the brutal expulsion of all Spaniards unwilling to work with the new regime and the seizure of their property. San Martín's rule did not prove popular with the wealthier citizens of Lima, with the clergy or the landowners, and he left Peru to its own devices in January 1823, after having a famous interview with the newly arrived Simón Bolívar. His place was taken by Riva Agüero, a Peruvian of noble birth, but the latter proved unable to end the war and was finally removed from office. Twice the Spanish reoccupied Lima, once in 1823 between mid June and mid July, and again in 1824, after a mutiny of the garrison of Callao, when they stayed in occupation of the capital until the August of that year.

Meanwhile Bolívar, who had arrived with a liberating army from Gran Colombia, was given dictatorial powers in place of the deposed Riva Agüero. Bolívar's victory at Junín in August 1824 caused the

Spanish to evacuate Lima and the last organized royalist force surrendered to Sucre the following December, after losing the battle of Ayacucho, though the Spanish garrison in Callao held out until January 1826. Upper Peru, that had formerly been part of the viceroyalty of La Plata, saw the defeat of the royalist force there in April 1825. It declared itself independent that August, elected Sucre its first president and gave itself the name of Bolivia, in honour of the liberator Simón Bolívar.[1]

The liberator left Peru in September 1826 to return to Gran Colombia and during the course of the next ten years anarchy and confusion reigned in Peru – by 1836 Peru had experienced six constitutions and no less than eight presidents. Understandably the country continued in great financial difficulty. Loans had been negotiated with English firms in 1822 and 1824, the money raised being largely employed in paying the army of liberation, but by 1826 they were no longer serviced.[2] It is scarcely therefore to be wondered at that the British who came to Peru at this period had a rather discouraging tale to tell.

Basil Hall visited Callao and Lima in the spring of 1821, both still held by the royalists, though San Martín's army was now at Huasco and Callao was blockaded by Cochrane's squadron. At Callao he found that all the shipping was crowded into one corner of the harbour, surrounded by a cluster of Spanish gunboats and protected by the guns of the fort and a boom. The customs house was empty, its door locked, there were no bales of goods at all on the quays and the road to Lima was completely deserted. In Lima he encountered deep distrust of any foreign visitor, especially if the foreigner were English, since it was known that Cochrane's ships were mostly officered by Britons. In consequence he found the task of helping British merchants extremely difficult, having to divide his time between Lima, Callao and his ship's cabin, to avoid falling under suspicion of spying for or siding with the rebel patriots. Two of his officers were arrested for spying, allegedly on behalf of Cochrane, and to get them acquitted was no easy task. The prosecution produced two false witnesses, who testified they had seen both these officers on board Cochrane's flagship, and only the good fortune of discovering a Spaniard once held prisoner on board that flagship, who swore that the officers had never been there, resulted in a verdict of acquittal. The viceroy then ruled that no one in future was to land at Callao from a foreign ship, and Hall therefore returned to Valparaiso.[3]

He went back to Callao the following June where he saw San Martín on board his yacht and exchanged views in a friendly manner, but shortly after he had to cope with the crisis caused by the viceroy's decision to pull his government and troops out of Lima. The viceroy had told the inhabitants that their best course of action was to leave for Callao, but Hall told the merchants to ignore this advice and stay in Lima beside their property. The next day the city appeared deserted, with doors barred and shutters closed, but the population was still there, hiding for fear of a slave rebellion. Hall thought this fear ridiculous, as the slave population was not united and consisted entirely of domestic servants scattered thinly about the city with rare opportunities to meet one another. In any case, very shortly after, San Martín promised freedom for all who were born after 15 July and for all who agreed to join his army. Hall represented the British merchants at a meeting summoned by the city's governor at which it was decided to invite San Martín to take possession of the capital. People, Hall recalled, were most afraid of the armed Indians surrounding Lima (*monteneros* as they were called), nominally under San Martín's orders but savage and undisciplined troops. He therefore eulogised San Martín for forbidding his troops to enter the city until total calm had been restored and an adequate system of policing established, and then only allowing in picked soldiers and selected officers. Hall witnessed the entry of San Martín when he proclaimed Peru's independence and was lavish in his compliments of the general's ease of manner and evident dislike of pomp and show. When Hall had met him previously, he had been much impressed by his unaffected charm, his appearance and his conversation. He found him both articulate and informed, animated and magnetic, a rather different impression gained from that of the shrewd Maria Graham when she met the Argentine general in Chile.[4]

Hall visited Callao and Lima again in December 1821 and noted the remarkable changes that had taken place since his last visit there. Now Callao's harbour was crowded with ships busy unloading their rich cargoes, while the sides of the bay were lined with more ships all awaiting their turn to unload. It was the first time he had landed there without apprehending he might be insulted.[5] However by the following year conditions had worsened considerably, when Farquhar Mathison visited Lima. He found prices rising, a scarcity of food, government spies everywhere and corruption rife among government officials. British property and persons were unsafe and wandering peasants and soldiers in disguise frequented the countryside plundering. Mathison thought it was imperative to appoint regular consuls in Peru in order to protect the merchants. His sympathies clearly lay with the royalists and he was outspoken in criticism of the way the Spaniards were being expelled, either forcibly marched to Callao (a distance of half a dozen miles) or, if infirm, strapped to a horse and then pushed on board a ship bound for Chile. 'It was [he wrote] my misfortune to witness this horrifying embarkation.' The decks of the transports were so crowded it was impossible to move on them and the stench, the heat and the shortage of water all added to the sufferings of the deportees. There were moving scenes of grief everywhere, since many of those who were left behind had been dependent on those expelled. Mathison registered his disgust at the official celebration on the 4th May (1822) to commemorate this political act. There was a procession organized in gratitude for what was officially described as this 'solemn act of expiation [and] sober example of vengeance'. 'A dozen dissolute women in finery' led the way with bands and torches to the palace of the governor where they were received by the supreme *Delegado*. A formal address was then delivered on behalf of all the women of Lima to which the *Delegado* made a suitable reply. Mathison thought the whole business an empty and vulgar exhibition, intended simply to delude and amuse the lowest section of the population. He paints a picture in his *Narrative* of a people who had become disillusioned by the painful experience of independence and now longed for royalist rule to return. 'Mines unworked, fields largely uncultivated, labourers especially negroes conscripted, the trade of the interior suspended, whole villages destroyed.' Lima, once a gay, rich city, the luxurious seat of the Spanish viceroy, had been 'exposed to the miseries of siege, famine, anarchy and military government'. He foresaw it would be a very long time before the country would be able to enjoy 'the blessings' of its independent status.[6]

William Tudor, the United States consul in Lima, also reflected in his dispatches on the disillusion felt by Limeños at the way 'liberation' had worked out. Caught up in all the euphoria associated with the patriots' invasion, they had first been blissfully unaware of the sacrifices that were entailed. 'Unfortunately for Peru [he wrote in May 1824] the invaders who came to proclaim liberty and independence were cruel, rapacious, unprincipled and incapable. Their mismanagement, their profligacy, and their thirst for plunder soon alienated the affections of the inhabitants, and prepared them to hail the return of

the royal armies.' He contrasted the characters of the royalist chiefs
with those of their patriot opponents – the viceroy, La Serna, humane,
moderate and upright, and his generals like Canterac and Valdez all
energetic and enterprising. It was unusual to find a North American
so strongly supporting the cause of the monarchists.[7]

Another observer, Robert Proctor, arrived in the Peruvian capital
on 23 May 1823. He was acting as agent for the contractors of the
recent loan that had been negotiated with the Peruvian government,
his aim being to get it ratified. Shortly after his arrival there was panic
in the city with news of a Spanish army approaching it – the
government and the foreign merchants packed everything and made
for Callao. Callao, which Proctor scathingly described as a miserable
collection of mud huts, became appallingly overcrowded with all this
mass of refugees, but he did manage to find accommodation for
himself and his family on board the *Medway*, a vessel of the East India
Company. This ship however was soon required to transport troops to
the Puertos Intermedios and he and his family had to move to another
East Indiaman, also overcrowded. Leaving his family behind, Proctor
then travelled by sea to Trujillo whence the patriot government had
departed, there had an interview with the president and witnessed his
political coup of freeing himself from control of the congress. Soon
after Proctor returned to Lima, when the Spanish army had withdrawn, and stayed there till 1824, when the Callao garrison mutinied
and handed the place to the royalists. Panic ensued once again,
especially among the community of British who had most of their
property in Callao; they were however able to negotiate to have their
belongings put on board some vessels, when a patriot frigate arrived
in the harbour. No one trusted the government and the regiment sent
to defend Lima mutinied as soon as it arrived there. Proctor was only
able to prevent his own horses from being requisitioned by leading
them up the stairs in his house, shutting them in a small room and
spreading litter to deaden the noise. As soldiers were then comman-
deering all green fodder at the city gates, he managed to keep his
horses alive with a diet of cabbages and melons.

When the royalists re-entered the town, as they did on 1 March
1824, Proctor endeavoured to leave Lima but his name was recognized
as the agent of the firm lending money to the patriot government and
the Spanish royalist general Rodil refused him permission to depart.
Through the mediation of Captain Martin, the officer commanding
HMS *Fly* lying at anchor at Callao, Proctor did get permission for his

family to embark on a merchant ship in the port, and he then got himself on board the same ship by successfully bluffing his way past the sentries.[8]

That anarchic political conditions continued in Peru for many years (long after the last Spanish troops had left) is borne out by the experiences of Charles Darwin in 1832. When the *Beagle* anchored in the port of Iquique (today within the boundaries of modern Chile), there was apprehension locally, since the rival political parties were each asking the town for a monetary contribution and the people thought 'the evil hour had come'. Darwin describes how not long before, when robbers had broken into some churches and had been successful in removing the plate, the enraged population had arrested some English and had then proceeded to torture them until the authorities intervened, the presumption being that sacrilege could only be the work of heretics. Shortly after, he visited Lima where he found conditions even more chaotic, with four *caudillos* contending for power. He recounts one dramatic incident when, on the anniversary of independence, with the president attending a solemn high mass and during the singing of the *Te Deum*, instead of each of the regiments present displaying the Peruvian flag, black ones with a death's head on them were unfurled. So lawless were the prevailing conditions that Darwin was not permitted to walk outside the boundaries of the city – the only place he could do so securely was on the barren island of San Lorenzo, just outside the limits of the harbour of Callao.[9]

Despite these difficult political conditions, British merchants continued to trade, at any rate during the 1820s. Joseph Andrews in 1825 found that Tacna, not far from Arica, was more like a British colony than a Spanish. He described a ball given there by the English to celebrate the victory of Ayacucho: 'the company not over attractive, amid dancing not over graceful', but a good supper was provided and the guests ate voraciously – 'no schoolboys ever crammed more inordinately, or with less ceremony, pocketing what they could not eat'.[10] When Samuel Haigh stopped at Arequipa during 1826 he found nearly half of the twenty Englishmen there had married or were engaged to creole women.[11] According to consul-general Ricketts there were sixteen British firms in Arequipa by the end of 1826, and in Lima, where the British merchants had begun to settle in 1821, there were by the end of 1824 twenty British commercial firms and 250 British subjects, including the keepers of public houses, shopkeepers and artisans.[12]

From the very start of the war for independence, British merchants had shown themselves ready to trade with anyone, Spanish or patriot. Lieutenant Bowers was quite open about this. He wrote in his book of *Naval Adventures* that though his sympathies lay with the patriots, he could only regret in commercial terms their victory at Ayacucho, the battle having effectively put paid to all his trading enterprises, for it left him saddled with a shipload of goods that were to prove unsaleable and a debt of £70,000. If all had gone well (by which he meant that the struggle had still remained unresolved), he would have made a profit of 50 per cent and this, with the freight to Europe he had been promised, would have been sufficient to redeem his fortunes and enable him to live in comfort for life.[13]

British merchants were pushing their trade with Lima well before 1821. Captain Sherriff of the British navy reported in October 1818 that though the viceroy would not permit the establishment of British firms in Lima, he was prepared to allow supercargoes to reside in the city and carry on business. The British merchants in Callao and Lima were much concerned at Cochrane's blockade and its effect on their trade in Peru, but Commodore Bowles, to whom they protested, was not prepared to break that blockade. He told the Admiralty that, in his opinion, the temporary inconvenience the merchants suffered was trifling when it was compared with the serious injury that would result from a misunderstanding with patriot governments, since these would jump at the chance of appropriating the 'immense mass of British property' there. He did however insist on the right of any ship of the British navy to enter and leave Peru's ports; there was much British property in Lima and the owners would suffer if they did not receive their regular remittances from England that were brought to them in the navy's warships.[14]

Cochrane's initial blockade of Peru in 1819 was soon called off, but then was resumed in 1820. This evoked further indignant protests from the British merchants to Commodore Hardy, then in command of the British squadron in South Atlantic and Pacific waters. Hardy took up the matter with Cochrane, complaining of the detention off Peru of eighteen British merchant vessels during the course of the previous twelve months. Cochrane replied that Peru's southern coast was now conquered territory, but ships might trade if they paid him a duty of 18 per cent of the value of their cargoes and 3 per cent of the return cargo, if it was specie they were carrying. He did however demand payment in cash as he had no customs officers with him. This was clearly a demand for protection from one who was merely a licensed brigand.

Richard Cleveland, a United States citizen and a tough and well-seasoned New England ship's captain, refused to recognize Cochrane's blockade, brought a cargo of wheat and rice into Callao after Cochrane's squadron had left the port and received from the Spanish viceroy a licence to trade all along the coast. On one occasion, when he sailed to Valparaiso, his vessel was detained by a Chilean warship but managed to escape being taken as a prize, since the cargo on board was, he explained, being carried entirely for an English account.

Michael Hogan, the commercial agent of the US government at Valparaiso, wrote home indignantly of Cochrane's plundering. The so-called 18 per cent he levied on neutral ships' cargoes was more like 25 and 'his low avarice [Hogan continued] produced acts of the greatest meanness. At one place after being treated with great kindness, more from fear than love, he took the Piano Forte from the Lady of the House after playing to him on it, and sold it for one hundred dollars to the captain of a vessel – in this manner he has secured to himself the execration of all classes. Did the feelings of his heart accord with his undaunted courage, he would be an acquisition to any country struggling for freedom, but in him they are at variance, and the Governmt that have from necessity employed him are ashamed of his acts.'

Cochrane justified his actions so far as British vessels were concerned – he paid no regard to those of other countries – by asserting that all the ships he seized were engaged in trade with the enemy: 'I will always facilitate the real trade of England,' he wrote in reply to Hardy's protests, but, he went on, the merchants' ships taken were involved in defrauding the patriot cause and as such were destructive of genuine trade. Hardy took his protests to the government of Chile, insisting that the cargoes Cochrane had seized were mostly British manufactures brought from Rio de Janeiro or Cadiz; the ships for the most part were insured at Lloyds and no adequate proof had been adduced of their being Spanish property. He got little change from Santiago, but he told the Admiralty he was determined to maintain British trade on the coast of Peru. Nevertheless he had to admit that he wished 'our trade was a more honourable one . . . As it consumes an immense quantity of British manufactures, I must submit to the appellation of smugglers which the Chili admiral attaches to us'.[15]

Before the arrival of the first British consul, appointed by Canning

in 1823, the interests of Britsh merchants in Peru, as elsewhere in
Spanish America, were looked after by British naval officers. The
commander of the British naval squadron stationed in South American
waters was the only constituted authority to deal with local governments. Basil Hall, himself a naval officer, commanding a frigate in this
squadron, is eloquent in his book of reminiscences on the subject of
the role the navy played in defusing explosive situations. It was, he
wrote, a task of great difficulty and importance, on account of the vast
extent of the command, the uncertainty and delays in communications
(a dispatch from Santiago to Buenos Aires could take as much as
eleven or twelve days), the instability and inexperience of governments,
and public agitation that often resulted in a lack of commercial
confidence. The commander-in-chief had to delegate to the captains
commanding the ships in his squadron and these ships were dispatched to every port where British trade was seen to be flourishing.
There was often the need to intervene in disputes that arose in the
course of trading, when for instance the merchants considered some
law or regulation to be oppressive, or were ordered to make a financial
contribution; or when a vessel was seized on the pretext of smuggling
or concealing Spanish property. Naval officers were required to
remonstrate and mediate, though not to use either force or threats
without the sanction of the commander-in-chief. Since however so
many disputes required to be settled immediately and there was no
time to await a reply to a message sent to the distant commodore, the
captain on the spot had to act on his own, interpreting as he best was
able the general principles laid down for his guidance.[16]

Such a situation had arisen at Callao in the summer of 1823, when
the Spanish general Canterac, then in temporary occupation of Lima,
had demanded that the British merchants hand over by 4 o'clock that
day $350,000 and send their property to his camp (ostensibly for its
protection) or face the risks a refusal incurred. Captain Prescott of the
Aurora, which was then on station off Callao, was asked by the
merchants to intervene and eventually succeeded in getting the levy
reduced to $150,000 without the merchants surrendering their prop-
erty.[17] A year later, when the royalist army was on the point of
abandoning Lima, Prescott got permission from the generals of both
sides to march a body of marines into Lima to protect British lives
and property there during the period of interregnum before the patriot
forces took over.[18]

Lieutenant Bowers, himself once a British naval officer, not unnaturally held a high opinion of the way British naval captains behaved in handling disputes of this character, citing in support of his contention two examples within his own experience. One occurred in 1821 when his brig at the Peruvian port of Ancón was plundered of $9000 by corrupt and venal customs officials. A short letter from Commodore Hardy resulted in the return of the money within a quarter of an hour and the officials in question being dismissed. The second was in 1824, when the Callao garrison mutinied and handed the fortress over to the Spanish. Fifty ships were lying in the port and were left in consequence without any papers. Captain Martin of HMS *Fly* risked his life by going ashore, breaking into the office of the captain of the port and rescuing the missing papers that would otherwise have been destroyed. 'Where [Bowers asked] is the consul who could have done as much?' In Bowers's view Britain would do better to let her commercial interests abroad be represented by the Royal Navy than by what he slightingly described as 'unfledged youths dispatched by the Foreign Office', ignorant of the customs of the country and its language.[19] Charles Milner Ricketts, the British consul-general sent out to Lima in 1825, was certainly not such an unfledged youth (any more than his predecessor Rowcroft, killed accidentally in 1824), but it seems he had little sympathy with the clamour of the local British merchants. When in 1827 he sent home to Canning a petition of complaint from British merchants about the seizure of their property, when Lima and Callao had both changed hands (their claims amounted to $12 million) he showed some indifference towards the merchants who had, when asked earlier to supply him with important statistical information, displayed unwillingness to assist him. Having (wrote Ricketts) decided to embark on speculations in Peru at a period of great uncertainty, the merchants had supported both sides in the war and at all times had been motivated purely by the hope of personal advantage. 'As a body . . . their pretensions to disinterested liberalism fall to the ground', even if particular individuals had shown themselves zealous in the cause of independence. Ricketts did not think that the British government could be answerable for their imprudence, particularly since they had made great profits. The claims being advanced dealt only with the government, but there were in addition further claims amounting to another $5 million against Peruvian and other merchants. The British were not popular locally, since their principal debtors were the state and its more influential citizens.

When two years later the British government instructed Ricketts's deputy Kelly to obtain documents or copies of them from the customs offices in Callao relating to the British merchants' claims for vessels seized and then condemned, Kelly replied that all the archives had been destroyed on the occasion when the Spanish reoccupied Lima and Callao. Since then, 'so iniquitous is the system carried on in the public offices, that it is not practicable to obtain anything like correct information: even the Government cannot procure documents on which it can rely, it being in the interests of those employed to falsify or withhold them in order to conceal their frauds'. Kelly held out little hope of any compensation being paid 'in the present totally exhausted state of the finances of the country'.[20]

Between 1821 and 1825 British merchants in Peru had done extremely well for themselves. Basil Hall in 1821, when dining with the governor of the town of Huacho, took note of the way political change had brought in so many European products: a roll of what was clearly English broad-cloth resting on a winecase that was French, on the table a bottle of champagne, knives and forks with a Sheffield stamp and a screen in the middle of the room that was made of printed cotton from Glasgow.[21] When Mathison arrived at Callao at the end of March 1822 he counted sixty merchant ships in the harbour, the great majority of which were British.[22] Stevenson described how, 'on entering Lima or in any other part of Peru I visited, almost every object reminded me of England; the windows were glazed with English glass – the brass furniture on the commodes, tables etc were English – the chintz or dimity hangings, the linen or cotton dresses of the females, and the cloth coats, cloaks etc of the men were all English: – the tables were covered either with plate or south American manufacture'.[23] Proctor was told by an English merchant, when he was in Lima in 1823, that the estimated value of British imports was £2 million a year, though this was a considerable exaggeration. The value of British exports to Peru had risen from just over £56,000 in the year 1821 to very nearly ten times that figure in 1825. 1826 however saw a notable slump in British trade.[24] Haigh witnessed the ruin of many merchants, their cargoes impounded for unpaid bills and sold at auction at one tenth of their cost. Many merchants he knew were destitute and a subscription was opened for them to give them temporary relief and pay for their passages back to England. Haigh thought that the markets of Peru, as indeed of the whole of South America, had been grossly overrated in England. They were widely scattered, the population was small and the goods that

Peru could offer in return were very limited in number (chiefly cocoa, cotton and bark) apart from bullion, whose supply was exhausted.[25]

As Ricketts told Canning in December 1826, British traders, when the revolution started, had enjoyed considerable success in Peru; gold and silver left the country in exchange for goods that were much in demand and the 'most exaggerated notions were entertained of the wealth of the country'. The Spanish capitalists were stripped of their property, the churches were plundered of their gold and silver, but now all that had gone to Spain or Britain or to pay for the armies of liberation: between 1819 and 1825 it was estimated that precious metal to the value of $26 million had been shipped from Lima in British vessels.[26]

But there were other obstacles to indefinitely expanding British trade in Peru, one being the high level of import duties. These, which in 1821 had stood at 40 per cent *ad valorem*, were doubled in 1826 so far as foreign textiles were concerned, and in 1828 a law was passed (though probably it was never enforced) forbidding for the space of the next ten months the import of any foreign goods that were prejudicial to local manufacture. The consequence was of course widespread smuggling and bribery of customs officials.[27] Trade (Ricketts wrote) was a gamble so far as markets in Peru were concerned and the whole system was corrupt.[28] Ricketts's private secretary, John Barclay Pentland, a scholar and a scientist, was sent to Bolivia to report, *inter alia*, on what were the prospects for expanding trade there, but the study he made and his prognosis were considered by Ricketts to be far too optimistic. So long (Ricketts wrote to Canning in December 1827) as the terms on which trade can be carried on fluctuate in the way they are doing, so long as feuds and anarchy persist and the system of contraband continues, the foreign merchant cannot hope to enjoy any security in commercial dealing.[29]

Another obstacle to trade was the difficulty in recovering a debt owed by a Peruvian to a foreign merchant. Recovery involved expensive litigation and the British merchant found it easier to resort to bribes and influence. A further obstacle was that foreign traders were subject to arrest or imprisonment by minor officials on frivolous pretexts and the minister with whom Ricketts raised these matters, though expressing sympathy, was not very helpful. Revision of the commercial code would need the approval of the national congress and that body was made up of men who thought that the foreigner had come to Peru merely in order to plunder the country. 'Ignorance, prejudice and jealousies are [wrote Ricketts] stubborn inmates of Peru.'[30]

John Robertson recounts two incidents that occurred in 1823, while he was resident in Lima, that illustrate this distrust and jealousy and the desire of Peruvians to squeeze the foreign merchant till he disgorged his loot. During a heated discussion in congress on the subject of granting religious freedom, one delegate reasoned that the argument that unless freedom of worship was granted, all the British would leave the country, was a totally fallacious one. The English, he said, were in Peru 'for our women and for our gold and silver'. Since existing laws provided against the marriage or seduction of Catholic women, what was needed was to give the English all the gold and silver that they desired and no more would be heard of their demands that they should be granted religious freedom. The congress there-upon passed a law denying religious toleration for any other than Roman Catholics. Shortly after, the same delegate proposed that all the English merchants should be subject to a monetary contribution amounting to $200,000, and that no English merchant might leave the country until the contribution was paid. Fortunately for the English merchants, the frigate *Aurora* was at Callao and, in support of the merchants' cause, began a blockade of the harbour and port. This prompt action by Captain Prescott proved to be surprisingly effective. Within two days he received a note to say that the government relinquished its claims and that English merchants might leave if they wished. Robertson, a man of considerable influence, who had helped to fit out San Martín's expedition and was, in the same year that this incident occurred, appointed commercial agent in London for the Peruvian government, had an interview with the president, the result of which was that English merchants made a voluntary 'loan' to the government. The merchants in turn were so delighted by the way the dispute had been resolved that they voted $1500 for a piece of plate to be given to Prescott.[31] The episode ended happily but it shows how vulnerable the merchants were. Four years later Ricketts was writing of their being forced to provide sea-transport for troops being sent to various ports without the normal remuneration; of native consignees being favoured in preference to British ones and of import duties being constantly raised. Ricketts summed up his feelings on the subject when he wrote in May 1827: 'It would be unreasonable to express surprise at the institutions of the country not embracing correct practical ideas of civil liberty, but considering the time that has elapsed since the opening of the revolution some improvements were to have been expected towards the security of personal rights and the impartial administration of the laws; in no country perhaps are they worse administered towards all parties, or worse calculated to protect a foreigner than in Peru.'[32] Nor could there be any improvement until a commercial treaty was signed between Great Britain and Peru, and that had to wait until 1837.

Complaints about his own treatment continued to be made by Admiral Cochrane while co-operating with San Martín in the liberation of Peru. Two attempts in 1819 by his squadron to capture Callao from the Spanish had been frustrated because of incompetence as well as adverse weather conditions. Cochrane bemoaned his inferiority both in guns and in well-trained gunners and of financial stringency that left his squadron short of equipment and of crews that were even moderately efficient. Most of his officers came from Britain, Ireland or North America but they could not bring the peasants, who were now turned sailors, to anything approaching seamanlike standards. When the second attack on Callao failed, Cochrane put the blame on defective rockets on which he had relied for success. These, he alleged, had been sabotaged by the Spanish prisoners compelled to fill them, so that they exploded prematurely before leaving the rafts they were launched from, setting fire to others and burning the crews, or steered themselves in the wrong direction because they were made of the wrong sort of wood, or sometimes failed to ignite at all; while a wind that blew intermittently prevented his fireships from entering the harbour.

Cochrane's strict enforcement of discipline in a squadron badly in need of it was shown in his punishment of looting. When a landing party of his marines looted a church in the town of Paita, he saw the articles stolen were restored, gave the priests 1000 pesos to repair the damage and ordered the marines in question to be flogged in front of the church they had desecrated. His comment on the incident underlines the kind of problems facing Europeans when in command of South Americans: 'Our thus refraining from plunder [he wrote] was almost beyond the comprehension of a people who had bitter experience of Spanish rapacity, whilst the undisciplined Chileños, who formed the greater portion of the squadron, as little comprehended why their plundering propensities should be restrained.'[33]

In the third expedition that Cochrane made, this time carrying on board the army commanded by San Martín, he managed to enlist foreign crews, but only by getting San Martín to join with him in a guarantee that they should receive their arrears of pay and in addition a further year's pay, an arrangement that eventually led to trouble. Cochrane's quarrels with San Martín were partly due to a disagreement over the strategy to be pursued. Cochrane wanted an assault on Lima, while San Martín waited seven weeks at Pisco, then made no attempt to take Callao and went north to the port of Ancón. Cochrane, ever the 'fiery Scot', became exasperated at what he called all this 'time lost in idleness'. His one consolation was his success in cutting out the Spanish frigate *Esmeralda* lying under the guns of Callao, a feat that Stevenson described as a death blow to the local Spanish squadron. When the royalist army abandoned Lima in July 1821, Cochrane was angry that all the credit was given to the army and not the navy that had effectively blockaded Callao.

Further occasion for the worsening of relations between Cochrane and San Martín was jealousy of each other's position. Two British naval officers, Captain Spry and Captain Guise, who had brought from England the sloop *Hecate* to join the Chilean naval squadron, had never wanted to serve under Cochrane, and when Cochrane dismissed Spry and accepted Guise's resignation after an incident of alleged disobedience, Cochrane was furious to find that both officers had found employment on the staff of San Martín. Bowers, in his book, describes Guise as 'haughty, unbending to those he despised, and unable to speak the language of the people which, from his contempt for their venality and corruption, he would never learn, was naturally no favourite among them'. Yet he must have possessed considerable talent to have earned the respect of San Martín and later to have reached the rank of admiral and commander-in-chief of the Peruvian navy.

Cochrane was also much put out when San Martín assumed the dictatorship with the title of 'Protector' of Peru, without consulting Cochrane first. The situation was made much worse when San Martín refused to pay the officers and crews of Cochrane's ships unless the squadron was made over to Peru, Cochrane himself being offered, as *douceur*, the title of Admiral of Peru. When asked by Cochrane to fulfil his promises, San Martín refused to pay a single *real*, telling Cochrane he could take away his squadron since a couple of schooners was enough for him. Cochrane makes out that San Martín denied in writing the previous commitment he had made to pay the foreign crews in the Chilean squadron, and Cochrane was convinced that San

Martín intended to starve those crews into deserting. Faced with the
threat of mutiny, Cochrane took his ships to the port of Ancón and
there seized all the silver bullion that San Martín had put in store,
both government and private property when the royalists had threatened to reoccupy Lima. To those who could prove ownership
Cochrane says he returned their silver but the rest that amounted to
the sum of $285,000 he used to pay his crews one year's arrears. San
Martín later claimed that Cochrane had appropriated all the silver to
himself and that his sailors deserted his ships, but Cochrane makes
out that what really happened was that the sailors went ashore with
the intention of spending their pay and then found that they were
prevented from returning, when they attempted to rejoin their ships.
San Martín also sent letters to the officers of Cochrane's squadron
stating he (San Martín) was rightfully their commander-in-chief, that
they ought therefore to obey his orders, and offering them commissions, titles and estates. Twenty-three accepted this offer, and Cochrane was left with a squadron half-manned and with an order from
San Martín to leave Callao immediately. He sent back half of his ships
to Chile, had the rest repaired at Guayaquil, then returned to Callao
to demand what he claimed as the pay of the crews still due to him,
while turning down a 'fraudulent' offer to assume command of a joint
navy to capture the Philippine Islands from Spain.

San Martín sent two envoys to Chile to accuse Cochrane of
committing fraud in seizing the silver at Ancón and requesting that he
be punished for this. When Cochrane returned to Valparaiso in June
1822 he was however not punished but honoured, though his attempts
to get O'Higgins to institute a court of inquiry into his conduct as
squadron commander failed to meet with any success; in any case
O'Higgins was displaced by Freire very shortly after this episode.

It is difficult to arrive at an impartial judgement about the rights
and wrongs of the question of the alleged use or misuse of the silver
seized by Cochrane at Ancón. Cochrane himself remained very
indignant that the patriot government of Peru awarded a pension to
San Martín to the value of $20,000 but gave him nothing but a vote
of thanks for the services that he had performed. It seems clear the
Peruvians believed that Cochrane had lined his own pockets with
Peruvian silver and they may well have been responsible for the story
that was put about in Chile (one that Cochrane got denied officially)
that he had stowed on a British ship a consignment of 9000 ounces of
gold,[34] destined wholly for his personal use. Perhaps there was a grain

of truth in the story. In the words of Salvador Madariaga, the biographer of Bolívar, Admiral Cochrane 'outNelsoned Nelson by all the Drake that was in him. His eye for gold was as keen as Drake's'.[35]

The other famous British mercenary who took employment under the patriots to free Peru from Spanish rule was the soldier William Miller, whom Robert Proctor described as being 'an excellent officer for dangerous services', a 'tall and gentlemanly [figure], his manner attractive, mild and unassuming', a man much liked by Peruvians. Miller was second in command of the troops on board ships sent to Callao in September 1819 and was badly wounded in the attack on Pisco that followed the failure to take Callao. He was then promoted to lieutenant-colonel and given command of a battalion that sailed for Peru in August 1820 – the only officer to hold field rank who accompanied that famous expedition and was also present on the field of Ayacucho.

Put in command of a Peruvian corps with a force sent to the Puertos Intermedios, he won the loyalty of his troops who were mostly Indian, mulatto or black. He wrote of the easy relations subsisting between his officers and his men, in marked contrast to those that obtained in the European armies of that time. The local people expressed their delight when he was seen to attend mass and was thereafter stamped throughout the country as being no heretic but 'a good Christian'. Later he was sent south with reinforcements to join Santa Cruz in a disastrous campaign and distinguished himself as commander of the rearguard that he managed to bring back intact to Lima. Bolívar paid tribute to his services by appointing him as chief-of-staff and temporary commander-in-chief and in May 1824 he was made general of Peruvian cavalry and served under Sucre in the campaign that culminated at Ayacucho. The Indians, we are told, were so impressed by his habit of chewing the coca leaf that many volunteered to join his forces. Indeed so popular did Miller make himself among the Indian population that an English merchant travelling in the interior found it enough to state that he was Miller's compatriot to be given the best accommodation and the best fare available in an Indian village.[36] One is reminded of the reputation that Byron made for himself in Greece.

The Indians, wrote Ricketts in 1827, were amiable enough but uneducated, slavish, feeble and inert and moreover hopelessly 'priest-ridden'. 'The withering effects of the sombre and sullen march of the Catholic faith are marked along the distant heights of the Andes.' The creoles were equally bigoted whenever religion was concerned, as witness their resolution in congress to forbid any worship that was not Catholic. There had been regulations in Lima under San Martín and later Bolívar for setting up schools, curbing clerical influence, suppressing the religious houses and selling church lands to pay secular clergy, remodelling the law courts, instituting a public library and freeing the press from clerical control, but nothing whatever had been done.[37]

When the Reverend Hugh Silvin, chaplain of the *Cambridge*, arrived in Lima in 1823, he visited a Lancasterian school there (200 little boys in attendance) kept by the missionary James Thomson whose activities in Chile and La Plata have been recounted in earlier chapters. Thomson had arrived in Lima in July 1822 and had been welcomed by San Martín whom Thomson found liberal-minded and intelligent, free from the usual Spanish prejudice against the advancement of public education. All the ministers in government supported Thomson in starting a school and a disused friary was made over to him. Popular hostility remained strong however, though this failed to surprise Thomson who was rather astonished at the several deputies who had dared to vote for religious toleration. Strangely it was the laity more than the clergy who were opposed to Thomson's school, linked as instruction in it was with readings from passages in the New Testament; and Thomson was pleased to find an archbishop who had actually forbidden a priest to preach against the reading of the bible in Spanish, copies of which Thomson himself had recently had distributed. Thomson made friends of two priests in Lima who were pleasantly surprised to find that he was not opposed to the Christian religion, having always assumed that all foreigners were either atheists or deists.

After San Martín left Lima for good, Thomson found his work more difficult through lack of funds, procrastination and promises that were not kept. It seems that the temporary reoccupation of the city by the army of General Canterac did not adversely affect the running of his school, save only that the ensuing chaos made provision of public funds impossible. When the state could no longer pay his salary he made preparations to leave the country but then his pupils' parents clubbed together to pay for his services to continue. That was in June 1824, but by September the number of his pupils had fallen from 230 to 200, due to fears of being recruited to fight in one of the opposing armies, and also because of the general poverty. The war had made it impossible for Thomson to continue his work in the country and he left Peru to go to Bogotá.

However in May 1826 he penned an optimistic report to the British and Foreign Schools Society, stressing the interest Bolívar had shown in the spread of Peruvian education. He had (so Thomson had been informed) instituted a Lancasterian central school in every province of Peru from which masters were to be sent out to all towns and villages in those provinces. Two youths from each province were to be sent to England to be educated, destined when they returned to Peru to fill important official positions, and ten young men had already been sent.[38] Unfortunately all these grandiose plans remained on the paper on which they were written. Bolívar himself left Peru four months after this report was written and, as Ricketts told the Foreign Office in December 1827, nothing whatever had in fact been done to establish a system of schools in Peru. This did not it seems apply to Lima, where Father Navarete, a Catholic priest who had taken over from James Thomson when the latter departed from Peru, told Thomson in 1847 that his schools were flourishing in the capital and their number had been increased to thirty.

Proctor, when he visited Lima in 1823 and 1824, shared the impression of most Englishmen that the people were priest-ridden, superstitious and bigoted. Most of the priests he considered depraved, willing to sell absolution for crime as well as the churches' sacred vessels, and drinking and gambling with the worst, though he did concede there were a few clergy (secular not regular), with enlightened views, who led pious lives. He mentions particularly the dean of Lima with whom he struck up a close acquaintance and who possessed a library that contained old editions of the classics and a few English books he especially cherished.[39] When Hugh Silvin visited Quilca he gave the priest a Spanish translation of a pious work by Bishop Porteous entitled *Evidence of Christianity*. The priest 'viewed it at first with a distrustful eye but at last accepted it'. One of the midshipmen from HMS *Cambridge* presented the local schoolmaster with a few religious tracts in Spanish (undoubtedly of an evangelical nature) and Silvin discovered a little later that the tracts were taken to the priest for approval,[40] but perhaps this need cause no surprise.

Two aspects of religious observance struck Proctor when he was in Lima. One was that religious ceremonies were carried out with the utmost parade. When a priest took the sacrament to the dying, the host was carried in a splendid carriage drawn by four horses, and followed by a procession with torches and candles. Soldiers lined the streets to keep order and on arrival at the house of the dying, the priest was received by kneeling relatives. The other was the noise of the church bells, something about which Haigh also complained when he was visiting Arequipa – the ringing there started at 2.30 a.m. The nuisance was such that Proctor found himself unable to attend to any other business. The bells, he complained, were not pulled in chimes but by boys who swung them by thongs attached to clappers and the sound thus produced was 'barbarous'. All attempts to regulate the frequency or duration of the ringing were condemned as profane or irreligious. More obnoxious however was the smell of corpses in the town. The dead were buried in shallow graves and bodies of small children awaiting burial were left near the churches till the sexton appeared. There were no inquests held in the city and Proctor suspected that child murder was an only too frequent occurrence there.[41]

Cleveland was very much impressed by the amount of time the Peruvians he met appeared to give to their devotions, in Trujillo even more than in Lima, families spending (though it is difficult to believe) as much as eight hours a day in prayer. He wrote slightly sarcastically, 'I have seen no people who appeared so devoted to religious affairs and none whose every rule of the Decalogue is so generally disregarded.'[42]

When Proctor had first visited Lima he was fairly favourably impressed. A city of 10,000 inhabitants, it contained some handsome private houses and those inhabited by the English were kept in a good state of repair. One British merchant lived in a house in many ways scarcely inferior to the palace of the Marquis of Torretagle, the man of most substance in the capital. Proctor was entertained by John Robinson and went to a ball where he remarked how some ladies were dressed in the European fashion. The scene he witnessed some months later, after the city had been occupied and then abandoned by the army of Canterac, turned out to be a very different one. Before leaving, the royalist troops had set fire to the royal palace, together with the archives in it, and the royal mint whose machinery they either destroyed or took away. The ground they had camped on was strewn with debris that gave off a most unpleasant smell and the countryside was like a bare plain, the troops having thrown down all the walls and used the bricks for building ovens. Life inside Lima was very much changed from what it had been a few months earlier and he complained, perhaps rather unreasonably, about the quality of the society with which he was now compelled to mingle. The ladies were chiefly illiterate and even the most respectable were brought up to be flirts and coquettes. They did not attend *tertullias* so the English found it hard to get up a dance, but instead came in crowds dressed as *tapadas* (women whose faces are hidden by a scarf or veil) to stare at the company through doors and windows. Despite the appearance of modesty this custom seemed to indicate, they were apparently in no way shocked by what the puritanical Proctor described as some of 'the most indecent dances' performed by mulattoes in public places, accompanied by the drum or guitar; indeed he saw 'most respectable ladies' watching and, what was worse, enjoying what he described as 'these gross exhibitions'. On the other hand he had to admit that though the ladies smoked, spat and gambled, they were otherwise well-mannered, kind and good-natured.

Cleveland also had cause to complain of the lack of intellectual life that he encountered on visiting Lima. If you lived passively, he wrote, and took care not to offend the clergy, you could live quietly and easily, but such a life he deemed 'stupid and worthless'. His views on the creole ladies of Lima were similar to those of Proctor – physically they were attractive enough but, save in the matter of music and dancing, 'as uncultivated as their last imported slaves'.[43]

Proctor could not help contrasting the humane way that the slaves were treated with their savage treatment in Brazil – he thought they looked happy and on no occasion did he ever witness a slave being whipped. As for the mass of the male population he held them in complete contempt. 'Never was a people more unfit for active or useful employment.' He found it incredible that there were in Lima only two or three native merchant firms and that Peruvians allowed their trade to be engrossed by foreigners – Chileños and Buenos Aireans for the most part. Charles Brand in 1827 shared this low view of the Limeños, describing the men as dirty and lazy, deploring their habits of smoking and spitting and the general depravity of their morals, and drawing attention to the fact that during his short stay in the city there were three murders and numerous robberies.[44]

Charles Ricketts on the other hand found Lima better on first impressions than he had been led to expect – 'the inhabitants free from the presumption of arrogance of the Buenos Ayreans'. It was a city unlike any other he had visited before, 'a mixture of Asiatic, Italian and African costumes', though the country outside seemed dreary enough. But six months later he wrote home plaintively that he 'heartily wished himself away from this place of poverty and consternations'. He would, he wrote, happily exchange his post for one a third less in value in Europe:[45] echoes here of the complaints that were made by Parish about Buenos Aires.

Transport Ricketts found was difficult – the roads were bad and mule carriage expensive; labour was scarce and therefore dear and the people appeared to him for the most part feeble, inert and ignorant. The comforts and decencies of life were unknown, capital had vanished with the Spanish capitalists; there were no manufactures of any importance save the cottage industry of weaving baizes and the coarse grey cloth that the peasants wore. The mines, the previous source of wealth, were inactive for lack of capital, with all their machinery destroyed and the miners conscripted into the armies.

Ricketts had found it difficult to get information out of the government about the exact condition of the mines, possibly due to jealousy, incapacity or disinclination, but it seemed no regular accounts had been kept regarding the output of the mines since the revolution had first broken out. Governments were prejudiced against the foreigner, though they dearly needed foreign capital and great caution, Ricketts thought, was required in investing money in Peru until a commercial treaty was signed that gave security to private property. The failure of British mining projects in the course of the preceding decade had been due either to faulty planning or deception practised on unwary investors and this story is a familiar one in other countries of South America, notably La Plata and Chile. So far as bad planning was concerned, excessively large salaries had been paid to employees brought out from England; miners, sometimes with their wives and families, hailing from Cornwall or Derbyshire could not stand the climate of the Sierra, or the fatigue of working the mines and then became obstreperous and demanded to be given a passage home; machinery had been bought that was totally useless, being far too heavy and bulky to transport through a mountainous terrain without any roads; a mine manager would discover on first arrival at the site that, before any ore could be extracted, an adit or chamber had to be cut to drain the water out of the mine, and this might delay the opening of the mine by anything up to three or four years. Finally the proprietors in England, alarmed at the growing expenditure and the threat of lawsuits about their title, would decide to discharge their workpeople and abandon the project altogether.

As for deception, Ricketts cited examples of people buying mines with a good past record of production which they then sold, without ever having had any intention of working them. This led to stockmarket speculation and eventually the bursting of the bubble, as happened in 1825/6. The Peruvian government itself, though it professed to have liberal views, had often shown a lack of good faith, granting title to British prospectors without the authority of congress, which alone could annul previous laws forbidding foreigners to deal with mines.[46]

The earliest example of commercial failure by Britons trying to mine in Peru was that of the Cornishman Richard Trevithick, pioneer of the steam locomotive. In 1814 Trevithick entered a partnership with a Swiss called Uville and two wealthy Lima merchants to exploit the silver mines of Cerro de Pasco – this with the full support of the viceroy. The mines, which were situated in the Andes at 14,000 feet above sea level and 160 miles from Lima, had fallen into ruin on account of flooding. They were extremely difficult to reach along a mule track sometimes two feet wide and cut into precipices that rose perpendicularly to 400 feet. Uville came to England to buy pumping engines and Trevithick agreed to provide nine of them, a mint and £3000 in cash. All the machinery and three engineers were sent out to Callao that September but it took a further eighteen months to get the machinery to the site and erect it at the formidable cost of £10,000. Trevithick himself arrived the next February and managed to get the machinery working, but there were delays and mismanagement and Uville and other shareholders put the blame on Trevithick for what went wrong. Trevithick therefore resigned his post and was given a pass by the viceroy to travel wherever he liked in Peru, inspecting mines and instructing miners in methods of mining employed in England. Trevithick managed to start up a silver and copper mine at Cataxambo, but then, when patriot forces arrived there, the miners fled to avoid being conscripted. Trevithick was forced to leave Cataxambo, 'robbed of all my money, leaving everything behind me, miner's tools and about £500 worth of ores'. Trevithick returned eventually to Pasco to take over control of the mines, but once more hostilities intervened. After the patriot victory at Pasco, the troops broke up the mining machinery and did all they could to damage the mines to prevent the royalists, if they retook them, from ever being able to use the ore.

When Simón Bolívar arrived in Peru his army suffered from a shortage of small arms, so he got Trevithick to design a carbine with a short barrel to fire bullets that broke up on impact and caused jagged wounds. He tried to make Trevithick serve in the army to prove the effectiveness of this weapon, though, as his son wrote in the *Life* of his father, Trevithick always disliked shooting and had never been a very good shot. Eventually Trevithick returned to mining but when royalist forces took over the mines he decided to leave Peru for good. He went to prospect in Costa Rica and after enduring many hardships returned to England in 1828, a pauper 'with only the clothes he stood in, a gold watch, a drawing-compass, and a pair of silver spoons', apart from having 'a hazy right in his Cataxambo copper mountain and an option on his Costa Rica mine'. All attempts by him to raise money to exploit these concessions proved unsuccessful, though another company in 1827 tried and failed to restart the Pasco mines. Trevithick in writing to a close friend was scathing in his comments about this attempt. He considered the engines sent to replace his (destroyed by the troops that had occupied the mines) were 'nothing more than playthings and the sheet copper pumps have all burst, and the englishe agents all turned oute, drunked and robbers, and the scheam have fallen to the ground with a total loss of all the property with oute even doing anything. So much for London engineering and mining knowledge.' Trevithick was not a literate man but was proud of his engineering skill and proud of being a Cornishman.[47]

If political conditions had been the cause of Trevithick's failure to mine in Peru with any prospect of making a profit, mismanagement in England and collapse of confidence in the money-market were the reasons for the failure of the Potosí, La Paz and Peruvian Mining Association. The tale is told by Edmond Temple in his book *Travels in Peru*, published in London in 1830 and in his *Brief Account* to the shareholders, and at rather less length by Joseph Pentland in his *Report on Bolivia*. The Assocation was, in Temple's words, 'one of the nine hundred and ninety-nine speculations of the all-speculating year 1825'. The company was formed in London on assurances given by two notable figures commissioned by the Peruvian government to encourage European investment in mining. The first Juan García del Rio was himself a Peruvian, the second an Englishman, James Paroissien, now a general in the army of Peru and who had served in San Martín's campaigns. Temple (though without any knowledge of mining) was appointed the company's secretary and he and Paroissien, the chief commissioner, Baron de Czetteritz (recommended by

Humboldt, the famous naturalist and explorer) in charge of mining operations, and a Mr Scrivener, a mineralogist, set off in a ship bound for Buenos Aires whence they planned to reach Potosí by land. They were accompanied by two servants, a spaniel and a highly fashionable carriage that proved unusable on arrival, its axle being too narrow and its wheels too low-slung to cope with the roads of South America. Meanwhile the company had appointed 'surveyors, engineers, mining officers, surgeons, secretaries, bookkeepers, clerks, assayers, chandlers, carpenters, gardeners, mechanics of every kind with a proportionate number of Durham and Cornish miners and no expense was spared in providing everything that could contribute to the comfort and even the luxuries of the officers of the Association'. All these, thirty-eight in number, together with mining machinery, were placed on a ship that was specially chartered and sent round the Horn to the port of Arica.

In 1803 Alexander Humboldt had visited Potosí and had found there forty active amalgam works producing at the very least 4000 pounds worth of silver a week. Since then the civil war had occurred, the machinery had been destroyed and the works plundered and the mines flooded. When Temple arrived at Potosí he found only fifteen amalgam works active and these on a very limited scale, but the agent of the Association had taken possession of nine mines and had made quite considerable progress in repairing the damaged amalgam works. Temple received the co-operation, indeed active help, of the local authorities, including an agreement to allow the ship sent by the Association to discharge its cargo free of all duties. All seemed to be going well until a letter arrived from the company warning of grave financial difficulties that meant no further funds were available. Temple was compelled to stop work in those mines that had been purchased and were now in action and desist from buying more mines and land, though he thought the opportunities favourable. The collapse of the money-market in London had placed the Association in jeopardy. When Temple met General Sucre, the president of Bolivia, the latter remarked perceptively, though apparently in a friendly way, that he found it strange that an English trading company should embark on so risky a speculation as mining in South America, not only without the required funds but without the means of obtaining them. He said he could not think who was more foolish, those who dispatched the expedition or those who had embarked on it. He thought that the English gentlemen involved must have been reading the history of El Dorado with more credulity than it deserved if they thought precious metals could be obtained without any labour or expense. It was true they abounded in Bolivia, but were not to be had for **nothing**, any more than were the materials with which people build their houses.

The Association, according to Temple, had expended £70,000 without seeing any benefit from it, and not a twelfth had been spent on mines or on the business of extracting ore. The cargo of the ship that carried the stores, provisions and equipment for the company and the thirty-eight employees engaged, was seized on arrival at Arica on the petition of the company's creditors. Among these was a rich merchant, the company's agent at Buenos Aires from whom Paroissien had borrowed money, backed by bills on the company in London which the directors now refused to honour. The cargo consisted very largely of what Paroissien described as 'rubbish' and had to be sold at below cost price. The employees who had sailed on the ship at first refused to return home until they were paid what was owing to them, but as no money was forthcoming were forced to sell everything they possessed merely in order to keep alive and finally accepted a passage to England.

Despite all this, the directors in London continued to send instructions from England as late as July 1826 telling Paroissien and Temple to help themselves to nineteen more mines situated in distant provinces, to hire technicians and to appoint an additional agent in Potosí. When Temple replied scathingly that these proposals were unrealistic, that the nineteen mines the directors mentioned were not worth nineteen shillings to 'us' and the letters of introduction sent to supposedly influential people were not worth the paper they were written on, he was severely reprimanded. Temple then rendered his accounts, wound up the company's affairs in Bolivia and resigned from his position. Paroissien, who acquiesced in all this, was so upset he became ill and died on the journey home to England. Part of the fault had lain with those directors who had failed to pay for the shares they took up and so brought about a loss of confidence and a deficiency of cash. The shareholders had been led to believe that their agents abroad had squandered their money in buying useless mines in Bolivia, but Temple contended this was not so. He later wrote to the directors assuring them that the Potosí mines could, if managed judiciously, produce a profit of 20 per cent on a capital outlay of £20,000.[48]

The other British mining company that tried to exploit Bolivian mines and about which a narrative was constructed was the Chilean and Peruvian Mining Association whose tale was told by Joseph Andrews. Captain Andrews, already referred to in connection with mines in La Plata and Chile, was sent to Potosí as agent of the company to contract for and buy up mines during 1825. His first sight of the place he found repulsive – 'it looks like the city of a prince of sin, strange, desert, solitary, mysterious, a place of evil enchantment'. It was there that he met Bolívar ('with all the heroes of the Andes'), who told him that he (Bolívar) was determined to thwart the attempts being made by two agents from Buenos Aires to purchase all the mines in the country for a sum of $2½ million. Bolívar expressed the hope that British companies would buy them instead and make an offer of $3 million. Andrews had already paid an instalment for some mines that he had inspected when told he had acted beyond his instructions and the contracts for purchase were never ratified.[49] His premonitions on first arriving seem therefore to have been justified. Miller, then governor of Potosí, pronounced his verdict on Andrews's company and of British mining associations generally when he wrote in his memoirs: 'Had he [Andrews] been sufficiently supported by the company he represented, he would have been able to have done more, at a comparatively trifling cost, than most of the rest of the mine-hunting brotherhood, who had gone to such enormous expense, particularly in sending out machinery that was never made use of . . . It would be a difficult task to decide whether the mismanagement of the directors, or the cupidity of the British public, was most to blame in these matters.'[50]

Pentland, writing only a year after the collapse of the mining companies, was convinced, as indeed Temple was, that there were great opportunities for British investment in Bolivian mines if only prudence was exercised. The production of the mines at Potosí was increasing and likely to go on doing so. What was chiefly needed was capital and the application of technical knowledge which Europeans could supply. There was little use for machinery but there was for smelting and amalgamation, again something that Temple reiterated in his book *Travels in Peru*. Bolivia, Pentland wrote, had a government that was anxious to protect the foreign investor, give him security of tenure for his property and unlike other South American countries showed no symptoms of xenophobia.

Ricketts, in forwarding Pentland's report to the Foreign Office in

London, again sounded a note of caution where mining investment was concerned, impressed as he was that so much money had been lost in this field so recently. He was preaching to those already converted. Capitalists in the United Kingdom had already burnt their fingers badly in the stockmarket collapse of 1826 and remained reluctant for many years to invest in Peruvian or Bolivian mines.[51]

One thing that had not been sufficiently realized by investors living in cosy England was the appalling difficulties of travel and transport in South America, more especially in the Andean region where virtually all the mines were located. Temple in 1827 stayed with Francis Burdett O'Connor, the Irish aide of General Sucre and at the time acting as commandant-general of the armies of the Bolivian frontier. O'Connor told Temple of his aspirations to found a colony of his native Irish in Tarija province of Bolivia, a colony to be called 'New Erin'. He had penned an address to the people of Ireland inviting them to come and settle in this beautiful and fertile country where the present population was so sparse and where they would have to pay no rent. Temple rightly adjudged this address to be 'the honest effusion of a generous, though rather too sanguine mind', since the chief impediment to immigration was not providing land for the immigrants but the sheer difficulty of getting to Tarija.[52] As Pentland found when he travelled in Bolivia, there were no wheeled carriages in the country (save a few used for religious occasions), no cart or carriage roads, and most of the 2000 miles he had travelled was made on mules up steep mountain tracks at heights of over 12,000 feet.[53]

Pentland had written his report before General Sucre had left Bolivia. Thereafter political conditions deteriorated very markedly. The British consul Masterman was to write in 1843 from the capital Sucre to the Foreign Office: 'Be assured that nothing awaits emigrants in Bolivia but sorrow and hopeless disappointment ... they will not only plunge into a sea of trouble themselves, but entail on their descendants the miseries inseparable from a state of society proceeding from bad to worse.'[54]

4 • Gran Colombia

Venezuela declared its independence on 5 July 1811, but it was to be another ten years before independence became a reality. The same applied to the declaration, made towards the end of that year, proclaiming the inauguration of the United Provinces of New Granada. During the course of 1812 Spanish reinforcements arrived from the West Indies and, linking up with royalist strongholds that had continued to resist the rebels, reasserted royal rule throughout Venezuela. New Granada continued in rebellion and helped Bolívar in 1813 to recapture Caracas and reestablish an independent Venezuelan republic. His triumph however was very shortlived and, after his defeat in June 1814 by a royalist army commanded by Boves, he abandoned Caracas to royalist forces. He then moved back into New Granada and captured Bogotá in December of that year, but a quarrel with other patriot leaders led to his withdrawal into the West Indies. Meanwhile France's armies were defeated in Spain and King Ferdinand VII restored to his throne. He was thus able to send over the ocean a well-equipped army of 10,000 men under the command of General Pablo Morillo who, by the end of 1816, had effectively crushed all rebel resistance in Venezuela and in New Granada. Only in 1817, when Bolívar, back once again on the mainland, took possession of Angostura, 200 miles up the River Orinoco but (important point) accessible by sea, did patriot fortunes change for the better.

In 1818 Bolívar endeavoured though without success to break out from the plains, where the patriot forces of General Páez had been waging guerilla war for some time, but in 1819 by a bold stroke of strategy he launched a campaign into New Granada, bypassing the royalists based on Caracas. After winning a victory at Boyacá on 7 August 1819, he entered the capital Bogotá without encountering any resistance. A truce followed in 1820 but that lasted only a matter of months and finally on the field of Carabobo in June 1821 the

Spanish army was completely defeated. It only remained for the patriot army, now commanded by General Sucre, to liberate modern Ecuador which it did in 1822.[1]

At a congress held at Angostura in December of 1819, it was declared that all the lands that constituted New Granada were to be united into one country, known to historians as Gran Colombia. Bolívar was, by a later congress, to be elected its first president but he was not successful in holding together a confederation of such diversity and by 1830 it had split into three states, Venezuela, Ecuador and New Granada, the latter being known today as Colombia and Panama. Gran Colombia, as described by O'Leary, Bolívar's secretary and chief-of-staff, was not a viable unity, either political or economic, once the yoke of Spain had been removed.

> Its geography [he wrote] is an important part of its history. When we behold two and a half million inhabitants spread over a territory of more than 112,376 square leagues, we can readily imagine how easy it is to defend and how difficult to subjugate. The influence of geographical location on the fate of Colombia must be examined in regard to its political consequences and its relationship to the social order. The great Andes chain divides various population groups that differ in origin, in customs, in feelings and in education. Most of the inhabitants of the warm regions are Negroes or descendants of Africans, whereas the downtrodden Indian race make up the mass of the population of the mesetas or cold regions. The creoles of pure Spanish extraction are separated from the Africans by racial pride of dominion; but at the same time they regard each other with mutual aversion, though there is no reason for it other than the difference in habits resulting from the difference in climate. This explains the rivalries between Venezuela and New Granada, between Cartagena and Bogotá, and between Quito and Guayaquil, all of whom have been so fatal in the annals of the revolution. Communication between the highlands and lowlands was difficult, and it was the policy of the Spanish government to favour the social isolation.[2]

Nearly six thousand volunteers from England, Scotland and notably Ireland went to South America to join the patriots in their fight for independence, once Bolívar had established himself with a firm base at Angostura. Initially a large proportion of these were officers of the British army who had recently received their discharge at the end of the wars against Napoleon, or restless civilians who were now commissioned in the patriot army of Venezuela; and a number of them were to write and get published, during the course of the next few years, accounts of their war experiences. These men were recruited in the first place by the London agent of Bolívar, a Venezuelan called López Méndez, who was then resident in London and was now given an official position as Venezuela's envoy extraordinary and minister plenipotentiary. The timing of his recruiting campaign, begun in May 1817, was nothing if not opportune for, in the wake of the recent wars, Britain was facing economic depression and rising and widespread unemployment, especially in industrial areas, and in Dublin 60,000 people were in receipt of poor relief. Conditions worsened in 1818 when the British army of occupation was withdrawn from France and demobilized. Thirty-three thousand were deprived of employment and the numbers were swollen by demobilized sailors, when the British fleets were reduced in size. There was therefore no lack of volunteers to go and fight in South America, a country about which almost nothing was known (save that it was extremely rich) by those who succumbed to López Méndez's blandishments. These last included a promise to pay one third above the salary earned by a soldier in the British army, a lump sum on landing on American soil and a grant of land when peace was made. Rapid promotion and financial inducements were offered to those who raised regiments and one lucky officer was informed he could become a divisional general and reap sufficient financial reward to provide for himself and his family for life.[3] Naturally many were disillusioned when, on arriving in South America, or on some small West Indian island with the hope of getting to Venezuela (for some never got beyond the West Indies), they found these promises unfulfilled. A modern historian would think it amazing that López Méndez should have inspired such confidence in guarantees given by a rebel government whose position must have seemed extremely precarious to people in Britain at that time. But those who enlisted (as opposed to their backers) were either desperate, simply reckless or extraordinarily ill-informed. One of the most embittered officers 'Lieutenant-Colonel' Gustavus Hippisley, accused López Méndez and his English assistant, a man by the name of William Walton, of being the most dishonest tricksters, and the accusation seems not unfair. As Eric Lambert has pointed out in his history of the volunteers, López Méndez must have known perfectly well that the volunteers' chances of ever receiving any sort of reward in cash, given the state of patriot finances, was bound to be slender in the extreme.[4]

Merchants however were excited at the prospect of reaping very substantial profits by supplying clothing, arms and equipment to the colonels raising regiments, and by cashing in on new lucrative markets, and were encouraged in their fanciful hopes by some editors of the popular press. Hippisley managed to sign a contract with the firm of Thompson and Mackintosh to supply his regiment with what it required and a certain wealthy Mr Graham, a member of the Ordnance Department, contributed £35,000 to equip Colonel Gillmore's artillery corps.[5]

The attitude of the British government was one of strict neutrality, as it had to be without breaking with Spain, which it certainly had no wish to do. But public opinion was behind the patriots and the press publicized the open letter that Bolívar had sent to López Méndez, agreeing to naturalize British subjects who went to fight with the patriots and to accord them the same civic rights as every South American. Though a Royal Proclamation was made in November 1817 forbidding all subjects of the British crown to take part in the struggle being waged between Spain and her rebel colonists, the government found that it could not enforce it in the existing state of the law. Fresh protests from the Spanish ambassador at the activities of rebel agents caused Castlereagh, the foreign secretary, to warn López Méndez he might be deported if he persisted in what he was doing. Yet no action was taken against him nor was any attempt made to prevent ships sailing from British ports carrying British and Irish volunteers, with equipment and arms to the patriots.[6]

It was not until August 1819 that the Foreign Enlistment Act was passed, but that served merely to close the door after most of the horses had left the stable. The bill was vigorously opposed while in the process of becoming law and 1700 London merchants, manufacturers and ship-owners petitioned parliament against it, arguing that the patriots were their best customers and that if the bill was passed into law the whole of the trade of South America would fall into the hands of the United States. One member of parliament, during debate, claimed that 'in our present commercial distress ... Providence seemed to have opened to us the markets of South America – a country of immense extent, and of unlimited wealth, whose resources would grow with the growth of its independence, and in a short time enable it to purchase and consume whatever we could export for its use'.[7] But whatever long-term prospects for trade were being opened by patriot successes, it can scarcely be urged that this Act of Parliament had any real bearing on the ultimate issue.

At the end of 1817 the first contingents of volunteers left England to join Bolívar's army. They were small groups, numbering 700 in all, officers and non-commissioned officers, commanded by so-called lieutenant-colonels: Wilson, Campbell, Gillmore and McDonald, Hippisley, English, Needham, Beamish and Blosset. Most of them were Irishmen. Henry Wilson had served as a lieutenant in the 9th Light Dragoons until 1810, when he returned to Dublin University to continue his academic studies. Peter Campbell, until he left England, had been a captain in the Buffs. Joseph Gillmore had served in Portugal and then in the 3rd West Indies Regiment while Donald McDonald also served in Portugal as aide-de-camp to General Ballesteros. Gustavus Hippisley was another junior officer never rising above the rank of captain, while John Needham, an Irishman, was a half-pay lieutenant who had served in the wars. James English (another Irishman) sailed as an officer in Hippisley's regiment but returned to England a year later to raise, at Simón Bolívar's request, fresh regiments for South America, this time consisting of rank and file and rather fewer officers. In doing this he was joined by George Elsom. They were each to be paid £50 for every new recruit they enlisted. Elsom, an unscrupulous businessman who had fled from England to escape his creditors, possessed no previous military knowledge but had enlisted in a hussar regiment and had obtained from López Méndez an introduction to Bolívar. Elsom was clearly a man with a presence, for he made an impression on Bolívar and, according to senior British officers, earned the respect and admiration of all.[8]

During the course of 1819 the regiments raised by English and Elsom arrived on the island of Margarita that lies not far from the coast of Venezuela and was now in the hands of patriot forces. When the first contingents had landed from England, the patriot general Arismendi had told them he had no need of them, having already sufficient officers, and Bolívar described these small detachments as more of a hindrance than a help. What he required were organized bodies of perhaps three to four thousand men, all suitably armed and equipped. It was for this reason that English and Elsom were sent back to England to find more recruits.[9]

Yet another Irishman, John Devereux, like Elsom a charismatic character, persuaded López Méndez to let him raise an Irish Legion in his native country, in return for which he was to have money and be given the rank of divisional general. Devereux was an adventurer, articulate and very persuasive. He managed to obtain £6000 by selling commissions to his fellow countrymen, inducing youths of eighteen or nineteen to buy majorities and colonelcies in regiments that never existed. He disposed of 116 colonelcies and commissioned (on payment) enough officers to command a force of 5000 men, though the strength of the legion that he enlisted was scarcely more than 1700.[10] Another Celt, Colonel Gregor M'Gregor, raised a regiment called the Hibernia that took Porto Bello in 1819, but when the Spanish counter-attacked he fled from the scene, abandoning his troops.[11]

What was the quality of the various commanders of these assorted regiments who had adopted impressive titles such as the 1st Venezuelan Hussars, the 1st Venezuelan Lancers, the Red Hussars, the Venezuelan Rifles? M'Gregor was an adventurer who had served for a time under Bolívar, but in 1816 had abandoned the patriots purely to forward his own ends. He led a filibuster against Florida two years before he attacked Porto Bello. He held no commission from the patriots, yet he chose to assume high-sounding titles. The American historian Francis Hasbrouck has little good to say of him, calling him conceited, lazy and timid, but the Scot Alexander Alexander, who encountered him at Margarita, described him as being a great favourite with the inhabitants of the island who appointed him to represent them in the patriot congress of Venezuela. He was also, according to Alexander, much respected by United States merchants and did a great deal to relieve the suffering of Britons who were destitute and left stranded on the island.[12]

Gustavus Hippisley was another commander whom Hasbrouck has little good to say about, describing him as nothing but a 'trifler'. Madariaga, in his life of Bolívar, writes him off as a lightweight soldier, a braggart though probably courageous, a man of enormous self-importance. He and Bolívar disliked each other and Hippisley in his *Narrative* has much to say about what he felt was the shabby way that Bolívar behaved over money Hippisley claimed was owed him and owed to the troops under his command.[13]

Colonel Wilson, early on in the campaign, was placed under arrest by Bolívar and then deported from Venezuela for trying to divide the patriots by intriguing to get General José Páez to assume the post of supreme commander.[14]

James English was an incompetent soldier who had calculated on making a profit out of the struggle the patriots were waging. After the failure of the attack by the British Legion on Cumaná, he behaved in a seemingly disgraceful manner, taking flight by ship to Margarita where he soon afterwards died of fever. The anonymous soldier-sailor author of *Recollections of Three Years' Service* thought he lacked energy and experience, though he credits him with generosity. He was obviously no military leader and George Chesterton, another officer who has left an account of his experiences, considered that it was just as well that English did not accompany his men on the crucifying march to Maturín en route to the Orinoco valley, as he was so hated that the men would have killed him.[15]

John Devereux was a remarkable character, really a most successful trickster who somehow, one suspects, through Irish 'blarney' (a quality with which he was well endowed) succeeded in convincing the American patriots that his services were valuable. He had in 1798 fought the British in the Irish rebellion, had been allowed to expatriate himself but must have been given leave to return from his exile abroad when peace was made. Despite the fact that in South America he was never known to have drawn a sword, 'except in making proclamations of wit', he ended up with $800,000 and the rank of a lieutenant-general. 'So much for address and speculation', was the comment made by Sir Robert Ker Porter, the first British consul to go to Caracas.[16] Devereux did not accompany his legion in its voyage across to Margarita – just as well, in view of the fact that the troops of the legion got out of hand when they found on arrival that the promises made them by Devereux were not to be honoured. William Adam, an officer who enlisted in a regiment raised by Devereux, does not spare his criticism of the latter: 'There was certainly [William Adam wrote] an unaccountable degree of blindness, stupidity or ignorance on the part of the general [Devereux] in granting the command to some whose days were passed over in idleness and debauchery, and whose nights were spent in drunkenness or the infatuations of the hazard table.'[17] When Devereux did eventually arrive, his legion by then having left Margarita, he managed to live in considerable style. Alexander saw him when he first arrived, and again on the mainland at Barranquilla, 'affecting all the pomp of a sovereign, and stalking about, a tall, vain figure, so covered with lace that he looked like a lace-merchant's pattern card' and surrounded by a new levy of officers, who were strutting around to show off their rank.[18]

The anonymous author of *Recollections* met Devereux in 1820 on board a brig called the *Mary Sunderland*. Devereux seemed to be deeply depressed till he realized that he was not going to be arrested but rather accorded a very warm welcome. To this he responded by making a speech that lasted for no less than an hour. The following day he chose to appear in a French field-marshal's uniform, having previously changed its red colour to blue by getting hold of an old silk dress from a woman on the island who covered it for him. At the banquet that was given that day in his honour by the patriot general Arismendi, Devereux insisted on making a speech (in English, which no one could understand) that went on for two whole hours. When the officer interpreting tried to translate, Devereux kept interrupting him, asking him to add something more: 'Tell 'em [he would say] I'll destroy every Spaniard in South America, tell 'em *that*; say that all Ireland is up in their cause, in consequence of my representations, tell 'em *that*.' Finally, the interpreter, exhausted, told Devereux he must tell them himself, as he, the officer interpreting, had never talked so much in his life.[19]

Later, at Rosario de Cúcuta, the author met Devereux again. Devereux made a number of claims that were rejected by the patriot vice-president who expelled the Irishman from his house and refused even to acknowledge him as holding a commission in the republic. Devereux, not to be outdone, accused the vice-president of attempted rape on the body of the widowed Mrs English. For this slander Devereux was imprisoned but later acquitted by a court-martial, his accuser by that time having been dismissed.[20] Colonel Brooke-Young wrote in 1821 of Devereux's extraordinary personality: 'Notwithstanding the failure of the greater part of his Expedition, the People of the Country actually adore him, calling him their Liberator. But his manner makes an impression wherever he goes.'[21] It is ironical that in modern Caracas, on the great monument fairly recently erected by the government of Venezuela in homage to all those officers and men who fought in the war for independence, the list of all the *foreign* officers, whose names are inscribed on one marble pillar, is topped by that of John Devereux. His name is spelled inaccurately as 'Juan Deveraux' (general of division), but it is unmistakably the mountebank hero.

Aside from all the adventurers and triflers, there were a number of distinguished soldiers hailing from England, Scotland and Ireland who did sterling service in the cause of the patriots. Apart from O'Leary and Ferguson, both of whom were Bolívar's closest aides, there were men of the quality of Colonel Rooke, a gallant and professional regular soldier who reorganized and disciplined the British Legion when its remnant arrived at Angostura.[22]

Of the several thousands of volunteers, whose home was either Britain or Ireland, and who crossed the Atlantic to fight with the patriots, only 160 men and perhaps 80 officers survived by the end of 1823 and these were incorporated on Bolívar's orders in the so-called 'Battalion of Carabobo'. The privates were paid a gratuity and presumably managed to make their way home, but a number of officers stayed on.[23]

The diverse accounts of their experiences, as volunteers in the patriot army engaged in liberating New Granada, amount to almost a dozen in number and vary greatly not only in length but also in literary quality. The best and most lively is by someone who served both as military and naval officer but preferred to remain anonymous; his identity has not so far been traced for certain, though he was possibly George Woodberry, former lieutenant in 15th Light Dragoons. Entitled *Recollections of a Service of Three Years During the War of Extermination in the Republics of Venezuela and Colombia*, it is the account of an officer who had served nine years in the British army and who, being given command of a ship by his relation, Major Beamish, sailed for the coast of Venezuela during the summer of 1818. Throughout the course of the next three years he served partly as a naval officer, partly as a soldier, with commissioned rank, being rewarded after Carabobo with the rank of general of brigade, a grant of land and citizenship within the state of Colombia. He continued to press without success for the payment of the debts of Major Beamish (who had raised, clothed and equipped a regiment of 300 Irish at his own expense and had then died when ten days out at sea), but finally resigned his commission and returned home to write his book.[24]

Another account, by an officer who chose to write under no name at all but who has since been identified as the Irishman Richard Longueville Vowell, is entitled *Campaigns and Cruises in Venezuela and New Grenada* [sic]. Vowell had inherited a fortune while studying at Cambridge University, so decided to leave the world of academe and adopt a life that promised adventure. He served in the campaigns that culminated in Bolívar's capture of Bogotá, fought under Sucre in Ecuador and then enlisted as a marine officer in Cochrane's squadron off Guayaquil, thus ending up in the service of Chile, in which he remained until 1829.[25]

A third long and lively account of campaigning with the patriot forces is given by a Scot called Alexander Alexander in his spirited autobiography. As a youth he had served as a bombardier in the British army in Ceylon; after that he travelled over much of the world, getting eventually to Demerara where he took employment on several estates. He did not however enjoy this life and at the age of thirty-six took himself off to Angostura, where he entered the service of the British Legion which was then being reorganized by Rooke. He managed without much difficulty to obtain a commission as a second lieutenant and was posted to Bolívar's guard of honour. Later he served as a captain of marines aboard a patriot brig-of-war. When Caracas finally fell to Bolívar, he seems to have resumed his civilian status and secured a passage back to England in the course of 1822.[26]

A fourth account is by George Laval Chesterton, a tough though very snobbish young man, who enlisted in the regiment of 'Colonel' English, raised in England in 1818. He had been employed in the Board of Ordnance who gave him leave to go abroad for an indefinite period, though whether his employment had been military or civilian is not clear from his narrative. He is chiefly renowned for having composed the anthem of the British Legion during his voyage across the Atlantic, was given a commission as a captain and appointed judge-advocate of the legion. In his book *Peace, War and Adventure*, not published until 1853, he gives a very vivid account of the patriot armies, the conditions they fought under, and thumbnail sketches of some patriot generals. Latterly he suffered much from illness and was eventually captured by the royalists, by whom he was treated with great humanity. When in reply to Morillo's questions as to why he had chosen to fight the Spaniards and what they had done to excite his hostility, he replied tactfully that he had been moved by the spirit of adventure and desire to roam, inspired by the accounts of the travels of Cortés, Ulloa and the naturalist Humboldt. Morillo had seemed quite satisfied, told Chesterton his motives were natural, and had then permitted him to go home.[27]

None of these four narratives give the impression of their narrators being particulalry aggrieved or writing to engage public sympathy. Not so most of the other accounts, the most readable being by Gustavus Hippisley and entitled *A Narrative of the Expedition to the Rivers Orinoco and Apuré*, published in London in 1819. A half-pay cavalry lieutenant who for five years had been captain and adjutant of the West Somerset militia (hardly an exacting post and certainly not associated with the hardships and rigours of active service), Hippisley, by his own account,

was persuaded to join the volunteers by a friend 'whose experience in
military matters was as distinguished as his name was honoured, loved
and respected'. He was given the rank of lieutenant-colonel and
appointed to the command of a regiment entitled the 1st Venezuelan
Hussars. His experiences in Venezuela were to leave him utterly
disillusioned, the pay and conditions being not what was promised,
and he finally resigned in disgust. On returning to England he was
instrumental in getting López Méndez arrested for debt, but failed to
obtain any compensation. Finally he retired to Guernsey, where he
was to write his scathing indictment of the patriot army and its
commanders.[28]

Captain William Jackson Adam was another British officer who did
not stay long with the volunteers, enlisting in July 1819 in the second
division of the Lancers regiment. Adam came home in 1820 and four
years later published his *Journal*, directed largely against Devereux
and the officers that he recruited rather than against the patriots.[29]
Not so James H. Robinson who enrolled as a surgeon in the patriot
army and was one of the first of the volunteers to reach Bolívar at
Angostura. He was involved in the fruitless campaign to break out of
the plains, in 1818, and in the subsequent chaotic retreat from San
Fernando to Angostura. The account of his experiences, *Journal of an
Expedition 1400 Miles up the Orinoco and 300 up the Arauca*, published
in 1824, is marred by its self-pitying tone and finally becomes a
tedious catalogue of all the malpractices of the patriots and the
seemingly disgraceful way they behaved towards British volunteers.[30]

Others who wrote with bitterness about their experiences as volunteers were James Hackett, Lieutenant C. Brown and George Flinter
whose narratives appeared in print in 1818 and 1819. Hackett openly
admits that his motives for enrolling himself were purely financial,
though he adds, rather sententiously, that he would not have adopted
the course he had, had he not thought that a gentleman of honour and
a British subject could consistently embark on it. He was given a
commission as a lieutenant in Colonel Gillmore's artillery 'brigade',
but the so-called brigade never succeeded in getting beyond a West
Indian island where shortage of money compelled its disbandment. A
few members of it did eventually succeed in making their way to the
mainland, but Hackett himself was not among them, for dismayed by
reports of the conditions to be expected in the patriot army, he decided
his best course was to go home. His avowed object in writing his
narrative was to warn others who might be contemplating doing what

he had recently done. In it he stressed the false hopes that were raised, the jealousy shown towards British officers by creole officers of the patriot army, and the brutal nature of a war to the death in which no prisoners remained alive, and though his evidence was entirely hearsay, it would seem it was not far removed from the truth.[31]

Brown, who was another young man who enlisted in the artillery brigade, showed more stamina than James Hackett. He actually got to Angostura, having on the disbandment of the brigade enlisted in Campbell's Rifle Corps. Eventually posted to Margarita, he fell ill and with great difficulty managed to obtain a passport to leave, though he had no success in recovering his pay. Like Hackett, he issued a stern warning to those who were thinking of volunteering to fight in South America. The promise of land in lieu of back-pay would, he wrote, probably be the award of a plot where the natives refused to settle, miles away from civilization and where one would have to employ Indians to keep out the 'savages' and wild beasts. There was very little hope of promotion – preference would always be given to natives who were very jealous of the heretic British. As the chiefs of the patriot forces had said: 'We do not want officers, but men who will carry the musket and act in obedience to those of our countrymen whom we shall be pleased to appoint to command them.' The Indians, of whom to a large extent the patriot army was made up, were men taken from their native 'missions' and the freedom for which they ostensibly fought had only an empty sound for them. The patriot forces were equipped with arms supplied by English speculators, but they had no conception of how to use them and threw them away to facilitate flight. These were then captured by the Spaniards who, as Morillo had publicly stated, needed no arms and stores from Spain since they were kept very plentifully supplied by those abandoned by the fugitive rebels.[32]

George Flinter, whose *History of the Revolution of Caracas* was published in London in 1819, was not a volunteer officer but, having served in the West Indies (presumably with commissioned rank), became an interpreter for the British admiral of the squadron stationed in those waters and subsequently for the Spanish in Caracas, having by then been discharged from the army. His sympathies were openly royalist and he wrote in a melodramatic style, but it is of interest nevertheless to read of 'atrocities' from the Spanish viewpoint. His book contains yet another plea to British subjects not to volunteer to join the army of the rebel patriots. He lists among the reasons for not doing so religious prejudice, a hostile climate, the extreme difficulty of obtaining food, the serious lack of medical attention for those who fell sick or suffered wounds, and the discipline and motivation of those who fought in the patriot army. They were not disciplined at all (he alleges) or fired with enthusiasm for the cause of liberty but 'a horde of naked savages, prowling in search of plunder, subsisting on the precarious food from the spontaneous production of the forest, and headed by a set of wretches who would disgrace a gibbet'. Even if they were to expel the Spaniards, the form of government these rebels would set up would resemble that of San Domingo, with numerous chiefs exercising a despotic sway over their slaves and quarrelling with one another. Flinter urged the British government to join Spain in quelling the rebellion and in freeing the seas of pirate vessels busy preying on British commerce and sailing under the rebel flag.[33]

The popular press of both Britain and Ireland joined in condemning the patriots during the course of 1818 and the author of an article in the *Annual Register* wrote of the disillusionment felt by the various volunteers when met by coldness if not actual jealousy – 'they have found an army of half-clothed and half-civilized soldiers, instead of men ardent and enlightened in the cause of liberty, and an army well-equipped and disciplined'.[34] The accusations were answered in a letter that was published in September in the *Morning Post*, signed by Rooke and thirty-two officers. Though Hippisley alleged the letter was a forgery, it helped English and Elsom in their task of recruitng for their respective regiments. Elsom, in a letter to the *Dublin Evening Post*, published on 2 December 1819, wrote of the irrational hopes of those who had earlier volunteered and their failure to realize that they were serving in a country that had suffered appallingly. In the course of a seven-year revolution houses, villages and whole cities had been burnt and removed altogether from the face of the earth, while the countryside had been continuously despoiled, often of everything it possessed. Allowances had to be made for all this and expectations not pitched too high. Daniel O'Leary later wrote in his memoirs that the greater part of the volunteers endured their hardships with fortitude.[35]

There is no doubt that the volunteers had been a very mixed bag indeed. Wilson's regiment, as described by Hippisley, was a prime example of the worst of its sort. 'Colonel Wilson [Hippisley wrote] was at the head of only a hundred men, and half of them deserters or mutineers from another corps; a drunken debauched lieutenant-colonel who could not dismiss a common parade; a still more drunken

major, but yet when sober a good soldier; a set of captains and
subalterns who, with the exception of two, had never served in any
regiment before, the whole of them, in point of horsemanship, had
been laughed at by all Páez's cavalry, either as horsemen or
swordsmen.'[36]

The Irish Legion's members were, if anything, worse. The author
of *Recollections* describes them as being either peasants or urban
proletariat, who were all physically unfit and had never seen a shot
fired in anger. The legion was sent first to Liverpool, where the men
committed various crimes, chiefly because they had not been paid,
and was then shipped off to Margarita. There the legion was half-
starved, many of its number were struck down by fever and 750 of
them died.[37]

Adam's criticism of their officers has been mentioned earlier in this
chapter. Alexander met some of these officers who told him that
originally they had purchased their commissions honestly but had then
committed highway robbery to obtain money to buy higher rank. Many
were old, some unfit for service and few of them 'could put their men
even through the manual and platoon exercises'. The men lampooned
the officers and showed themselves openly disobedient, going round
shooting pigs and poultry and breaking into houses and stores; and
when their officers fought their frequent duels, they gathered round
in hundreds to witness the 'sport'. Little wonder the people of the
island disliked them, said they should be fighting on the mainland and
contrasted their undisciplined behaviour with that of the regiment of
Colonel Blosset. General Montilla who had come to collect them said
that never in his life had he seen such a body of 'unsoldier-looking
men' and decided to leave the island without them. As has been
mentioned earlier, they were eventually sent off to Rio Hacha under
the orders of Luis Brion, the admiral commanding the patriot fleet.
The royalists withdrew from that city which the mutinous Irish then
set fire to, all becoming impossibly drunk. Still unpaid, the men asked
to be sent home, so the legion was then shipped off to Jamaica where
the soldiers committed further crimes. From there the legion sailed
back to England, the British governor of the island being unwilling to
continue to pay for its food. One hundred and fifty men from the
legion had left Rio Hacha for Cartagena there to form part of a
battalion under the command of Colonel Ferrier, and its survivors
were in the end incorporated into the British Legion.

Alexander while at Caracas, after the victory of Carabobo, saw the remnants of the volunteers (a mixture of British and Irish soldiers) and thought they looked a sorry sight. They were billeted in an old barrack, without bed, bedding, knapsack, uniform, shoes or any sort of cooking utensil. Living under these conditions they mounted guard over the president (Bolívar), with red straw hats, shirts and trousers, 'having only a passeta a day to lay out as they pleased . . . all were sallow, all sickly pale. Had it not been for their tongue, no one would have known them to be Englishmen [sic]'.[38]

Captain Adam thinks the great mistake had been to choose Margarita Island as the rendezvous for the volunteers – the responsibility had been Colonel English's. The climate he (surprisingly) alleged was bad, so was the quality of the water and there was no adequate supply of either food or accommodation. Bolívar could hardly be expected to make arrangements for the reception of these troops while engaged in fighting a campaign on the mainland, and when the movements of his army were uncertain and it was not known from one month to the next what places would be held by either side. Adam thought there had been special pleading made on behalf of the Irish Legion which, though its members had been tricked by Devereux, had received the same treatment as everyone else.[39]

What was the treatment they all received? The troops who arrived at Margarita found not arrangements for their reception. There was no bedding and the quarters were verminous. Brown describes the men living in tents used by the British in the Peninsula and since condemned as unserviceable. There was not sufficient nourishing food (they had to subsist on salt-fish and bad biscuit), and no money to pay the troops. Not surprisingly there was a mutiny though it seems it was very rapidly crushed, the ringleaders being publicly flogged without a murmur from the rank and file. Even so discontent persisted, especially when the British contingent was kept inactive for the next four months. When campaigning began on the mainland opposite, the troops suffered much from the tropical rains as well as the continuing shortage of rations. The British Legion was involved in attacks on two of the Venezuelan ports, Barcelona and Cumaná, the first a success, the second disastrous. It then took part in a gruelling march over the mountains to Maturín and thence eventually to Angostura.[40]

The anonymous author of *Recollections* describes the hardships of that march. Numbers were drowned in the flooded streams, 400 died of sheer exhaustion, many lost their footwear and had to march barefoot, all were bitten by vicious insects and some suffered lacerations to their legs from ray fish in the shallow lakes. Rain extinguished the nightly campfires and the ground on which they had to doss down was covered in 6 to 9 inches of water. When the remnant arrived at Maturín there was no medical attention to be found, no medical supplies, a filthy hospital and only hovels in which to shelter. The food situation was as bad as ever and only 233 effectives ever got as far as Angostura.[41]

Later, when the legion was reorganized, and formed part of Bolívar's army that advanced to capture Bogotá, it suffered, as did all the patriot troops, in the long march across the *cordillera*, again in the middle of the rainy season. Vowell has left a graphic description of what conditions were like on the march, when the rain descended night and day. Huge pinnacles of granite overhung the passes, enormous chasms yawned below. He experienced a sense of extreme loneliness, with no sound save only the scream of the condor or the murmur of distant waterfalls. Clouds frequently obscured the path and to lose the way meant certain death. Sometimes he was compelled to lie down, when the strength of the wind made standing impossible; many of his companions died. Two years later it was much the same story, in the march that led to Carabobo. Only the hardiest survived.[42]

What chiefly irked the volunteers was their inability to get paid for their services. Alexander relates how at Angostura in 1818 there were promises made of great rewards once Caracas was taken – each soldier was to get $500, a lieutenant $4000, a captain $6000, and those who distinguished themselves in the field were to be made a grant of land, given a vote in the Venezuelan congress and allowed to enjoy two years' leave in England. All this was pie in the sky and no satisfaction to the volunteers. There was nothing but meat for the British to eat, since they could not afford the rice, salt and ham that was sold in small quantities in the market. Eventually Colonel Rooke managed, after making many representations, to get the officers an allowance of table money, and shortly after Bolívar ordered that all ranks of the British Legion were to receive meat and salt rations and laid down a scale of pay for them.[43]

Hippisley recounts how in 1819 all but six of his regiment, and all the Red Hussars regiment, refused to swear allegiance to the republic until they were paid at least part of the $80 promised them ($200 in the case of officers). The crisis was averted by the timely arrival of a ship from England with stores on board that had been dispatched as a speculation, to make a profit by being sold on the spot. The officers remained very discontented when they found they were getting only $10, but the local merchants were much relieved when the congress rescinded a previous order that every merchant should pay a forced levy. One British merchant had refused to pay and in consequence had been sent to prison. Clashes over pay between Bolívar and Hippisley leading to the resignation of the latter will be dealt with later in this chapter.[44]

The anonymous author of *Recollections* was sent from Margarita to the mainland on a vain quest to get money from congress to pay the volunteer forces on the island. When he finally came back empty-handed, Admiral Brion, a man of means, advanced some money from his private purse (having previously refused to do so) to supply the needs of the British contingent. Later the author recounts how Bolívar was at last persuaded by Colonel Blosset to make a partial payment to the British, who up to then had not received any reply to their various petitions. One of the patriot brigadiers accused the British of never being satisfied, was challenged for this by Colonel Blosset and severely wounded in the duel that followed. More such accusations brought on more duels, but the author thinks this display of *machismo* increased respect for the British contingent.

In 1820 the author seized a favourable moment to ask Bolívar if he could be paid the arrears he was owed. Bolívar, in a receptive mood, gave him an order for $1000 – 'the only pay I ever received for a three years' harassing service and a broken constitution'. He tried again, after Carabobo, and the surrender of Caracas, but was still unable to obtain any pay, though, as he declares, more money was available than was required to satisfy every man in the British contingent; instead of which it was thrown away 'on a profusion of banquets and ridiculous pageantry'.[45]

It was lack of pay that led inevitably to serious lack of discipline and sometimes desertion to the Spanish side. After the capture of Barcelona, Colonel English failed to ensure that the men he commanded were confined to barracks, and in less than three hours (the same author bears witness) there was no man sober in the whole division. Three days of riot, debauchery, plunder and wholesale destruction of property followed, until the author and Colonel English eventually got the troops out of the town and placed a strong guard on the bridge leading to it. But having prevented the drunken soldiers from desecrating the cathedral, the British officers proceeded to loot it. Colonel English set the example by removing a picture of a battle scene between rival forces of Moors and Spaniards, that he thought might be a valuable antique. His officers helped themselves to treasures hidden in boxes behind the high altar – gold salvers, massive gold knives and golden crowns studded with jewels. Colonel Blosset was heard to exclaim: 'Here's a pretty thing! I will send it to my wife. Fine finish to a full dress, by Jove!' Officers carried away their spoils in bags they got their servants to make from the clothing of the statues of the saints. What was perhaps most disgraceful of all was the plunder of the body of (allegedly) St Laurence, patron saint of Barcelona, after breaking the glass case containing the corpse. 'It wore a loose dress of white satin, in the Roman form, and round its neck was a golden collar of great weight, set with emeralds and pearls, to which was fastened a chain of the same metal, each link being elegantly chased. On its wrists and anklets were bracelets similar to the collar, to each of which a chain was also affixed, and a crown adorned its head, whereon its name was enamelled at full length. It is needless to say his appendages were removed, but we carefully replaced the carcase.' Chesterton, among the others, helped himself to 'some trifling silver relics'. The following day the British soldiers, seeing what their officers had done, stormed past the guards and ransacked the cathedral, despoiling it of everything that was left worth taking. The women of the town, though somewhat surprised that they had not been raped or sexually assaulted, reprimanded the officers for their sacrilege, saying that their priests had been right about the English, save only that the English had no tails. They were so insistent in their scolding that the angry officers had to warn them that if they did not soon desist, they (the officers) would take away even the bones of the saint they revered.[46]

The inevitable lure of permissive looting (never allowed by Wellington in Spain) induced most of Hippisley's regiment to desert and join the forces of Páez who licensed the plunder of enemy property.[47] But it was usually lack of pay and lack of food that caused the desertions. During the period of inactivity following the taking of Barcelona, forty of Chesterton's men deserted, despite his impassioned pleas to his company. Two were caught and executed and this seemed to have had the desired effect, for without it Chesterton was sure that two hundred soldiers would have deserted. Yet Chesterton and three other officers, on his own admission, tried to desert (not indeed to the enemy) when General Urdaneta refused to accept their resignations from the patriot army. Urdaneta became so angry at the numbers of

British officers applying to resign that he threatened them with imprisonment, but the officers kept up their recriminations at the way in which they were being treated, until Chesterton received a reprimand from the chief-of-staff for his violent language. Chesterton now became so enfeebled by attacks of malaria and yellow fever that Bolívar was induced to relent and allowed him to go home with a draft for $40.[48]

The impressions left on the British chroniclers by Simón Bolívar were extemely mixed. Vowell, who met him in 1818, described Bolívar's polite reception of him and his fellow British officers. Bolívar was very apologetic about the poor accommodation he was able to afford but told them he was pleased to see European officers who were capable of disciplining troops and inspiring *his* officers by their example.[49] The anonymous author of *Recollections* met him three years later at Bogotá. He seemed as anxious as General Páez to supply the wants of the British troops, even sharing his private food store with them. But, having said that, the author confesses he was not particularly impressed by the physical presence of the liberator, nor by the manners he displayed. A very large head, very thin legs, and in conversation very obscene. The author was shown into a dirty room containing very little furniture; on the floor was O'Leary with a small writing desk, taking dictation from Bolívar. The latter, at the other end of the room, was sitting stark naked on the edge of a hammock, on which he swung himself to and fro, alternating between dictating and whistling a republican tune. He spoke to the author in excellent English but his friendly attempt to embrace the latter had to be tactfully resisted. Later the author was given dinner, when toasts were drunk to the British armed forces, and invested formally with the republican orders of Bolívar and the liberator. After that the party became disorderly – everybody had drunk too much – and Bolívar's manner degenerated into the coarse and boisterous.[50]

Chesterton first encountered Bolívar at a levee held in 1819 and shared with Colonel Stopford, his companion, disappointment at Bolívar's physical presence, exclaiming, 'Is this the great Bolívar?'. Chesterton describes him as short and slim, with small features and expressive eyes, prematurely grizzled and with careworn features. His voice was dissonant and unattractive and his address to strangers shy and awkward. 'He always appeared [Chesterton writes] to be awaiting an unfriendly communication, for his looks were suspicious, and his eyes usually downcast.' This rather unprepossessing manner was also remarked on by General Miller and to this defect Chesterton attributes (it must be added rather naïvely) much of the hostility shown to Bolívar. However his activity of mind and body Chesterton thought were unsurpassed.[51]

The most unfavourable impression of Bolívar is given in the narrative of Gustavus Hippisley, who managed to quarrel bitterly with him, having first met him in 1818 not long before the patriot army withdrew in disorder from San Fernando. 'General Bolívar [wrote Hippisley] is a mean looking person, seemingly (though but thirty-eight) about fifty years of age. He is about five feet six inches in height; thin, sallow complexion, lengthened visage, marked with every symptom of anxiety, care, and, I could almost say, despondency. He seemed also to have undergone great fatigue. His dark, and, according to report, brilliant eyes, were now dull and heavy, although I could give them credit for possessing more fire and animation when his frame was less harassed. Black hair, loosely tied behind with a piece of riband, large mustachios, black handkerchief round his neck, blue great coat, and blue trowsers, boots and spurs completed his costume. In my eyes he might have passed for anything but the thing he really was. Across the chamber was suspended one of the Spanish hammocks, on which he occasionally sat, lolled and swung whilst conversing, and seldom remained in the same posture for two minutes together.' Later, after his quarrel with Bolívar over the settling of his accounts, Hippisley in his comments on the liberator adopts a much more acerbic tone.

Hippisley found the greatest difficulty in getting paid what he thought he was owed. After an unsatisfactory interview, he described the replies he got from Bolívar as being 'unworthy of himself – full of subtility, evasion, deceit, dishonour and base ingratitude'. What Bolívar had told Hippisley was that he did not for a moment doubt the accuracy of Hippisley's account, but it lacked the signature of López Méndez. Why, he asked, had López not advanced the requisite money to Hippisley in England, or obtained credit for it from wealthy merchants? A second angry interview followed, with Rooke acting as the interpreter. Hippisley asked for a pass to England and said he would only return to Venezuela to give his services to the patriots if Bolívar ordered his expenses to be paid and would grant him the rank of a general of brigade. Bolívar became extremely angry and told Hippisley that neither he nor his government would be influenced by any threats. Hippisley thereupon resigned his commission, sold his belongings and returned to England, determined to prosecute López for fraud, though before leaving (with a touch of farce) he managed to get Bolívar to purchase his cocked hat and his feather and cap.

Hippisley in his *Narrative* concludes by saying that Bolívar possessed no gratitude, honour, liberality or indeed humanity. Brave (Hippisley continues), but not qualified to be a general, let alone a commander-in-chief, he made numerous mistakes in his campaigns and any of the repeated surprises he had experienced as a commander 'would have disgraced a corporal's guard'. 'Bolívar would willingly ape the great man. He aspires to be a second Buonaparte in South America without possessing a single talent for the duties of the field or of the cabinet. He would be king of New Granada and Venezuela, without genius to command, consequence to secure, or abilities to support the elevated station to which his ambition most assuredly aspires. In victory – in transient prosperity – he is a tyrant and displays the littleness and feelings of an upstart. He gives way to sudden gusts of resentment and becomes in a moment a madman, and (pardon the expression) a blackguard ... In defeat, in danger, in retreat, he is perplexed and contemptible even to himself – weighed down by disasters, which he has neither skill nor strength of mind to encounter, to enlighten or to remove.'[52] Hippisley's disparaging assessment of Bolívar as leader in the field was made, of course, before the astonishingly successful campaigns culminating in the freeing of all of New Granada. Moreover, such scathing criticism sounds impertinent if not absurd, coming as it does from an officer who had never held any senior rank and had never had the responsibility of commanding a body of troops in the field. It may well be that Bolívar saw himself as being a kind of American Napoleon: 'We know how deeply Bolívar admired and imitated the Corsican,' wrote his biographer Madariaga, but his aspirations for his country were noble, lofty and very far from selfish. In fairness to Hippisley, it should be added that some years later, in a letter to Bolívar, he retracted his earlier allegations.[53]

Sir Robert Ker Porter, who was appointed the first British consul in Caracas, gives a picture in his private diary of the frantic welcome accorded Bolívar when he arrived in Caracas from Peru in January 1827. 'Crowds of rejoicing people all wild in screaming "Viva Bolívar, Viva Páez, Viva Columbia", firing pistols, guns and rockets.' The rejoicings continued over several days, 'mobs, morning, noon and night clinging to the iron rails of Bolívar's mansion, like clusters of monkeys'. Porter found Bolívar's physical presence infinitely more prepossessing than any of the writers already quoted. 'A fine black small piercing eye, an expression of solemn reflexion without a smile, but much sweet tranquillity and goodness in his countenance.' Porter was clearly carried away in his admiration for the king-like liberator and had little love for democracy. In tones worthy of Thomas Carlyle he inveighs against 'These Republican infants – these envious party-spirited creatures – these would-be Legislators! These actual unprincipled blockheads'.[54]

Perhaps the most balanced view of Bolívar comes from the pen of an officer who had served for some years in Colombia, witnessed some of the principal events of the revolution in that country and had published in 1827 his book *The Present State of Colombia*. He describes Bolívar as being 'neither a Napoleon in war, nor a Washington in Council', but whose services to his country were not just important but indeed essential. He pays tribute to his firmness and decisiveness, his amazingly robust constitution and his energy and ability to cope in what were often the most difficult circumstances. Most of the chieftains (the officer writes) respected him and, as Porter's earlier account bears out, he was regarded by the soldiers and people with little short of religious veneration. In contrast to the impression conveyed by Hippisley, and one or two others, about the way Bolívar behaved towards the foreigners in his service, the officer describes his attitude as 'uniformly marked by care and attention to their wants'. He did not at first have the means to pay them, but when the circumstances improved 'he honourably redeemed his pledges'.[55]

After Bolívar the most important of the patriot leaders was General Páez. None of the British and Irish chroniclers has anything but good to say about him. The anonymous author of *Recollections* pays tribute to his heroism and magnanimity. A man of neither birth nor fortune, Páez had risen by his own merits to command the *llaneros* or native cavalry of the Apuré Valley and the province of Barinas – by far the most effective force the patriots were able to put into the field. Initially uncouth and uncivilized in manner, he changed dramatically once he made contact with the officers of the foreign legions, mingling with them socially and adopting their customs, dress and manners. Indeed he became very Anglophile and checked any of his own officers who were inclined to abuse the British. He was one of the very few patriot officers (the author thinks there were not more than four) who acknowledged the benefits they had received from the presence and actions of the British Legion, and he alone proposed to the congress that it should be given a public testimonial. He was also the only patriot officer who was able to restrain the *llaneros* in their rapacity and passion for murder.[56]

James Robinson in his narrative pays Páez a generous compliment on his almost superhuman activity and Hippisley shared in this admiration. 'He will [wrote Hippisley] for amusement, as he did before some English officers, single out a wild bull from the herd of cattle, and ride him down, pass his lance through and thus slay him, or gallop up to the animal's rear, and grasping the tail firmly in his hand, twist it so suddenly and so strongly as to throw the beast on its side, when, if some of his followers do not come up at the moment to pierce him, he will, by a cut of his sabre, hamstring and leave him, until the arrival of his people puts the finishing stroke to life, and the flesh is prepared for cooking.' The feat, had Hippisley only known, was common among all the cowboys (*llaneros*, *gauchos* or whatever their name) throughout the length of South America. Even so, it was perhaps unusual to find a general performing it.

Wearing only a coarse linen jacket and a coarse linen pair of trousers, with no stockings and no shoes, Páez appeared nearly always on horseback, admired and respected by all his men. Hippisley thought him the only man who could inspire him with feelings of friendship after only the first encounter. He describes Páez as ready to share his moments of leisure with his troops, ready to dance and smoke with them, and taking his drink from the same cup as theirs. He certainly had the common touch.[57]

O'Leary's *Memoirs* reinforce this impression and add a number of significant details. 'He was [wrote O'Leary] of middle height, robust and well shaped, though the lower part of his body was not proportioned to his bust; his chest and shoulders very wide, his neck short and thick, a big head, covered with dark auburn hair, short and wavy; dark, quick eyes, straight nose with wide nostrils, thick lips and a round chin. His clear complexion told his good health ... Caution and mistrust were the chief features of his physiognomy.' Wholly illiterate – (Alexander describes how with great care he could scrawl P A E Z on official papers) – 'he knew nothing about the theory of the profession he practised so much, and was unaware of even the simplest words of the craft; the slightest emotion or contradiction gave him strong convulsions which for a time deprived him of his senses ... As a guerrilla chief, he was without rival. Rash, active, brave [to a fault – Alexander pictures him rushing into battle], fertile in stratagems,

quick in conception, resolute in execution, swift in movement, he was
the more formidable the smaller the force under his command . . .
Lacking in method, knowledge, moral courage, he was valueless in
politics. Without being cruel, he did not spare blood . . . His ambition
was boundless. It and his cupidity were his dominant passions. He
was able to acquire an exceptional hold over the *llaneros* by allowing
looting and by relaxing discipline.'[58]

The British narratives also contain some distinctive portraits of the
other generals with whom volunteers were brought into contact.
Rafael Urdaneta was for a time given command of the British Legion
but was eventually removed from that post after British officers
complained about him. Chesterton had no liking for him, describing
him as 'of diminutive stature, pale, effeminate and a slave to indolence', 'a miserable sensualist' who kept two mistresses in the field and
spent his time lounging in his hammock. Chesterton thought him unfit
for command. Alexander on the other hand described him naïvely as
a noble fellow whose only fault was dislike of foreigners, a dislike for
which he had ample cause. The anonymous author of *Recollections*
gives a rather more balanced account of the man. He thought him
admittedly an intriguer, two-faced and a hater of the English race, but
a brave and able commander of guerillas, though useless at other
forms of command.[59]

Urdaneta was replaced in command of the legion by General
Santiago Mariño, a popular and attractive figure. Chesterton describes
him as 'a stout fair-haired man, of winning countenance and gentle
manners, a man of the European school'. When he visited the British
sick and wounded in the dreadful hospital at Maturín, he wept at the
sufferings of the soldiers and so endeared himself to the troops. Even
Hippisley was won over and calls him talented, brave and generous.[60]

General Juan Bautista Arismendi was another of the patriot generals
with whom the volunteers came into contact when they first arrived in
the Caribbean, as he was the officer-in-command of the garrison of
Margarita Island. A native chieftain, ex-fisherman, half creole and
half Indian, aged fifty-four but looking more, he was idolized by the
people of the island for the bold and ruthless way in which he had rid
the place of the Spanish troops. The anonymous author of *Recollections*
found him open, sincere and very pro-British, and also much attached
to the Irish, whom he described as 'brave blunderers'. 'His person is
large [the author continues], athletic and muscular, though spare and
thin; and he is capable of enduring almost incredible fatigue and

privation.' He had a peculiarly ferocious expression 'which his smile only increases ... his laugh, like an excited hyena, never fails to create a momentary shudder ... his displeasure is always signified by this demoniacal grin, accompanied by a low lengthened exclamation resembling the suppressed roar of a tiger'. Hippisley thought him ferocious, blood-thirsty, cunning, treacherous and vindictive, 'the general butcher of the army'. Clearly he was not a man to be crossed.[61]

General José Francisco Bermudez, the officer commanding at Angostura, was also a man of ferocious appearance, though Hippisley thought him to be humane, and found him both kindly and polite. Unfortunately for the British officers, he was very jealous of foreign competition, unless the officers proved to be surgeons. Hippisley describes him in field dress looking more like an escaped convict, 'a dirty pair of trousers and an old pair of shoes, an old hat with a long white feather at its side, a short piece of dirty blanketing thrown over his shoulders, with a hole cut in the centre through which his head protruded'. Europeans like Hippisley were not accustomed to seeing generals in 'battle-dress'.[62]

The other leader of the patriots with whom the foreign volunteers had some dealings and of whom the author of *Recollections*, being employed as a naval officer, had very vivid memories, was Luis Brion the patriot admiral, the officer commanding the Colombian navy. Hippisley who also encountered him described him in the following terms: 'A native of the island of Curaçao; in stature about five feet five inches; thin make; his limbs firm, and well put together; rather a round face, much sunburnt, and pitted with a few marks of small-pox; short, black hair, dark penetrating eyes, and good teeth; a Jewish cast of countenance, which, however, is rendered more expressive of his real situation by the full moustachio which he wears on his upper lip. In person and manner he displays a good deal of ease, and on a first appearance he is even rather prepossessing; he speaks English, and understands it well; he is as good a Frenchman as he is a Spaniard, and speaks the latter tongue with true Castillian pronunciation.' According to the author of *Recollections* Brion had known nothing of naval affairs before entering Venezuelan service and was only given command of the fleet because he agreed to pay to equip it. In consequence he lacked the talent and experience to command professionals, and for this reason was violently jealous of British officers serving under him. At a dinner at which the author was present, Brion uttered the grossest invectives against such naval officers, deplored their being given commissions and announced his intention of getting rid of them. Jealous because the author had succeeded in capturing a Spanish merchantman and performed well in a naval action, he tried, though vainly, to get the congress to deprive the author of his commission. Brion himself had failed to destroy a Spanish naval squadron in an action off Cumaná, thus losing the chance, the author believed, of ending the war in less than six months.

The same writer goes on to describe Brion's obsession with uniforms and rank. 'Officers in the Colombian Navy are entitled to a comparative rank in the army, by which they may be addressed on all occasions, and to wear its uniform if they please. According to this regulation, Admiral Brion ranked as Captain-general; and was usually seen on his quarter-deck, attired in an English hussar jacket and scarlet pantaloons, with a broad stripe of gold down each side, a field marshal's uniform hat, with a very large Prussian plume, and an enormous pair of dragoon boots, with heavy gold spurs of most inconvenient length. He always signed himself Captain-general and was so addressed by his officers and men, and if any of them neglected this title, or substituted that of Admiral, they seldom regained his favour.'[63] He appears a vain and dress-conscious man, in marked contrast to the patriot generals.

So far as uniforms were concerned, it was the British officers who dazzled by their extravagant dress, and Colonel Macdonald who had sailed from England in command of the 1st Venezuelan Lancers had been murdered soon after his arrival by Indians who were tempted to steal his bright clothes, elegant sword and novel equipment. Hippisley has left a proud description of the uniform of his own regiment, the so-called Venezuelan Hussars, though forced to admit it proved quite unsuited to the hot and humid climate of the Venezuelan plains. The dress uniform was a dark green jacket, with scarlet collar, lapels and cuffs; figured gold lace round the collar and cuffs with an ornamental knot on the arm; a laced girdle round the waist and two small gold-scaled epaulettes; dark green trousers with gold lace down the sides and a *chaco* (or shako) worn on the head. The field uniform was a dark green jacket with a red cuff and collar without facings though trimmed with black lacing nevertheless, dark green forage cap with grey overalls, Wellington boots, crimson sashes, black leather pouch, belt and sabre. The officers wore in addition to this a blue scarlet cloak that was lined with red baize.[64] What a contrast this parade of peacockery was with the dress of the patriot forces! Vowell describes

Buenos Aires (landing place and Almeida)

Plaza de la Independencia, Santiago, Chile

An early view of Valparaiso, Chile

View of Callao and

distant view of Lima

Angostura

View of the city and valley of Mexico, from Tacubaya

Rio de Janeiro (1809)

a group of officers surrounding Bolívar when he first set eyes on him near Calabozo in 1818. Bolívar himself was simply dressed and carrying only a light lance, on which was a banner with a skull and crossbones and the patriot motto '*Muerte o Libertad*'. Few of the officers had jackets but they wore a shirt (quite often check) outside white trousers that reached below the knee, and a hat of split palm leaves in which was stuck a plume of variegated colours. Almost all of them were barefoot, but they wore spurs of silver or brass with rowels at least 4 inches across. Under their hats they wore a handkerchief as a protection from the sun, but one of them had a gold helmet, another wore a silver one. Many had silver scabbards and stirrups and silver ornaments on their bridles. The rank and file were less well equipped. Vowell found that Bolívar's guard were the only ones with uniform. This consisted of jackets that had been designed to be worn by English marines but since condemned as unserviceable, trousers of a variety of colours and hussar caps captured from Spanish loyalists.[65] Páez's guard of honour also had the benefit of uniforms and Robinson thought them smartly dressed, very similar to English troops: a dragoon cap, a red jacket, turned up on the inside with yellow, blue cuffs, blue cape and blue trousers with yellow seams. He thought however the red colour unwise, in view of the presence of so many wild bulls.[66]

Many of the patriot forces had virtually no clothes at all, mostly ragged blankets or pieces of carpet. The fire-arms they carried were antiquated or often in very bad condition – some were quite unserviceable and seem to have been carried only for show. Many had lances or bayonets on poles. Robinson described the troops' excitement on the arrival in 1819 of a ship carrying uniforms from England. 'Never did infant survey with more astonishment and satisfaction the trappings of its doll than did these individuals contemplate the mighty alteration to be made to their persons.' They had no conception how to use such clothes. 'Some put their legs in the arms of their coat and brought the skirts up and buttoned them round their loins. Others tied the arms of their coat round their loins, while the skirts were allowed to hang before like an apron. Others again tied the legs of the pantaloons in the same manner, allowing the upper part of them to hang before like the skirts of a coat.' It was found impossible to make the men wear shoes. When the first pieces of artillery arrived, the troops tried to drag them by the tails of their horses and were amazed when they saw horses yoked to and drawing carriages.[67]

Robinson's supercilious attitude towards a poor and primitive
people is not one that commands much sympathy. He was contemp-
tuous of their ignorance. One officer asked ingenuously if there were
any women in England, apart from those sent there from South
America, and thought the English people must starve without meat
supplies sent from South America. Others thought London was an
island and the West Indies were part of England, though none of this
strikes the modern reader as being in the least surprising, given the
remoteness of Venezuela and the almost total lack of public education.
Robinson found himself repelled by what he terms a 'corrupt, stupid,
mean, beggarly and dishonest set of beings, chained in ignorance and
swayed by superstition and the most gloomy bigotry'. He was particularly disgusted by their culinary and eating habits, nothing prepared
separately and all beaten together and eaten with fingers. He was also
very indignant when the Indians gathered round to watch the Europeans eating, at the same time delousing themselves and each other,
as if they had been a crowd of monkeys. And the scene he paints of
the patriot camp (one he confessed that depressed his spirits) is
reminiscent of Shakespeare's Prologue to the fourth act of *Henry V* –
the armies encamped before the battle of Agincourt: 'The wild howl
of the Indian song, which broke on the silence of the night from
upwards of twenty different groups, all assembled round the fires, the
lowing of thousands of bullocks and the neighing of as many horses,
the braying of mules, the clashing of arms, and the watchword passing
along the various parties on their station.'[68]

Brown found the patriot troops on Margarita, save for one battalion,
almost naked. They arrived for what was supposedly a grand parade
that Brown considered ridiculous, two or three deep, father and son,
followed by grandson carrying their provisions, most without muskets
and even bayonets.[69] The same was the case with the cavalry that
Hippisley saw at San Fernando. The soldiers were of all sorts and
sizes, aged anything between thirteen and forty, riding mules or half-
starved horses, and most of them without a saddle. 'Some without
trowsers, small clothes, or any covering except a bandage of blue cloth
or cotton round their loins ... others with trowsers, but without
stockings, boots or shoes ... In their left hand they hold a pole from
eight to ten feet in length, with an iron spear very sharp at the point
and sides and rather flat ... a blanket of about a yard square, with a
hole or rather slit cut in the centre, through which the wearer thrusts
his head, falls on each side of his shoulders ... sometimes an old

musket (the barrel of which has been shortened twelve inches and forms his carbine) with a large sabre ... or even a small sword, hanging by a leather thong at his side, together with a felt cap, a tiger-skin or hide cap on his head, with a white feather, or even a piece of white rag, stuck to it.' All these troops had hard, fierce looks and Hippisley thought them more savage in nature than the wild beasts in the forests and mountains.[70]

The British officers had their come-uppance when starvation forced them to sell their fine clothes in order to keep themselves alive and the creoles mocked them, telling them they had come to South America merely to sell their second-hand clothing. Captain Hippisley, son of Colonel Gustavus, wrote of the people deriding the English 'as slaves purchased for hide and tallow' and saying that the troops had been sent from England in exchange for some Venezuelan mules and bullocks.[71] His father the Colonel described it as 'galling to behold the generals and native officers of rank living uncommonly well, and the British officers and men, to whom the government owed such considerable arrears, starving or stripping themselves naked to pur-chase the absolute necessities of life.' Alexander relates how the creole officers insulted those British who could not speak Spanish (and that went for most of them) and showed active dislike of the foreigners. These creoles, he thought, were a very rough bunch, thieves, liars, mostly illiterate, gross and immodest in their speech, but nevertheless brave patriots who endured every hardship for the good of the cause. On the other hand he was deeply critical of the attitude and behaviour of British officers whom he encountered in Angostura and later on in Margarita. 'Nothing but animosity reigned among them, and low petty jealousy about rank and precedence ... they brought their aristocratic notions into this country of freedom and equality, where all men were citizens alike. These sticklers for rank and gentility were most of them runaway clerks, or old lieutenants of militia, cashiered officers and others who found it convenient to conceal as much as possible what they had formerly been.'[72] Alexander was sensitive on this point, not wishing to disclose the fact that when he had served in the British army he had been only a humble bombardier.

Hippisley wrote of the patriots' savagery and all accounts by those so far quoted register the shock felt by Europeans at the ruthless policy of extermination pursued relentlessly by both sides, and dating from Bolívar's announcement, made as far back as 1813, that this was to be a 'war to the death', and that any Spaniards who refused to join in the patriot struggle for independence must not expect to be spared their lives. The Spaniards not unnaturally gave as good as they got. The anonymous author of *Recollections* cites Morillo's dispatch to Ferdinand VII, relating the measures he had taken when he retook Bogotá in 1816: 'Every person of either sex, who was capable of reading or writing, was put to death. By this cutting off of all those who were in any way educated, I hoped to effectually arrest the spirit of revolution.' At Margarita, which Morillo tried but failed to seize, counter-atrocities were committed. The author saw 7000 skulls heaped together in one place, all bearing the cut of the machete. When he once captured a Spanish schooner he was, on his return to port, ordered to hand over all the prisoners so that they could be executed, a task he disliked but could not refuse. When the patriots attacked and took Barcelona (an action the British Legion took part in), he was forced to witness the cold-blooded massacre of 1300 of the garrison and, together with other British officers, was reprimanded for not participating, and warned he would be expected to do so, if he wished to continue in patriot service. It usually fell to the officers to execute the prisoners of war with a sword and 'when the head fell at the first blow, the spectators applauded and laughed.'[73]

Alexander wrote that when Angostura was finally abandoned by the Spaniards, 200 of them who failed to escape were taken away to an island and killed – their bodies then being thrown into the water. For months afterwards the local people refused to eat fish that were caught in the river, but the man who had superintended the massacre was promoted to be a lieutenant-colonel. Robinson wrote: 'Travel where you may, in the bush or the mountains or the plain, your sight is perpetually arrested by piles upon piles of human bones, of both sexes and all ages.' Vowell, on arrival at Guyana la Vieja, recently taken by General Bermudez, recounts seeing the ground covered by the unburied bodies of the members of the garrison, all of whom had been killed in cold blood. It 'gave us [he writes] the first specimen of "*Guerra a la Muerte*".' Chesterton at Cumaná was disgusted at the sight of Spanish prisoners being speared to death by Indian troops. When he and other British officers had pleaded for the lives of these wretched captives, General Urdaneta had replied that if he were to spare the lives of the prisoners he would not be able to rely on the continuing loyalty of his men. 'That scene [Chesterton wrote] was a deathblow to all my past enthusiasm in the Republican cause.'[74]

Once the Spanish were expelled from Gran Colombia various

attempts were made by Britons to exploit and develop the wealth of
the country or what, misguidedly, they took its wealth to be. Accounts
were written of what was attempted and achieved or not achieved, as
the case may be, by Captain Charles Cochrane in his *Journal of a
Residence and Travels in Colombia*, published in 1825, Colonel Hamilton's *Travels Through the Interior Provinces of Colombia* published in
1827, John Hankshaw's *Letters Written from Colombia* published in
1824, *The Present State of Colombia* by an officer of the Colombian
army published anonymously in 1827, *Colombia in its Present State* by
the hydrographer Colonel Francis Hall, published in 1824, *Notes on
Colombia Taken in the Years 1822–1823* by Richard Bache, who
described himself as an officer in the army of the United States, the
private diary of Sir Robert Ker Porter, not published until 1962, and
James Thomson's already quoted *Letters on . . . South America*. Captain
Cochrane was a naval officer who obtained leave from the Admiralty
to examine the resources of Colombia with a view to commercial
exploitation and to secure an exclusive concession to carry out pearl-
fishing off the coast, employing modern techniques if possible. He
travelled widely in Colombia in 1822 and in 1824, succeeded in
obtaining the grant of a pearl fishery for the firm of Rundell, Bridge
and Rundell, and signed an agreement to work a gold mine, fallen
into disuse through lack of capital. He was much impressed by the
Anglophilism he encountered wherever his travels took him. A local
taste for English goods was one that dated back many years, since a
flourishing contraband trade had existed between New Granada and
British Jamaica. English merchandise, merchants and soldiers, customs and manners were the most approved; English newspapers from
abroad 'establish and guide public opinion', and English vessels
increased trade as well as acting as its protector: 'in fact to be an
Englishman is a *passe par tout* throughout the republic'.[75] Richard
Bache also had cause to remark on the all-pervading English influence. Everyone who did not speak Spanish perfectly was immediately
regarded as English. People he met were 'constantly referring everything to England, as the standard of perfection, extolling her power
and riches, giving the name English to all goods, whether manufactured in France, Germany or the East; they have produced a belief
among the uninformed creoles that everything not Spanish must be
English'.[76]

Cochrane cited the opinion of the Scotsman Rennie, whom he met
when he was in Cartagena, that there was every prospect for successful

investment in a country as rich as Gran Colombia, once the country was properly organized. Cochrane hastened to endorse this opinion, stressing the need for capital, machinery, craftsmen and technicians; the improvement of the appalling roads, of which he had had many gruelling experiences, and the introduction of steam navigation. Once these arrived he was convinced that Colombia in a very few years would rank among the richest and most productive of the nations of the modern world. He also saw prospects for immigration and settlement of farming communities, bringing in English farm machinery, together with English grain and plants. 'Few speculations in the small way [he wrote] would pay better than taking a small estate or farm close to Bogotá and laying it out as kitchen and fruit gardens.'[77] In the same vein John Hankshaw wrote of Merida, 'What might not be made of it, if peopled by European families of enlightened ideas, with sufficient capital to rebuild and beautify the city as its situation deserves?' All reasonable people with whom he conversed agreed that the government ought to encourage the inflow of European industry, skilled workers and settlers, to relieve the country's current state of poverty and wretchedness.[78]

The optimism of Cochrane and Hankshaw was shared by Colonel John Hamilton, the leading commissioner sent by Canning to report on Colombia's condition, with a view to extending British recognition of its new republican government. He praised the climate and the fertile soil which seemed suited to European settlement and forecast the immigration of considerable numbers once a stable government had been established and religious freedom guaranteed. He himself had bought a farm 2 or 3 miles outside Bogotá, had brought out English ploughs and harrows, an English ploughman and an English blacksmith and intended to supply the capital city with fat meat, good butter and other provisions scarcely known in that area up to then. He added, however, that it was most necessary to change the prejudices and bad habits fostered by the Roman Catholic clergy, who encouraged the poor people in their xenophobia; to improve the conduct of public finances and particularly to reform the condition of the ports where corruption, delays and endless vexations had to be endured by foreign merchants, despite the lowering of customs duties.

Everywhere on his travels in Colombia, Hamilton experienced Anglophilism. For example, when visiting a priest in a village, he was greeted by the farmers he passed on his way with three hearty cheers for the English nation. The priest had a portrait in his house of King

George II of England on horseback and Hamilton noted that, not long before, no priest would have defiled his house with a portrait of a heretic prince. At another place (the town of Bonga) he was welcomed by the corporation, the town band and crowds of people greeting him with shouts of '*Vivan los Ingleses, viva la Colombia y nuestro Bolívar*'. The town band then struck up and there were displays of rockets and fireworks as well as other joyous celebrations. Despite Hamilton's dislike of the clergy generally, he confesses to have been well entertained by all the village priests he encountered on his journeys.[79]

Colonel Francis Hall had also much to say on the prospects for European immigration. Commenting on the sparse population, and the desolation wrought by war that had reduced fertile provinces like Guyana, Cumaná and Barcelona to destitution and poverty and their towns to 'grass-grown wretchedness', he thought that 20 million emigrants could very easily be absorbed. The lack of people meant that labour was dear and the creole labourer performed *badly* in a week what a European could do *well* in a day. Everything constructed was badly done, whether a house or an artefact. The finishing of dwellings was always defective – no right angle or straight line of wall, no beam or rafter planed or squared and doors and windows that 'would be inadmissible in an English stable'. There was no machinery, not even a wheelbarrow. This meant workmen would have to be imported from Europe if the settlers wanted a decent house to live in.

Many emigrants from Europe went to North America, but Colombia offered greater attractions. There was no need to trek inland in order to find land to cultivate; not much work was involved in clearing the light woodland covering the landscape; the climate demanded little clothing and produced three crops a year from the soil; food was abundant and very cheap. The government had now passed favourable laws in order to encourage immigrants and had authorized the distribution of 2 to 3 million *fandegas* (a *fandega* being an area of 2000 square yards) at only $2 a *fandega*, or one if in the interior. Hall did however sound a note of warning. Foreign settlers, he wrote, must come to Colombia prepared for the worst. There was always local jealousy; the natives were prone to break their bargains or any promises they might make; to lie was not thought reprehensible and religious toleration was purely theoretical. Bigotry was only sleeping because it had not yet been provoked and though the 'solitary Protestant traveller may be an object of curiosity, but not of dread or suspicion', the case could well be very different with hundreds or thousands of foreign settlers. Hall also dwelt on the danger of disease and of drinking to excess in a tropical climate – three-fifths of the English soldier-volunteers had perished solely on account of drink.[80]

Writing in 1826, the anonymous officer author of *The Present State of Colombia* paints a very much more pessimistic picture of the prospects for European immigration and for commercial development. Attempts to open up the river traffic had so far met with no success. A concession had been granted to a German national to navigate the Magdalena River, by which Bogotá could be reached from the coast, but conditions had proved so difficult that only one steamboat had been launched on the river and that had made only a maiden voyage. A colonel by the name of James Hamilton had succeeded in obtaining a ten-year concession to run steamboats on the Orinoco in its upper reaches above Angostura, but being unable to fulfil the contract to put boats on the river within two years, had forfeited the concession gained and had to pay a penalty of $20,000. The pearl fishery concession arranged by Cochrane had resulted in the flotation of a company with a capital of $350,000 and known as The Colombia Pearl Fishery Association. It had operated two ships for some months but had found no pearls of any value and it seemed unlikely it would find any. As for mining, a Mr Thomson had paid the government the sum of $150,000 for the lease of salt mines near Santa Marta, but as he failed to pay his deposit he forfeited his right to the lease. A certain Captain Cochrane had obtained a concession to roll copper on the north coast of Colombia but abandoned the project on returning to England.[81] Sir Robert Ker Porter in 1825 met in Caracas the American consul who had invested in copper mines bought from a Captain D. Cochrane, an agent of the liberator. The mines proved to be rich in ore but the cost of running them made the profits slender. It was alleged that this Cochrane, who had died, had obtained as much as $12,000 (some said $25,000) by disposing of his mining shares to willing dupes. 'Like most of these *jobs* in London [wrote Porter], whatever advantage on the speculation is obtained by the first share-holders disposing of their shares.' Between 100 and 200 English miners together with mining machinery were sent out to work these mines, but many perished of yellow fever.[82]

The other mining venture in Colombia that acquired some notoriety was that of the Colombian Mining Association linked to the names of George Stephenson, the pioneer of British railways, and his son Robert Stephenson, the celebrated civil engineer. George had been commissioned by one of the projectors (Thomas Richardson, whom he knew) to recruit miners, technicians and inspectors, and ship tools and materials to South America. His young son Robert was keen to go out to act as an agent for the company's agents (the firm of Herring, Graham, and Powles) and eventually went, against the wishes of his father, having first taken a course in mining and learnt enough Spanish to hold down the job.

His first task was, on arrival at La Guayra, to advise on the practicability of constructing a breakwater and a pier there and of building a railway through the mountains to Caracas. Only the project of erecting a pier seemed to him to be feasible. He then proceeded to Mariquita in January 1825, where the principal silver mines were located, 12 miles from the river-port of Honda, the last point on the River Magdalena accessible by boat. The place was in a state of almost total ruin, as a result of recent earthquakes, the wars of independence and the flight of the inhabitants; its original population of 20,000 had fallen to a mere 450.

Stephenson's principal tribulations were the Cornish miners who had now joined him, and the difficulties of ever getting the heavy machinery sent from England the last 6 miles to the site of the mines, over roadless mountains and across bridgeless rivers. The Cornishmen's behaviour was similar to that witnessed everywhere throughout South America. Their high wages to which they were unused they spent on getting very drunk and their dissolute conduct offended the creoles. They also proved insurbordinate, unwilling at first to accept orders from a young man of twenty-one years who had not learnt his mining at the pit-face and was not even a Cornishman. Though later he did succeed in getting on better terms with his staff of miners, he never managed to cure them of what today is referred to as 'the English disease': 'to the last [wrote his biographer] he could never get from any man more than half a day's work each day, and he always had nearly a third of his hundred and sixty subordinates disabled by drink'. The directors continued to ignore his advice not to send out more heavy machinery, none of which could of course be used, and complained when no silver arrived in England. Stephenson stuck it out for three years, though himself realizing only too well that the concern could never make money, before finally resigning his post. In those three years the company had lost the best part of £200,000. As Stephenson's biographer commented, had Robert been able to work the mines with slave labour, as the Spaniards had done, they would have yielded as much profit as they had to the previous owners.[83]

The author of *The Present State of Colombia* was also very dubious about the prospects for immigrants. He did not know of twenty (he wrote) who had even tried to farm, let alone made a success of doing so. The Colombian Association for Agriculture and other purposes, with a capital of £1,300,000 had managed to acquire a million acres, two-thirds of which were given by the government, with the usual concessions of exemption from taxes, import duties, tithe and military service, but he did not think it could ever pay, given the state of the roads in the country.[84] Porter, in his diary, relates the fate of a colony of Scottish settlers brought out to farm an estate at Topo, 8 or 9 miles outside Caracas, by the British firm of Powles & Co. When Porter first visited the settlement in December 1825 he was impressed by the health of the immigrants, most of whom had served in the army, but the following year he had changed his mind. The settlers had become discontented when they found that, though they had been informed they would be able to grow grain and vegetables and graze cattle on the land, they had first to clear the virgin forest and then grow coffee, indigo and cotton. What was worse, the contours and nature of the ground did not allow the use of the plough, nor the climate permit the growing of cereals, and three years would have to elapse before they could hope to see a crop of coffee. Porter was not very sympathetic. He likened the settlers, rather unfairly, to the early Spanish colonists who had thought to grow rich without having to work, since Nature had been so prolific in her gifts to South America. By October 1826 Porter was writing of them in his diary as '200 idle, drunken Scotchmen' who were now in their present plight entirely because of their laziness. They had turned down offers of employment from established colonists like Colonel Stopford and had asked instead for a passage home. 'In fact, so bad and worthless a set never left Great Britain' was Porter's comment.[85]

There was however another side to the story. It seems (according to Joseph Lancaster who was then in Caracas in charge of a school and who interested himself in the plight of the Scots) that Topo was an area renowned for its sterility. The settlers had cleared 120 acres and reaped 200 bushels of maize of very indifferent quality and 30 bushels of green beans to feed 143 people, 80 of which were children. They had been, in Lancaster's own words, 'allured, deceived and deserted in foreign lands', and if they now declined to work on the estates it was because they were unwilling as free men to labour with slaves.[86]

The problem of getting the Scots provided for vexed Porter for the best part of a year. He quarrelled violently with Lancaster for taking the part of the wretched Scots, and encouraging them to refuse offers of jobs on the grounds that the Venezuelan government would soon make them a grant of more suitable land. Lancaster accused Porter of not doing enough for the immigrants who wanted to go to the USA, and Lancaster managed to raise through subscriptions, including 500 pesos from Bolívar, sufficient funds to prevent them from starving. He told Porter that he had petitioned both Houses of Parliament for money to pay their passages home and requested that the people of Britain should be warned against similar deceptions. He also wrote to Lord Harrowby, the Lord President of the Council, who had been an admirer of his achievements as a successful educator, requesting his support in the matter. Porter however remained unmoved, describing Lancaster in his diary as a 'hypocrite and evil-tongued' and in a letter to his sister as 'a sad, backbiting, vain, envious Quaker, superficial in the extreme', while the Scots were an 'idle, drunken race'.[87]

This colony was not the only one presenting Porter with problems. Another bunch of Scotsmen, the MacAlpin family, had agreed with the Agricultural Association to take over some land near Maracaibo. Mismanagement and ignorance had, according to Porter, resulted in the same sort of failure as had occurred in the Topo settlement. He conceded that MacAlpin had been deceived, having like the others been led to believe that all he had to do was plough and sow, and now he was totally bankrupted. Porter's explanation was not quite accurate. In fact what had happened was that Powles & Co, who had sponsored the Maracaibo settlement and the Agricultural Association, had run short of cash on account of the crisis that was hitting the London financial market, and had therefore had to abandon the settlement. Canning, to whom Lancaster had also written, decided the government in London must help, though as a result of a petition received from a Scottish pastor and not from Lancaster, and told Porter to arrange the passages of all the Scots at the government's expense. Porter noted despondently in his diary that 'this ill-managed first attempt at colonisation will check for many years to come the emigration from England and Scotland'.[88]

He was now willing to concede that the colonists had been sorely deceived by the Agricultural Association and by its agents working in

Britain, but could not help adding with a certain venom: 'They [the Scots] are a worthless, drunken set, mostly weavers and mechanics. Scarcely ten out of the whole know anything of agriculture.' The fact that at that time the handloom weavers throughout Britain were in desperate straits, driven to accept starvation wages or face unemployment and destitution on account of competition from the new machinery and were therefore ready to do anything if it offered the prospect of improving their lot, seems to have escaped the consul's attention. The last of them were shipped off to Canada in April 1827. There were no vessels making the passage to Britain and Alexander Cockburn, the British minister appointed to the Colombian government who was staying in Caracas at that time, advised they should be sent to British North America. They founded a settlement in Upper Canada and there apparently made their home.[89]

Porter records that in 1826 he had encountered one English planter who gave the appearance of prospering. He was paying $6000 a year for the lease of a coffee estate near Caracas, was the first to distil rum in Venezuela and the first to drive a cart to the capital from the port of La Guayra over terrible roads. Two years later Porter remarked that this planter's estate was the only one in the Caracas valley that looked to be flourishing. The planter, who hailed from Cumbria, 'a most industrious and clear-headed' man, had spent nearly $14,000 in trying to make his estate pay its way, working with 180 slaves 'whose idleness and freedom his good management has properly curbed'; yet even after spending all this time and money it was still not clear if the farm would make a profit.[90]

Porter believed the English public had been disgracefully deceived about the people of Venezuela and the latter's political situation through the propaganda of unscrupulous merchants in pamphlets, books and newspapers. But, he continued, unless foreign colonists came in their thousands to do the work the local people were unwilling to do ('ignorant, bigoted, prejudiced' as they were), and take up farming, build public works, promote places of education and improve the means of transportation, the natives might just as well stay lazy and the speculators remain at home.[91]

The work of public education had begun in 1822 and Colonel Hamilton in his travels in the south and west of New Granada noted that in every village there was a primary school of a kind which 'although small . . . [was] well managed'.[92] A decree of January 1822 had provided for the establishment of primary schools in every town of any size and of normal schools for training teachers in Bogotá, Caracas and Quito. A Franciscan friar called Sebastian Mora had pioneered implementing the scheme and a Frenchman called Pierre Commettant had been brought to Colombia to assist. Lancaster who had been working in Philadelphia where he had fallen seriously ill had been invited to come to Caracas through the good offices of Colonel Brooke Young (once an officer in the Irish Legion and later the town major of Caracas), not only to improve his health but to build on the initial work of Mora and of Commettant and set up a teacher's training college. Difficulties however soon arose after Lancaster's arrival in 1824, over the inability of the town council to pay Lancaster's salary or for the scholastic equipment he needed, for it was in serious financial straits. Eventually Bolívar, who was then in Peru, sent a letter welcoming Lancaster's presence and a draft for 20,000 pesos drawn on the London agency of the Peruvian government. Lancaster ordered all sorts of equipment and received many gifts of books and prints from his numerous admirers in England, but soon fell foul of everyone through his inability to pay his bills and his refusal to allow the authorities responsible for financing him to carry out an inspection of his school. Lancaster was a jealous and obstinate man who could have learnt a useful lesson from James Thomson in tactful behaviour.[93]

Lancaster's school (no grandiose college, as he had optimistically planned) with not more than a dozen pupils continued to function in Caracas, and when Bolívar entered the city, as he did in January 1827, the school took part in the celebrations. Porter recorded in his diary that 'Mr Joseph Lancaster on a mule, in all the pomp of pedagogism, his boys bearing the flags of those nations who had adopted his system of education [marched] in solemn order at [the] tail' of the procession that came out to welcome the liberator. Later a dispute arose about the ownership of the school equipment that Lancaster claimed belonged to him and not to the municipality. Lancaster, always a difficult man who had quarrelled with so many people in England, made accusations of bad faith against Bolívar whom in later years he described as being 'this dictator, this man of blood'. Lancaster left Venezuela hurriedly on 18 April 1827 in fear of his life (though he was not threatened) and glad to escape from what he described as 'that land of deceit, revolution and blood'. He was under pressure to leave the country partly because of the scandal he had caused by striking a lady in a general's house for drenching him with water at carnival time, partly because another scandal attached to the publicity of his recent marriage, conducted according to the Quaker rite, with Bolívar present in person as a witness, and partly on account of financial embarrassment. The Peruvian government (no longer the same as it was when Bolívar was in Peru) was now in serious financial difficulties and Bolívar's draft on it could not be met, while the town council of Caracas refused to pay Lancaster what he thought was owed him. Bolívar himself had now become thoroughly disillusioned with Lancaster and was not best pleased when the latter asked for a passport to leave Venezuela for good without having made any provision for a substitute to run his school. He felt that Lancaster had not fulfilled his promise to set up a training college, was now unwilling to produce accounts and to hand over the school equipment he had bought with the money entrusted to him. All this occurred ironically at a time when Bolívar had become very interested in expanding a free education system throughout the whole of Gran Colombia.[94]

While Lancaster was still at Caracas, James Thomson arrived in the city, having travelled from Lima via Quito and Bogotá. He was more concerned with his missionary work, distributing copies of the Bible in Spanish, than in setting up Lancasterian schools and was now acting officially as an agent for the Bible Society. In all his journeys through Gran Colombia he records having found only one person who showed hostility to his work and that was the bishop of Popayán who would allow only bibles with notes. In Bogotá, after much debate, he managed to found a Bible society whose meetings were held in the university and which gained support from Colonel Hamilton (Canning's first commissioner there) and James Henderson, the consul-general. British merchants provided funds and army officers like Colonel Forsythe, Colonel Stopford and Colonel Young (all settled in Caracas) gave their active support to it. According to Hamilton's account in his *Travels*, the founding of this Bible society also received strong support from the minister of foreign affairs and from the minister of finance and was opposed mainly by two priests who tried unsuccessfully to insist that the bibles contain appropriate notes as laid down by decree in the Council of Trent. Significantly, the society's first secretary was a member of the Dominican order; but, despite these very auspicious beginnings, it did not flourish for very long. In 1826 Colonel Forsythe's firm, which had agreed to distribute the bibles, was forced to go into liquidation, and the receivers gave back to the society eleven cases of bibles, saying they could not dispose of them – there was apparently no market for them and those people who showed any interest already possessed copies. When in 1832 James Thomson paid another visit to Venezuela he had to admit that clerical opposition had succeeded in killing the society's work, coupled with the fact that dire poverty denied people the means to pay for a bible.[95]

The widespread distribution of bibles was something that John Hankshaw very much favoured as the best benefit that could be bestowed 'on this tractable but priest-ridden people'. Much impressed as Hankshaw was by the Indians' natural sweetness of disposition, meekness and willingness to oblige, despite their poverty and degradation, he regretted (like so many other Britons) that they were exposed to 'so idolatrous and disgusting a system' (meaning by that the Catholic religion).[96] But as a French traveller in the region pointed out in his *Travels in Colombia*, Catholicism was the one unifying factor in a country utterly diversified and the parish priests, who held absolute sway within the dominion of their parishes, were for the most part good men, co-operating with the patriot government and active in the legislative assembly.[97]

The task of uniting all the peoples of Gran Colombia under one administration, with a free constitution based upon examples of all the most enlightened governments, was one that Bolívar set himself but in the end was unable to complete. Robert Stephenson in July 1827 drew attention to the current political turmoil: 'One day we hear of nothing but civil war, another brings forward some displeasing decree from Bolívar, whose character as a disinterested man has lost ground very much among his own people. The laws in many parts are held in contempt, and a disposition for changing the present Constitution is pretty general throughout every department. A division of the republic into states appears inevitable.' Stephenson did not however believe that all this would lead to a civil war, since the country was too exhausted for that and the people remained too apathetic.[98]

But with or without civil war, the unstable political situation was one that appeared disheartening to more than one foreign representative. Thomas P. Moore, United States minister to the government of Colombia, wrote to van Buren in March 1830 that 'the condition of this beautiful country is to be most deeply deplored. Revolutionary movements succeed each other with a rapidity that threatens utter ruin to the Republic; paralyzing industry, annihilating all confidence between man and man, and filling society with distrust, despondency and despair'.[99]

Porter was convinced that some form of dictatorship was necessary to govern the country, chiefly because of its scanty population. Even Venezuela, its most valuable department, had relatively few inhabitants, 'and *such* inhabitants – the greater part blacks and coloured people, ignorant, lazy and full of vice', so only a government bordering on the despotic was 'best fitted for their noviciate'. He fulminated at what he regarded as a flagrant abuse of the free press – 'these Republicans are like children with new playthings'. Very fortunately (he continued) few could read the one-page weekly newspapers which he found abusive and violent in tone and 'written with the most superficial sophistry . . . like the effusions of discontented schoolboys'. He waxed indignant at the lack of moral sense and the injustice in public life, citing the wrongful condemnation of half the cargo of a British brig, detained by a Colombian privateer on the grounds that the cargo was Spanish property. 'The trial is of a piece with almost every other in Colombia – where bribery and want of either virtue or common moral principle is general'. He advised the owner to leave the port, taking with him the remainder of his cargo. He (the owner) would get no justice on appeal and would see the cargo and the vessel detained for at least a period of six to eight months, possibly even double that time, pending a decision of the court.[100]

He also complained bitterly of the lack of civilized society in Caracas (this was in the late 1820s) – 'the manners and usages of the people resemble truly the general appearance of their city . . . fair remains . . . choked up . . . with rank weeds'. He was shocked at the boorishness displayed by the company at a ball he attended, given in honour of Bolívar's birthday. 'A sad mob of finery, dirt, uniforms, niggers and people smoking cigars. I never saw such a bear garden and so disagreeable a crowd of notable republicans.' There were imitations of Peruvian dances but he could not see them as the smoke was so thick. Later he confided to his diary his disgust at the lack of personal hygiene as well as the deep religious prejudices among even the better class of people. He recounts a visit that he had paid to the widow of a general and her daughter. Porter writes he would have liked to have kissed the latter, a little girl of twelve years old, but 'we are heretics and they are disgusted too frequently in touching your hand'. On leaving, his hostess said they would dispense with the normal custom of shaking hands – 'indeed [added Porter] I did not regret it, for theirs was not of the most cleanly'.[101]

Porter eventually grew to like Caracas, stayed there as consul for fifteen years, became a popular and well-known figure and established very friendly relations first with Bolívar (whose portrait he painted) and later with Páez whose firm autocracy in Venezuela Porter admired. The Caracas that he had first encountered on arrival in December 1825, when still shattered by the 1812 earthquake and by ravages of war, improved itself greatly over the years; but then (as he confided to his diary), 'whole streets [were] fallen and in grass – the houses without roofs, and already fine grown trees were seen bursting through their moulding windows, overshadowing the buried remains of whole families whose domestic walls had become their mausoleum'. He took rooms in the city hotel, 'a sad miserable hole – filthy and fleay', and the dinner he was served was unsurprisingly 'in full unison with our quarters'. He then became ill with a bowel complaint and found the hotel 'a wretched place for an invalid. Not a *chaise percée* in the estab^t. The necessary is through three courtyards – and such a place! Besides all its niceties, the visitor is kept on the alert by a large rat or two darting from the unoccupied seat, either to the right or left.'[102] This very unsavoury three-seater latrine seems symbolic of all of the backwardness of a country the British found hard to love.

132

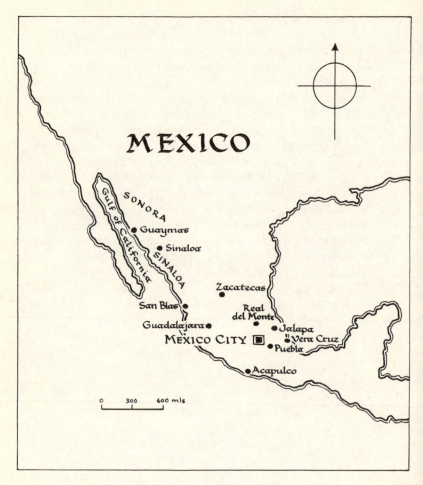

5 · Mexico

After fourteen years of sporadic warfare, revolution and counter-revolution, the Federal Republic of Mexico was established in 1824. The cost of the struggle for independence was enormous in purely material terms. Ten per cent of the population had died, per capita incomes had been reduced by a quarter, mineral production by as much as three-quarters, agricultural production by a half and industrial output by two-thirds. Imports from the United States and Britain came in to fill the economic void created by this state of affairs, but Mexico could not supply enough goods to correct the ensuing trade imbalance. Loans were therefore obtained in London amounting to 32 million pesos but current expenses quickly absorbed them and for four years after 1827 the bondholders received no interest.

By 1828 the constitutional order of the federal government had collapsed and 'the army became the arbiter of power'. Any economic recovery was inhibited by lack of confidence, insecurity and uncertainty: not until 1836 did the Spanish government recognize Mexico, nor indeed did the Holy See. Banditry and political violence, the privileges asserted by a military caste and the refusal of regional governments to accept the control of the central power all combined to perpetuate backwardness.[1]

Canning in 1823 had sent missions to Colombia and Mexico to ascertain if the new governments were in fact independent of Spain, controlled the country, enjoyed popular support and were capable of resisting invasion from Europe. One of the two commissioners sent to Mexico was Henry Ward who has left probably the most informative and vivid account of the country's condition as he saw it in 1827 (Ward has been described by Professor Donghi in the *Cambridge History of Latin America* as 'a well-informed and acutely aware, if not disinterested, observer'). Canning also sent consuls-general to three ports in Mexico; Vera Cruz, San Blas and Acapulco, and decided at the end of 1824 to sign a trade treaty with the Mexican government. Though the Mexicans at first refused to accept the terms of the treaty offered, it was eventually ratified and Canning was able to get his way on every point excepting that of the free exercise of the Protestant religion.[2]

Impressions of life as they found it in Mexico in the third decade of the nineteenth century are conveyed in the reminiscences and journals of a variety of authors, some American but mostly British. Apart from Ward, whose *Mexico in 1827* was published in 1828, there was Lieutenant Hardy, a British naval officer, commissioned by a private trading company to obtain for it an exclusive concession for pearl fishing in the Gulf of California, who travelled in the north-west provinces of Mexico between 1825 and 1828. Another British naval officer, Captain George F. Lyon, spent a year in Mexico during 1826 as commissioner for a mining company and published his journal in 1828. William Bullock, an amateur naturalist, antiquarian and company promoter, spent six months in the country in 1822 and wrote an account of his residence and travels, which was published in 1825. Basil Hall, the naval officer in command of the British frigate *Conway*, called at San Blas in 1822 (the first English warship ever to call there) and gave an account of what he found in his *Extracts from a Journal*, already cited in the chapters in this book on Peru and Chile. And Mark Beaufoy, a scientist and soldier who spent two years travelling in Mexico between 1825 and 1827, recorded his impressions in a very readable but prejudiced book entitled *Mexican Illustrations* and published in 1828. Also published in 1828 was *A Sketch of the Customs and Society of Mexico* by a man of business who remains anonymous and who travelled in the interior of the country between 1824 and 1826.

Of the three North American citizens who have left a written record of life in Mexico in the early years of independence, Joel Roberts Poinsett, a fine linguist who had travelled widely and has been described by his biographer J. Fred Rippy as 'an amiable and versatile Charlestonian,' has been met in earlier chapters of this book when he was acting consul-general in Buenos Aires and Santiago. He was sent to Mexico in 1822 by the government of the United States to report on the general condition of the country and advise on what policy that government should adopt towards the Emperor Agustin I. One of the results was his *Notes on Mexico* made in the autumn of 1822 and published in 1824, with a London edition in the following year. Poinsett was, in 1824, to be appointed the first minister the US

government accredited to Mexico and he held that post for the next
five years.

Edward Thornton Tayloe was a traveller who visited Mexico out of
curiosity. He stayed for thirty-three months in the country between
1825 and 1828, though his edited *Journal and Correspondence* was not
published till 1959. Finally there was that splendid writer, Madame
Calderón de la Barca, whose *Life in Mexico* was first published in the
USA in 1842 and has recently been republished in Great Britain in
an edited paperback edition. She was in fact a Scottish woman, born
Frances Erskine Inglis, whose family migrated to Boston, Massachu-
setts in the year 1831. She married in 1838 the Spanish minister to
the USA, the Marquis Calderón de la Barca, and in December 1839
accompanied him to Mexico in his posting as the first ambassador
from Spain. The two remained in Mexico City until January 1842
when political upheavals compelled them to leave.[3] Though strictly
speaking her experiences refer to a slightly later period than that with
which this book is chiefly concerned, her observations about life in
Mexico, graphically descriptive as they are, demand inclusion in any
résumé of 'gringo' impressions of that country in the early years of
independence.[4]

Ward, in the introduction to his book, contrasts the absurd optimism
evinced by Europeans in 1824 about the prospects for Mexico's future
(based as it was on inadequate data) with the deep pessimism of 1828.
At first speculators had imagined that capital was all that was needed
to render Mexico a flourishing state. When the fallacy of this theory
was exposed, opinion swung to the opposite extreme. 'Unexampled
credulity . . . was succeeded by obstinate disbelief'. Ward states that
in writing his book he is trying to strike a sober balance between these
two extremes of opinion and to present the true facts as he saw them
in 1827.

Firstly, he emphasizes the difficulty of travel and transport in a
mountainous country in which no adequate roads existed. Communications were not only difficult between the coast and the central
plateau, but also between the interior provinces. Everything had to be
carried by mule and as a result the cost of food in Mexican cities was
extremely high. The great stone causeway from Vera Cruz had been
destroyed in the revolution, though a road connecting the port with its
mines had been built by the Real del Monte company, in order to
carry its heavy machinery. Ward and his fellow commissioner had
arrived in 1823 accompanied by three English carriages, only to realize

on arrival how unfitted these vehicles were for the roads and that when they broke down, as they very soon did, there was no one capable of repairing them.[5] William Bullock in 1822 describes the hardships of his journey from Vera Cruz to the town of Jalapa, on the route leading to Mexico City. It took four days to travel a distance an English stagecoach on English roads would have covered comfortably in twenty-eight hours, carrying double the weight his party was carrying.[6] Not surprisingly the trials of travelling north of the city of Guadalajara, as discovered by Lieutenant Hardy, were even worse than those experienced by William Bullock en route to Jalapa. 'The width [of the road] scarcely admitted the passing of a mule. Every step of the animal was a leap of at least eighteen inches or two feet, and the juttings of the rock on either side made it necessary for the rider to sit with his heels on the animal's neck.' 'Roads in many parts of Mexico [Hardy wrote] and particularly in the interior provinces, are merely paths traversed by horses and mules, but never by a coach or waggon. And it requires a great knowledge of travelling, constant observation, and nice discernment, to make out the tracks which distinguish a high road from one which merely leads to a *rancho* or to the open country . . . or even from a rabbit track.' Hardy got lost on at least one occasion.[7] Bond Head had ridden on similar roads when he was prospecting for mines in the Andes. Nor were Hardy's and Bullock's encounters with resthouses or hotels (so-called) very much better than those of Head in his several journeys across the La Plata provinces. One night Bullock spent at San Rafaél he slept in a shed resembling a bird-cage. It had to be shared with a number of others and the beds were just planks on which mattresses were placed. Sleep proved quite impossible due to the noise of braying donkeys, dogs barking, horses champing maize, the pack-mules kicking each other and fighting and the chorus of cursing of the muleteers. He was bitten all night by fleas and mosquitoes and was made a target for the droppings of fowls.[8] Even in the best hotel in the capital Hardy was appalled by the dirt and squalor. In his bedroom there were holes in the floor and the walls, both of which were very far from clean. The dining-room was scarcely more hygienic and the sight of the cook put him off his food: wearing dirty clothes, no shoes or stockings, filthy hands, hair dirty and dishevelled and, to crown all, smoking a cigar.[9]

Beaufoy remarked on 'the slovenly, dirty and beggarly appearance' of the Mexican people. Few wore either boots or stockings, shirts were torn and a *serape* or blanket with a hole through it was all their clothing, apart from a cloak wrapped round them like a toga, though not in a manner that Beaufoy found graceful. All their clothes, including their bedclothes, were handed down from father to son and, not surprisingly, they stank. Their houses he found equally distasteful, utterly bleak and comfortless. 'Four walls whitewashed, an opening for a window, with a shutter but no glass, a mattress thrown on some boards in one corner, two or three low, long, narrow rush-bottomed seats, a rough-made table, half a dozen brown jars to stir their victuals in, and a floor of brick or plaster compose the interior arrangements of almost all the houses.' A few relieved the monotony of whitewash by sporting a coloured border of paint and the walls were on occasion hung with 'miserable daubs', allegedly the portraits of saints. Many of the rooms had no windows – only the door to let in the light – and 'all are equally spit over; for as both sexes smoke cigars, they must get rid of the saliva, and are too idle to walk to the door'. As to the matter of personal hygiene, Beaufoy found they generally washed only their hands – occasionally their eyes and mouth – and the men shaved only every five or six days.[10]

Poinsett in 1822 was horrified at the poverty and misery that he encountered in the town of Quelitán and at the mud huts in which people lived: 'I certainly never saw a negro house in Carolina so comfortless.' However, despite their poor living conditions, the Mexicans seemed to him an amiable people, good natured, naturally polite, 'virtuous', 'orderly' and pious and 'observant of their moral duties'.[11]

The anonymous author of *A Sketch of Customs and Society in Mexico* draws attention to the strange mixture of squalor combined with luxury that he encountered in many houses in Mexico City. In one house belonging to a well-to-do Mexican the windows and doors were insecure, the dining room smelled of smoke from the kitchen, and its walls were stained yellow by the smoke; all it contained was a greasy deal table, some rush-bottomed chairs and a dirty brick floor. The *sala* on the other hand was fitted out with great magnificence. The bedrooms lacked chairs, a table or a wash-basin but the chamberpot was solid silver. There were no knives provided for eating but the spoons and forks were all of silver. The owner of the house, when ready to leave to attend a ball, was dressed in a printed cotton jacket, a black cravat and dirty boots, unshaven and smelling strongly of tobacco, while his wife who was accompanying him was adorned with jewels of enormous value.[12] Ward's wife found it impossible to mix socially with a people whose 'Manners – mode of Life, and Ideas' were so different from her own. 'No English woman ever will, or can get on much with these People,' her husband wrote in 1825. 'Our Dinner and Evening Parties go off well and are allowed to be better than anything that has been seen yet in Mexico, but they do not bring us a bit nearer to the Natives, who never give anything in return, and are hardly to be seen anywhere out of their own Houses, except in the Theatre.'[13]

Ward noted in 1827 the growing prosperity of Mexico City and compared it with its state of only a very few years before. The ubiquitous and numerous class of beggars had almost disappeared from the streets;[14] Poinsett in 1822 thought they numbered as many as 20,000 in a population of 150,000. He depicted them sleeping where they could and then issuing forth from their hide-outs at daybreak to steal, beg or possibly work. Having got enough to feed themselves they would then get drunk in a *pulquería* (usually nothing but an open shed) round which they could be seen lying prostrate on the ground, sleeping off the effects of their recent debauch. He found them lively and very civil but also dexterous pickpockets and their idleness offended his Puritan soul; he compared them unfavourably to the Naples *lazzaroni* who worked more readily, stole less frequently and were very seldom addicted to drink.[15] These crowds of beggars struck Ward, on first arrival, as 'exhibiting a picture of wretchedness to which no words [of his] could do justice', but however wide the gap between rich and poor, the great and vital distinction in Mexico was, Ward noted, always between Americans and Europeans.[16] This term 'European' embraced North Americans, and all these gringo travellers tended to be puritan in their outlook. Lieutenant Hardy noted disapprovingly the sluggish character of the Mexican people. 'Idleness and cards are their chief occupation ... hence their deficiency of education, want of good moral principles and ignorance of domestic comforts.' The socially-minded democrat Tayloe was shocked by the crowds in Mexico City of beggars and half-naked Indians carrying loads of 300 pounds on their backs, and so much ignorance, filth and vice.[17]

These sentiments were echoed by Poinsett in a dispatch he wrote to Clay in March 1829: 'The want of means of acquiring knowledge, the absence of all incitement to exertion, the facility of procuring the means of subsistence almost without labour, a mild and enervating climate and their constant intercourse with the aborigines, who were and still are degraded to the very lowest class of human beings, all contributed to render the Mexicans a more ignorant and debauched people than their ancestors had been.' Lack of education he was sure was responsible for the low living standards obtaining among the Indian peasants. A nation needed a free peasantry, if it was to be one that was strong, and politically and economically Mexico seemed to him desperately weak. 'Seven eighths of the population [he wrote] live in wretched hovels, destitute of the most ordinary conveniences, the only furniture a few coarse mats to sit and sleep on, their food Indian corn, pepper and pulse.' What prevented these people from enjoying a better material existence was not low wages but rank improvidence – they gambled away what money they earned or spent it on festivals of the church – the latter being particularly abhorrent to a stern moralist like Joel Poinsett. 'All these evils [Poinsett concluded] if not cured entirely would be greatly mitigated by education', thus evincing an ingenuous belief that if men are only shown the light of reason, they will necessarily be guided by it.[18]

Impressions of Mexico City differed. Lyon found the city an attractive place, because of the regular pattern of its streets (the usual checker-board pattern adopted in all New World cities founded by Spain), well paved and far cleaner than he expected, and moreover adequately lit. Bullock, two years earlier, had been suitably impressed by the city's size, its long regular streets and the magnificence of its churches. Not so Beaufoy (not easy to please) who complained of having been badly misled by the rosy picture painted of it by Alexander Humboldt and more recently Bullock. Mexico City 'may be taken [he wrote] as no inapt illustration of the Spanish dominion in South [sic] America; vast and magnificent to the eye, but almost entirely destitute of the real attributes of order and security'. Beaufoy, who was a mass of prejudices, took a dislike to the bleak, swampy plain on which the city was situated, and to the half-naked, miserable Indians and the mestizos who crowded the streets. He also disliked the fruit and vegetables – peaches resembling green almonds, rotten turnips and small, stony grapes. Ward had a different tale to tell. He admitted that in 1823 the city was still suffering from the effects of the recent war: streets unlit, pavements destroyed, all the principal houses shut, the population poor and wretched-looking and hardly a foreigner resident; but within two years all that had changed, though not it appears for very long.[19] Madame Calderón in 1839 found beggars everywhere in the city and the streets 'so ill-kept, the pavements so narrow, the crowd so great and the *léperos* [in modern parlance, louts or 'yobbos'] in rags and blankets so annoying' that no one who was a respectable woman walked, save to mass or to do early shopping. Even so, she could not help admiring many features of the capital city: 'The air of solidity and magnificence which distinguishes Mexican edifices and which, together with the width and regularity of the streets, the vastness of the public squares, the total absence of all paltry ornament, the balconies with their balustrades and window-gratings of solid bronze and iron, render Mexico [City] inspite of its insufficient police, one of the noblest-looking cities in the world.' Unfortunately lack of public money had left public monuments badly decayed, 'sad proofs ... of the melancholy effects produced by years of civil war and unsettled government'. The Botanical Garden was one sorry example. When she saw it it was 'a small ill-kept enclosure, where there still remain some rare plants of the immense collection made in the time of the Spanish government, when great progress was made in all the sciences, four hundred thousand dollars having been expended in botanical expeditions alone'. Bullock had written seventeen years earlier of there being no money to pay the salary (a trifling sum) of the Italian curator of this garden that was laid out so handsomely. Madame Calderón found the garden pretty but also rather melancholy, a proof of the decay of science in Mexico since its independence.[20]

The same story, she continued, could be told of the Academy of Fine Arts and pointed at the contrast evident between 'the remains of these beautiful but mutilated plaster casts' (Greek and Roman sent from Spain and the splendid engravings which still exist) and 'the present disorder, the abandoned state of the building, the non-existence of these excellent classes of sculpture and painting', reflecting as it did unfortunately 'the low state of the fine arts in Mexico'.[21]

The low state also of education among the Mexican people generally was something that most observers remarked on, and often unfairly ridiculed. Mexicans had a pathetic belief in the greater wisdom of the foreigner wherever science was concerned. A friar asked Hardy to mend his watch, as all foreigners were supposed to be proficient where anything mechanical was concerned. And he found that his services as a quack doctor were everywhere in great demand. 'Every stranger [he wrote] who arrived brings with him an assortment of lancets, blister-salve, emetics, narcotics, cathartics, dieuretics etc.; and the natives are so accustomed to believe all foreigners well-instructed in [what he terms] "the healing art" that they submit to be killed by them, as though they were licensed man-slayers, by a Decree of the

Congress.' He succeded in effecting a number of cures but more apparently to his own surprise than to that of the patients he healed. Lyon was also called upon to display his medical skills on his travels, once his fame had spread for having first bled and then set the dislocated wrist of an injured boy who was brought to him. He refers in typically facetious manner to the cures he effected upon rheumatic old women, chiefly he alleges through the application of nothing more drastic than soap and water.[22]

Ignorance of the basic principles of hygiene was by no means the only form it took. Few even of the better-to-do knew anything of geography. Lyon met the owner of one estate who thought Spain and Europe were the same country; that London was an independent nation; that England was merely a province of London and that both were dominions of the King of Spain, while France was another name for Panama.[23] Bullock found that the people of Jalapa believed that Spain's king appointed the governors of all the west European countries and that only the riches Spain drew from Mexico kept the poorer parts of Europe alive. They had hardly heard of the Duke of Wellington and were amazed when shown Ackerman prints of some of the public buildings in London. Yet Bullock very sensibly comments that Englishmen were just as ignorant of the geography of South America and few had heard of Guatemala or Puebla which are 'superb, populous and wealthy cities'.[24] Inevitably it was the women who were the worst educated of all. Madame Calderón could not help contrasting the education of the female sex in the USA and in Great Britain with the education of women in Mexico, even among the better class. 'When [she wrote] I say they read, I mean they know how to read; when I say they write, I do not mean they can always spell; when I say they play, I do not say they have generally a knowledge of music.' And if the *men* wanted a proper education they had to travel abroad for it.[25]

Primary schools using Lancaster's methods flourished in Mexico after 1822 when the first was started in Mexico City, but only when they were run by Mexicans, and the education that they dispensed was of so rudimentary a nature it scarcely began to satisfy the demands of someone like Joel Poinsett. James Thomson travelled for three years in Mexico from 1827 to 1830 trying to establish Lancasterian schools but gave up owing to the bishops' opposition. His son-in-law, Richard Jones, went to Guadalajara in 1827 to direct the schools in the province of Jalisco but was forced to leave in 1834 when its government changed and became less liberal. The bishops were unwilling to tolerate the use of the scriptures in the schools when supervised by a Protestant and when the scriptures were not annotated.[26] Religious tolerance was, wrote Ward, more widely practised by 1827 and popular prejudice was on the wane. By the treaty Britain concluded with Mexico the British were entitled to a Protestant burial and to be interred in a Protestant cemetery though they did not as yet possess the right to the exercise of the Protestant religion, whether in public or in private. But old prejudices died very hard especially in the country districts, not surprisingly since till 1822 no foreigner was admitted to Mexico. Henry Ward's wife wrote home to her father in August 1825 that even the horses they brought from England were the object of popular religious prejudice. 'At La Puebla the enlightened and tolerant mob endeavoured to stone the horses, because they were "*Hereges*" [Heretics] and not "*Christianos*", and would have done it had they not procured a very strong escort.' She did however go on to say that, 'In spite of this disgraceful fanaticism amongst the Lower Ranks, there are many of those who have the direction of affairs, who are of a very different opinion, and would willingly encourage the building of a Protestant Church, were it not for that article in the constitution which forbids anything of the kind.'[27]

Lyon in his travels found the priests he met encouraged the people to regard all foreigners as being either Jews or heretics (the two terms were really synonymous). Many believed that foreigners had tails and that the stirrups they used when riding were placed more forward than the local custom to allow the rider to stoop a little, thus preventing the friction of the saddle from inconveniencing the rider's tail.[28] Hardy met a friar who was much concerned at the presence of so many Englishmen having the effect of spreading heresy – he called Protestantism 'Jewish paganism' and an invention of the Devil. He became very emotional when Hardy told him of the congress's decree to extend religious toleration, though later when given entertainment on board the ship from which Hardy was prospecting, he drank a liberal quantity of cognac and 'indulged much less in his favourite polemics'.[29] The legend of foreigners having tails only persisted where foreigners were rare, that is in the country districts where the priest was still a petty despot to whom the villagers doffed their caps and whose hand they kissed as they genuflected. Until foreigners became more numerous it was, Beaufoy wrote, amusing to see how, when

Europeans were bathing or undressing, the women and children gathered round to catch a glimpse of the dreadful tail.[30]

The anonymous author of *A Sketch* encountered considerable religious prejudice on first arriving in Guadalajara as late as 1826. Protestants were liable to be murdered by *léperos* and only two Englishmen had tried to settle there. One had been asked to leave the town within twenty four hours of arriving because he talked too freely about religion, and the other apparently felt so unsafe he decided to sell his business and leave. The author and his companions however were accepted and treated with respect by the mob, because they were seen to attend mass on Sundays and on holy days, though, once accepted, the author confessed he became less regular in his devotions. The local senators had thought at first that he and his companions were foreign spies and the priests were afraid they would have the effect of undermining their influence, but a letter from the minister in the capital to give them protection and encourage them soon led to a total change of attitude.[31] It was the enlightened governor of the province that helped overcome the native prejudice first felt towards the mining companies when they arrived in Guanajuato. Ward in November 1826 found there no trace of religious ill-feeling; and though the Marquis of Rayes still refused to employ any heretics in his mine, he was very polite when Ward visited him.[32]

Beaufoy, with his usual prejudice, considered that the lower classes in Mexico had no true conception of the Catholic religion and used its ceremonies and holidays as an excuse for idleness and drinking.[33] Madame Calderón thought very differently, being much impressed by the popular devotions and the really gruesome penances she witnessed. At one public penance in a church, where she was present incognito, she described the women kneeling for ten minutes with their arms extended in the form of a cross, while the men scourged themselves so viciously, with iron scourges sharpened into points, she could hear their blood splashing on the floor. After half an hour of this self-inflicted torture, during which a monk encouraged the penitents to be even more severe with themselves, a bell was rung to tell them to stop; 'but such was their enthusiasm, that the horrible lashing continued louder and fiercer than ever.'[34]

Despite his widespread condemnation of almost everything Mexican (he would surely have been horrified at the penitential scene Madame Calderón witnessed), Beaufoy did have some good to say about the soldiers in the Mexican army. Almost all were clothed in British cloth

and 'cut a much better appearance than I had expected; far superior
to the officers, who are sometimes decked out more like tragic heroes
than men disciplined to uniformity'. Mexican soldiers, he was convinced, had the makings of very good light cavalry and would prove
the equal of their European counterparts, but only provided they were
'permitted to scratch, spit and smoke their cigars on parade'.[35] Twenty
years later they were to be beaten by the armies of the United States,
but this was not because they lacked courage or skill but through lack
of any proper equipment, organization or leadership.

Lawlessness was one topic eliciting comment from every observer.
Hardy wrote of the incidence of crime he met with while staying in
Mexico City and the uselessness of the urban police. Murder, Lyon
wrote, goes unpunished in Mexico and maiming is not a criminal
offence. The country boasted a penal code and trial by jury but these
were not followed. Everybody went about armed, noted Beaufoy: those
who could afford it carried a sword and a sharp pointed knife in a
deerskin sheath; the poor carried a stick and knife, which they carefully
concealed in their sleeves. And whenever one travelled abroad with a
servant, the latter would always carry a musket. Madame Calderón in
her letters home makes frequent references to robbers, a fruit of the
civil war in Mexico and an evil never eradicated. An attempt had been
made in 1824 to subject robbers to military law but the measure
proved to be ineffective. While the country remained disorganized, as
it did still as late as 1840, the scourge of banditry would persist.
William Parish Robertson wrote in 1846 that in a country that
possessed on the face of things all the elements of power, you could
not pass from one province to another without being waylaid and
robbed on the roads and even in the public streets of the cities.[36]

Criticism of the government was another topic which united all
observers. Hardy, in reflecting on the federal constitution, thought
that Mexico had 'acted as if she was trying to make the clothes of a
grown person fit an infant, without alteration'. The democratic process
appeared a mockery if typified by such scenes as he witnessed at a
meeting of the congress of Sinaloa. He heard 'the most extravagant
rhetoric that was ever uttered by a corporate body', witnessed a deputy
sink exhausted by the vehemence of the language he used and heard
the tale of one deputy who was so exasperated by his opponent's
reasoning that he dropped dead of a paralytic stroke. Hardy wrote,
somewhat superciliously, that his reactions to this scene were first
laughter and then disgust.[37] Ward wrote home privately to his father-

in-law in September 1825 of 'a most lamentable lack of Talent and Probity in those who are at the head of affairs . . . I assure you that to preach the necessity of Honesty, Liberality and Fair dealing here, is no sinecure. I have never seen more paltry Intrigues, – more Corruption, – and more bad faith here, in four months, than I did in four years in Spain.' Mexico he continued was 'a country where Bribery is very much in fashion'. 'They have however some good men, whose exertions give hopes that they will improve by Degrees; and really when one considers the last Legacy of Fanaticism and Prejudices bestowed upon them by Spain, and the existence of a strong Spanish party here still . . . one cannot wonder that so much remains to be done.'[38]

Commenting on the series of coups and the general political instability, a witty Mexican quipped with Madame Calderón: 'Some years ago we gave out cries [*gritos*, with reference to the "*grito de Dolores*" that heralded the revolt in 1810] – that was the infancy of our independence – now we begin to pronounce [*pronunciamos*, with reference to the seizures of power or *pronunciamentos*]. Heaven knows [the Mexican concluded] when we shall be old enough to speak plain.'[39] Ten years earlier Joel Poinsett had been uttering the same lament. 'The higher orders [he wrote to Clay] have lost all confidence in the Government, from the Corrupt and scandalous conduct of those who are in command; and that the experience of every day evinced the impracticability of a representative system [in?] a country where the people, besides being too ignorant to be governed by democratic Institutions, have in the last twenty years learned nothing more than disorder and anarchy, and a contempt for the laws, and those who administer them.' Poinsett, whom Fred Rippy has described as 'a flaming evangel of democracy', made himself very unpopular with powerful conservative forces in Mexico as a result of his attempts to support the spread of democratic ideas and in 1829 the Mexican president, under pressure from the press and state legislatures, petitioned successfully for his recall.[40]

One aspect of the disillusion felt by the public with their governments, whether they were federal or provincial, was resentment at the financial skulduggery and incompetence of public officials. In regard to the two north-western provinces of Sinaloa and Sonora, one Mexican told Hardy that the only benefit he derived from the change from Spanish rule was that he formerly used to pay 3 rials duty on certain articles and now he was having to pay 4, adding somewhat sardonically, 'the benefit is to come, I suppose'. All the states of Mexico had (Hardy added) been guilty of extravagance, paying salaries to generals and congressmen out of all proportion to available revenue. Merchants had been forced to disgorge so-called voluntary contributions and this, by impoverishing the capitalists, meant less revenue for the state.[41] Edward Tayloe professed himself shocked at the wasteful extravagance of the federal government, especially where the armed forces were concerned. An army numbering 60,000 was costing 12 million dollars a year, a figure that exceeded by 3 million the entire receipts of the treasury; while the navy that consisted of a few gunboats and vessels, purchased at an exorbitant price from Britain and from the USA, was costing 2 to 3 million dollars.[42] This was the navy that Beaufoy considered contemptible and a waste of money, shamefully neglected and generally hated. Its conscript sailors were Indian peasants from the interior provinces who could not stand the climate of the coast and died of the fevers contracted there.[43]

At independence, Hardy wrote, Mexicans had fancifully imagined that 'riches and abundance would flow from thousands of hidden and obstructed sources', and only later realized how utterly foolish that expectation had been. As William Robertson was to remark on his brief visit to Mexico as a member of a committee of Spanish-American bondholders, one was struck by the fact that at every step one was confronted by evidence of riches and abundant resources, mineral, cereal and pastoral, and yet one learnt that the country was 'beggared and bankrupt in public men and in public credit', and that its revenue was unable to meet its natural expenditure.

For those who sought not so much to invest as to establish commercial relations with Mexico, once it was opened to foreign trade (as it was in 1821), there were the usual difficulties met with in every Latin American country – difficulties of transportation in a mountainous country without proper roads, high import duties and corrupt officials, a glut on the market caused by the influx of too many, often unsuitable, wares and always the jealousy of local merchants. Ward thought the British had made the same mistake as the Spaniards had made in Mexico in trying to supply a huge country from a single point, namely Vera Cruz. The cost of land carriage very often meant that goods sent must be sold at a loss.[44] Vera Cruz in any case was not a location to linger in. Bullock in 1822 described it as 'the most disagreeable place on earth ... surrounded by arid sands, extensive swamps and savannahs', a thoroughly unhealthy spot, 'a painted

Golgotha, the headquarters of Death'. The merchants of the United States were the beneficiaries of this mistake. They landed their goods at many small ports and then sold them easily in nearby provinces with the result that by 1827 they controlled the best part of Mexico's commerce. The practice of smuggling was extensive and most European goods shipped via North America paid virtually no import duty.[45]

Import duties were absurdly high in the opinion of all foreign observers. The anonymous author of *A Sketch of Mexico* cites an example of the tax levied on a single length of printed cloth. It cost 8 shillings in Manchester, paid 24 shillings on entering Mexico and was subject to a further charge of 8 shillings, so that if it was to be sold at a profit it had to be priced not below 40 shillings. Nevertheless he found British merchants (there were then five in Mexico City) to be fully occupied with business, their profits from commissions being considerable. Local opinion of them was improving since their code of honour and good faith in business were qualities that were appreciated, even if they were objects of pity for being 'Jews and heretics'.[46]

The old problem of market research, or rather the lack of it, hampered merchants in the first years of trade being opened. It was the same mistake that had been made with every Latin American country. Bullock describes how 'grates, fire-irons, fenders and hearth-rugs have been sent to people who never saw a fire-place or a chimney, and knives and forks to people who scarcely know the use of them'. He pointed out that even the wealthy used few table-knives and no steel forks. 'I have seen a good dinner for a large party, with only one knife on the table.' Again, watches sent by Roskells of Liverpool were English products that were well enough thought of, but people simply could not afford them. They must, he continued, have time to recover from the effects of the recent struggle before they were in a position to buy such expensive luxuries. On the other hand there were certain British articles that he had found very much in demand: hundreds of crates of blue and white china had been sold in a matter of weeks at great profit; English muslins and calicoes were also very popular, as were both English beer and porter. Breweries were about to be established but he did not think beer would ever replace the local and traditional drink of *pulque*.

He described the jealousy of the local merchants he met when trading in Guadalajara and the pilfering and dishonesty of some – it was necessary to suspect everyone until one had knowledge to the contrary.[47] But in Mexico City the foreigners flourished and by 1826 there were said to be, according to the consular report, twenty-six merchant houses there, with eight permanent establishments in Vera Cruz.[48] Things were different on the coast of the Pacific. Acapulco, in 1825, according to consul-general Charles Mackenzie, was nothing but 'a scene of ruin and wretchedness', due to the wars and the recent earthquake, and no British merchant vessel had arrived there as yet, sailing directly from an English port. While Eustace Brown, consul-general at San Blas, bewailed the enormous import duties that stood in the way of developing commerce. There was also, he wrote, a deep distrust of the foreigner as smuggler and heretic. 'Everyone [he wrote] who has lived in South [sic] America since the commencement of the revolution well knows in what light they consider the British nation . . . and in regard to her merchants, they consider them as interlopers and monopolists who come to deprive their citizens of their daily bread and other traders of their gains. They believe this country will be ruined by the introduction of articles of necessity and luxury and that they are impoverished by the extract of the precious metals, which they consider the only thing of real value.' As a result he was unable to report much progress in developing trade.[49]

Some British, according to Beaufoy, had been foolish enough to imagine they could make a fortune out of agriculture. Many, he wrote, had bought vast tracts of land with the intention of growing wheat, not realizing that there were no roads, and canals could never be built in Mexico. One landowner had assured Beaufoy that to make it worthwhile growing cereals he had had to become a carrier, buy his own mules and then freight them at his own expense 100 miles to the capital. Beaufoy blamed Humboldt for having conveyed through his popular writings on Latin America too rosy a picture of the prospects offered to enterprising Europeans. 'It is [he wrote] by having attempted so much, and trusted so often to the report of others that notwithstanding the vast mass of valuable and interesting information contained in his volumes, he has gained the appellation of Baron Humbug'.[50]

The attempt to exploit Mexico's mines was another source of disappointment. Ward, in his book, analyses systematically the results of British mining enterprises in various areas of Mexico that involved an investment or expenditure in machinery, stores and quicksilver and the payment of salaries to employees of very nearly 3 million pounds. Robertson in 1846, twenty years after Ward was writing, put the figure

as high as 4 to 5 million.[51] As in Chile and Peru, the long struggle for
independence had left the mines in a parlous state. They had been
abandoned and had then become flooded, Spanish capital had vanished abroad, quicksilver had become expensive and it had proved
impossible to raise more money. Between 1810 and 1820 the output
of gold and silver from Mexico had fallen by as much as half. It was
to remedy this situation that the new government in 1822 passed
measures to encourage foreign investment. Many duties on mining
metals and on quicksilver were now abolished and foreigners might
become joint proprietors with Mexicans of Mexican mines. The
British were, according to Ward, over-eager to invest and in consequence submitted to terms dictated by Mexican mine-owners that
proved to be a grave handicap. By 1827 there were working in Mexico
seven great English companies, as well as one German and two North
American, the most progressive and important of which was the Real
del Monte Mining Company.

Ward in his book lists several reasons why disillusion soon set in.
There was a failure to realize that the sums invested came nowhere
near the amounts invested under Spanish rule, perhaps being only
one-third of that sum. False hopes had been raised that the produce
of the mines would be the equivalent of what had been mined in the
best of the pre-revolutionary years. As the only knowledge that
Englishmen had of conditions obtaining in Mexico had been gained
from Humboldt's *Essai Politique* depicting the country in its years of
splendour, no allowance had been made for the serious effects of
fourteen years of civil war, the dispersal of the labour force, the
deterioration of the land, the destruction of the mining stock, and the
difficulty of reorganizing an industry dependent on other forms of
economy, more especially on agriculture. As had been the case in
Chile and Peru and in Gran Colombia, nearly every British speculator
had imagined that the only obstacle to opening the mines and then
drawing a profit from them was the flooding to which the mines had
been subject and that this could be cured by the use of machinery.

The speculators had had no experience of the skills and methods of
Mexican miners and so drained Cornwall of half its population to
substitute a new method of mining. This had proved to be a total
disaster. The typical working man from England was not an adaptable
character, as was shown also in South America, and was soon
corrupted in his manners, especially in the larger towns. 'Indolence,
obstinacy and insolence [Ward wrote] take but too soon the place of

those qualities by which our working-class are distinguished at home', and the English working man was as prejudiced in his attitude towards foreigners as was his Mexican counterpart. The Mexicans moreover were disinclined to co-operate with the mining managers when the boasted new improvements produced no real advantage or proved to be unworkable. This had been evident in the attempts to substitute the practices used in Cornish mines for Mexican methods in the washing and dressing of mineral ores and those of amalgamation and smelting. The result had been that the mining companies had had to reorganize their system, making their direction solely European and the labour force solely Mexican, entailing an enormous waste of resources. By September 1826 the Anglo-Mexican Mining Company had spent £30,000 on the salaries of employees who had now been dismissed and £100,000 on machinery, nineteen-twentieths of which was unusable. The Real del Monte Company had also had to reduce its workforce, though because its operations depended on steam, it continued to use only Europeans for tasks involving the use of machines; the United Mexican Mining Company on the other hand had got rid of all its European employees. In other cases money and work had been expended on mines that proved to be completely unworkable. Adventurers in London had bought and sold mines without any up-to-date knowledge of the country and relied on Humboldt's information. Too high a price was paid for a mine once celebrated for its high production but which had long since passed its best, and companies were saddled with having to pay a fixed yearly rent to the owners of the mine.

All however was not gloom and despondency. Most of the mines owned by the companies were known (wrote Ward) to be of good quality and great progress had already been made to get them into working order, especially in replacing machinery. Ward praised the work that had been done by all of the British mining companies and more particularly by Captain Vetch, director of the Real del Monte business. Vetch had transported from Vera Cruz 1500 tons of machinery over a period of five months, using in the process 700 mules and between seventy and one hundred men. And the Anglo-Mexican company had between February 1825 and November 1826 completely rebuilt the works and machinery at twenty mines in Guanajuato. Other companies could claim similar achievements. Conditions for mining in Mexico were much more favourable than they were in either Chile or Peru. Temperatures in Mexico were very much higher than in mining districts in the Andes; compulsory labour was unknown in Mexico where some Indian tribes had been working as miners for a period of several generations; a mine in bonanza was sure to attract labour from the surrounding districts due to the system of profit-sharing; and in any case miners' wages were high. At Guanajuato, within a year of the establishment of two companies there, the Anglo-Mexican and United Mexican, the population had shot up from 30,000 to 45,000. At Tlalpujahua, a ruined village before the arrival of the mining company, the population had increased from 1000 to 5000 within a year, eighty houses had been rebuilt or put in a proper state of repair, and it now had a market that was well supplied as well as a shop selling European goods (run by the English firm of Green & Hartly) with an annual turnover of $6000. Lyon noted that at Bolaños the population of 1000 had doubled since the British started mining there, though the increase was only relative: in its great days its population had amounted to as much as 35,000.

Ward enthused about the good spirit prevailing in the Mexican mines, where the church blessed every piece of machinery and the introduction of each innovation was regarded as excuse for a festival, those erecting the new work being paid a bonus for doing so. He described a ceremony at Tlalpujahua when a new pump was inaugurated to which he and the French consul agreed to become the godfathers. Before a raised altar that was surrounded by flags and silver candlesticks, the priest solemnly blessed the pump and sprinkled it with holy water, accompanied as he did so by the godfathers. The ceremony ended with a firework display and the distribution of wine and cakes.

There were also stories of failure to be told, as Ward discovered during his travels when he covered over 3000 miles visiting the various mining districts. At Zinapan for instance the mines were abandoned, the company concerned (Anglo-Mexican) having unwisely entrusted the management to a Cornishman who ignored local warnings about the site where he chose to build works. These were on the edge of a torrent and when the rains came they were swept away. This misfortune, combined with the panic that shook the London Stock Exchange in 1826, made the company decide to abandon the site.

There was also the disastrous enterprise involving Bullock and the Mexican Mining Company. Bullock had been appointed manager with a salary of £700 and was joined by his family and fourteen Irish miners, a smelter and a gardener, all paid for by the company. Bullock was allowed to build a house in a beautiful situation with a garden attached, only to find that in the mine there was not a vestige of a vein of ore. Thus between £15,000 and £20,000 had been thrown away on a useless mine that the local people always said was worthless. According to Ward, it appears that Bullock was more influenced by the scenic attractions than he was by the value of the mine.

Ward continued to be pretty scathing about the miners brought over from Cornwall and expressed the hope that the British as a race would not be judged by the way these men behaved. Though he admitted that some of them were useful and conducted themselves in a proper fashion, 'the generality of the Cornish have left behind them a character for ignorance, low debauchery, insubordination and insolence, which has materially diminished the respect the Mexicans were inclined to entertain for the supposed superiority in intellectual acquirements of the inhabitants of the Old World'. He praised the people of Guanajuato for the indulgence they showed these men when six or seven drunken Cornishmen were picked up lying in the street; they were not charged with a criminal offence but allowed to cool off in an *hacienda*. Had they been Mexicans they would have been jailed; and, adds Ward, these very men were being paid enormous salaries for work that was often badly done.

Generally speaking, Ward discovered that the local authorities and the clergy were favourably inclined to the mining companies. Only at the mines at Zacatecas were foreigners treated with active hostility. This was partly due to the clergy in the area but also to the fact that, unlike other areas, Zacatecas had never felt the distress suffered by others in the revolution and the mines there had continued active even during the most troubled times. In consequence the foreign companies there were looked on merely as interlopers, bringing with them unwelcome change. The people were rude to Ward and his wife, who accompanied him on this his third tour, calling out to them that they were Jews, and when Ward and his party left the town they were hissed at, abused and threatened with stoning, causing the men to draw their pistols.[52]

Lyon confirmed the unfriendliness of the Zacatecan miners (mostly creoles, not Indians). He too was hooted at as a Jew and stones were thrown at him. There was no garrison in the town, so murders were frequent and went unpunished, but the disorder that was prevalent here was not present in other towns that Lyon called at in Mexico. The mining town of Real del Monte he found a model of orderliness, having become a near-English colony: many British were living there, the houses were built in the Cornish style and English carts, waggons and tools were everywhere in use on the premises. There had originally been racial strife, due Lyon thought to British xenophobia, but by the time that he visited the town mutual ill-feeling was a thing of the past, the Cornish by then having been sent home.[53]

When Madame Calderón visited the place she expressed her admiration for the mine and its buildings and more particularly for the road that led to them, 'the first broad and smooth road I had seen as yet in the republic. Nearly all the men working the machines were British (Scottish people being preferred) and the miners were all of them Indian'.[54] Yet this model mining enterprise was still not paying in 1847, according to William Robertson. Though it produced large amounts of silver, there was after twenty-three years of activity, a deficit of 5 million dollars.[55]

Attempts to wrest wealth from Mexico in another field by a British firm is recounted by Lieutenant Hardy in his *Travels in the Interior of Mexico*. He was acting as the agent of a firm known as the General Pearl and Coral Company and, in December 1825, after having an interview with the president, he obtained a licence to fish for pearls in the Gulf of California. The company had sent two vessels round the Horn, carrying on board diving bells and all the supposedly required equipment, but it soon became clear that the rocky seabed made use of the diving bells impracticable. The first cruise Hardy made lasted six weeks, during which very few pearls were discovered and these were all of them damaged and misshapen. A second attempt, equally lengthy, also yielded nothing, so the scheme was abandoned. Hardy reported that the only pearl oysters to be found in the Gulf were located at Guaymas and warned future speculators against 'embarking on so wild an enterprise'. Ward, who saw Hardy before he set out, was critical of the way in which the whole enterprise had been undertaken. The fault he considered was in not ascertaining what the local conditions for pearl fishing were, since in the Gulf of California there were abundant pearls to be found of the finest quality, if rather small.[56] This was therefore yet another example of British money thrown away in the quest for wealth in Latin America through lack of prudence and proper reconnaissance.

R. Amazon

● Belem

● São Luís

PARA

MARANHÃO

BRAZIL

Pernambuco ●
(Recife)

BAHIA

● Bahia
(Salvador)

0   200   400 mls

MINAS GERAIS

São José ●
(do Rio Preto)

● São João del Rei

RIO DE JANEIRO ■

SANTA
CATERINA

Porto Alegre ●

6 · Brazil

First accounts of British experiences in early nineteenth-century Brazil date from the arrival of the Portuguese regent together with his court and government in Rio de Janeiro in 1808. John Mawe, a scientist and author who had earlier been in Buenos Aires, came to Rio well provided with a letter of introduction to the viceroy. He found himself taken under royal patronage, allowed to travel freely about the country, and provided with a military escort and all the necessary recommendations.[1] He wrote a book about what he saw, published in 1823, entitled *Travels in the Interior of Brazil*; it is a record of his experiences in Rio and the province of Minas Geraes in 1808 and 1809, a work of considerable contemporary interest since no foreigner hitherto had been allowed such liberty to move about.

Shortly after the regent's arrival, British merchants appeared in Rio, one of the first being John Luccock, a clothier from the West Riding of Yorkshire, who was later joined by his wife and family and who stayed in Brazil until 1818. In 1820 he published a book entitled *Notes on Rio de Janeiro and the Southern Parts of Brazil Taken During a Ten Years' Residence in that Country from 1808 to 1818*. Most of his narrative is concerned with the trading conditions he encountered while he was resident in Rio, but in 1817 he set out on a tour to visit the various planters and rancheros with whom he had been trading for the past nine years, as also some of the mining areas, and the impressions gained on this tour are also recorded in his book.[2] Another British resident at this period, a wealthy invalid Henry Koster, travelled to Brazil in 1809 and stayed in Pernambuco for the sake of his health.[3] He travelled freely in the northern provinces and in 1816 wrote his *Travels in Brazil*, which was published in the following year. James Henderson, a young man with some means, sailed to Brazil in 1819 in the hope of finding public employment. Having had no success in securing this, he decided to discover as much as he could about the country in which he now found himself, journeying from Rio via Bahia and Recife (or Pernambuco as it was still called) and getting as far north as Maranhão.[4] The result was his *History of Brazil*, which was published in 1821.

Meanwhile in 1817 there arrived briefly in Rio de Janeiro the frigate *Congress* bearing on board the US commissioners sent by their government to report to Congress on the state of affairs in the provinces of the River Plate. The commissioners' secretary Henry Brackenridge whose book, published in 1820, has been referred to in an earlier chapter, devoted nearly 200 pages to describing life as he found it in Brazil, though his visit was confined to the city of Rio and the port of call of Santa Catarina.

The two Scotsmen already mentioned in the chapters on Chile and the provinces of La Plata, Alexander Caldecleugh and Farquhar Mathison, both spent a little time in Rio (in 1819 and in 1821) and a description of their impressions can be found in the early pages of their books. Maria Graham whose observations on Chile have already been alluded to in an earlier chapter resided for over two years in Brazil between 1821 and 1823 before and after her visit to Chile: her *Journal of a Voyage to Brazil and Residence During Part of the Years 1821, 1822 and 1823* was published in 1824.[5] Always eminently readable, she gives the reader perceptive insights into life as lived by someone of means in the three principal towns of Brazil: Pernambuco, Bahia and Rio de Janeiro.

The other British resident who recorded his views on his life in Brazil in the early decades of the nineteenth century was an Anglican clergyman, Robert Walsh, chaplain to the British embassy in Rio in 1828 and 1829. Unsurprisingly, he has more to say than others about the nature of religious observance and the attitude of the Brazilians, whether clergy or lay, towards the foreign Protestants.[6]

There were also two British naval officers whose experiences of Brazil were very different, the first being Admiral Thomas Cochrane. The second volume of his *Narrative* deals with his remarkable exploits in command of the navy of Brazil in 1823 and 1824; it is a tendentious but absorbing account of his services in the cause of Brazilian unity and the almost predictable disputes that arose over his right to keep naval prizes and to his financial remuneration. The other sailor was William H. Webster, a British surgeon in the Royal Navy attached to the frigate *Chanticleer*. His ship called at Rio, Maranhão and Para between 1828 and 1830 and his *Narrative of a Voyage to the South*

Atlantic, published in 1834, conveys such impressions as he gained of these ports that he got to know only very briefly.[7] As to United States observers, Captain Richard Cleveland (already referred to) in 1817 called at Santa Catarina of which he records a brief impression in his *Narrative of Voyages and Commercial Enterprises*, while the naval chaplain Charles Stewart (again referred to earlier in this book) has left a description of Rio de Janeiro as he found it in 1828 in his book *A Visit to the South Seas*.

Brazil when the regent first arrived there seemed to offer British merchants even more dazzling prospects of markets for the sale of manufactured goods than any other part of South America, since Spain still ruled her American colonies and kept legitimate commerce with them out of the hands of the foreigner. Unfortunately the same mistakes as had been made earlier at Montevideo and at Buenos Aires in 1807 and were to be made again elsewhere (at Valparaiso and at Callao) were made at Rio in 1808: overestimating the size of the market, a failure by firms to obtain information about kinds of goods that were likely to sell, and a failure to realize that the ports affected did not have the required facilities to deal with an influx of merchant ships, all clamouring to unload their cargoes speedily.

John Mawe conveys a vivid picture, in a passage much quoted by historians, of the glut of goods arriving from Britain, once the Portuguese court was installed in Rio. The population of the whole of Brazil amounted to only 800,000, exclusive of the negro slaves who made up as much as one-third of the total, so the market was very soon overstocked. The rent of warehouses escalated, the customs house was overflowing, 'even salt, casks of ironmongery and nails, salt fish, hogsheads of cheese, hats, together with an immense quantity of crates and hogsheads of earthen and glassware, cordage, bottled and barrelled porter, paints, gums, resins, tar etc. were exposed not only to the sun and rain, but general depredation'. The local people pilfered freely the articles strewn along the beach, and the numerous watchmen employed to guard them profited amply from their employ. A large proportion of these goods had eventually to be sold at the customs house for the benefit of the underwriters, and as their value continued to depreciate they were auctioned often at a gross discount, resulting in heavy losses to the merchants.

Many quite unsuitable articles had been sent out in the vain hope of achieving a profitable sale (the same story as in Buenos Aires and a little earlier in Montevideo): stays for women who had never heard of

them, skates for use in a tropical climate, coffins that were never used
by Brazilians, iron stoves, fire-irons and candles, elegant services of
cut glass for those who were accustomed to drink out of either horn
or coconut shell, chandeliers for creole houses in which only a
primitive lamp was employed, lengths of superfine woollen cloths that
were essentially luxury items, immense quantities of high-priced
saddles of a kind that was never employed in Brazil and thousands of
whips for a country in which the horse's reins were so long that they
always did service as a whip.

However, as Mawe went on to point out, there *was* a market for
certain commodities: iron- and steel-ware, salt, common woollens,
cotton goods especially if they were cheap, hats, boots, shoes and
leather, earthenware and glass, bottled porter, Cheshire cheese,
butter, cheap furniture, tin plate, brass, lead, powder, drugs, books as
well as low-priced paper, watches, telescopes, salted meats and most
of all goods from India for eventual resale in Africa, silk and cotton
hosiery and fashionable dresses.

Those who purchased goods in return too often found they had
made a bad bargain, for far too little attention was paid to the state of
articles sold in bulk; for instance, hides were found spoilt by drying or
had been eaten away by grubs; or precious stones, bought at asking
price, were later sold for a trifle in London or bought indiscriminately
without any consideration of their intrinsic quality. Rio was full of
young supercargoes, with grandiose ideas about becoming merchants,
who lived in a style they could not afford without realizing that the
only way to make money out there was through pursuing the retail
business.[8]

John Luccock gives a graphic description of the inadequacy of the
port of Rio to cope with the multitude of merchant ships. There was
not a single wharf that was able to serve an ocean-going vessel and
there were only two lighters available to ferry ashore the numerous
cargoes. Ships had to wait for weeks to unload, while they saw the
port dues mounting daily. The customs officers were quite incapable
of carrying out detailed examinations and consequently made valuations that were entirely arbitrary. If a merchant decided, having
landed his wares, that he must remove them elsewhere for sale, he
was unable to obtain a refund on the 24 per cent duty paid, let alone
the 4 per cent export duty. Only after the British Foreign Office and
a committee of British merchants had put pressure on the authorities,
and the necessary sums had been paid in bribes, was the customs

situation regularized and Luccock was able to write home, as he was
to do in June 1809: 'I am happy to say that the English have become
masters of the Customs House, that they regulate everything and that
orders are given for the officers to pay particular attention to the
directions of the British consul.' In 1810 a commercial treaty was
signed between Britain and Portugal reducing the duty on British
goods admitted to Brazil to 15 per cent, with valuations henceforth to
be made by a joint committee of English and Brazilians. But already,
even before the treaty, the picture for merchants had changed for the
better so far as the market was concerned, and they were no longer
reduced to returning unwanted goods to British ports or trying to sell
them in Buenos Aires. 'Our trade [wrote Luccock] is very good, we
cannot produce goods fast enough.'[9]

There were continuing difficulties of course, some caused by the
war against Napoleon but more on account of the war with America
and attacks by United States privateers, that meant vessels had to sail
in convoy and were often delayed for months at a time waiting for a
convoy to be assembled. Even so, Luccock's business turnover was
$100,000 a year. But not all the merchants were so successful.[10]
Henderson, in 1819, recorded great losses being made by merchants,
often due to an overwillingness to grant credit to purchasers. When a
debtor defaulted on his payments the legal processes involved, in
order to recover what was owing, could take several years in Brazilian
courts, and even when an order was secured for the seizure of property
belonging to the debtor, it was found that by a fictitious sale the debtor
had conveyed the property elsewhere. The appointment of a judge
conservator, secured by the treaty of 1810, was of little benefit in such
cases; the judge's decision could always be questioned when the case
was referred to a higher court. But having said that, Henderson
admitted that great individual fortunes were made, and in 1819 there
were sixty British firms already operating in Rio and British imports
into Brazil were valued at as much as 3 million pounds, half of them
into the port of Rio. The British also did well at Recife, where
Henderson found sixteen British firms whose members had been able
to accumulate a common fund of £5000 to build themselves a church
and a hospital.[11] Maria Graham wrote of eighteen British firms
possessing establishments in Bahia, while there were only two French
and two German firms doing business in the same town.[12] Caldecleugh wrote in 1824 of Brazil importing everything it needed from
abroad (save only wine) from British merchants. And Henderson

mentioned that Brazil was purchasing most of its military and naval stores from two or three English mercantile houses.[13] When Maria Graham was staying in Rio she remarked on the numerous English shops there – saddlers, bakers, food and drink stores – and noticeably English public houses or taverns, 'whose Union Jacks, Red Lions, Jolly Tars, with their English inscriptions, vie with those of Greenwich or Deptford'. Most of the streets she passed along were lined with displays of English goods, textiles and crockery but especially hardware. While Robert Walsh, in 1828, found the shops in Rio so overstocked with goods from Europe (meaning, seemingly, from Britain) that they sold more cheaply than they did in London's Cheapside.[14]

The British seem to have been looked on by Brazilians as a useful and necessary evil. British goods were naturally welcome and Portugal (of which Brazil remained part until declaring its independence, which it did in 1822) needed the support and protection of Britain, not only during the wars against Napoleon. And even after Brazil was independent it still needed British official recognition, although that meant having to make concessions in regard to bringing an end to its slave trade. But as was regrettably so often the case with British communities in foreign countries, their standard of behaviour was unendearing. Lord Strangford, British ambassador in Rio until his recall in 1815, told Wellesley the foreign secretary that Brazilians looked upon the English as being 'usurpers of their commerce' and were 'offended with the haughty language and proceedings of our consuls and (certainly not without reason) of the insults daily offered to their Prejudices, Customs and Religion'.[15] The drunkenness of the English sailors in the streets was the source of a complaint to the royal court by certain Portuguese officers but, according to Graham, the Empress of Brazil showed herself remarkably indulgent, passing it off with 'Tis the custom of the North, where brave men come from. The sailors are under my protection.'[16] More offensive than the sight of drunken English sailors in the midst of a people who are seldom drunk was that of British and United States seamen openly begging in the streets, the only beggars Robert Walsh ever saw.[17]

Maria Graham found little in common with the English colony while staying in Bahia. Their only interest seemed to be in trade and those she spoke to showed little interest in the country that they were living in – often ignorant of the names of plants that were seen to be growing around their doors or of the countryside 10 miles outside

Bahia. 'Society [she remarked wistfully] is at a low, very low, scale here among the English', though they did themselves well enough for food and drink. Her social snobbery was once more in evidence when she described the English in Rio – 'much as at home in their rank in life ... the ladies very good persons doubtless, would require Miss Austin's [sic] pen to make them interesting' though charity compelled her to concede that they were mostly good-humoured and hospitable people.[18]

Walsh found the English community in Rio outnumbered by the French by two to one (700 British to 1400 French) and they did not seek to assert their presence with any display in their houses and shops. They ran a circulating library, used briefly to run a newspaper and had their own Anglican church building, designed as all such buildings were at that period in a simple neo-classical style, like the Anglican church that was built at Funchal or the garrison chapel at Corfu. Walsh described it as 'small but elegant' but in a very neglected state. It was unfurnished and showed marks of decay, with a roof not waterproof, windows broken, blinds stained and soiled and the place far from clean. It was in fact the first English church to have been built in South America since the signing of the treaty of 1810 that permitted the British to have Protestant worship. Henderson records that he was present at the laying of the foundation stone on 12 August 1819 and that the building was dedicated jointly to Saint George and Saint John, in honour of the sovereigns of England and Brazil. According to Walsh, some Brazilians had opposed the erection of the church, but the Catholic bishop had replied perceptively: 'The English have really no religion; but they are a proud and obstinate people. If you oppose them, they will persist, and make it an affair of infinite importance; but if you concede to their wishes, the chapel will be built and nobody will ever go near it.' 'Brazilians [Walsh continued] say he was right, for the event has verified the prediction.'[19]

The privileged position of the British and the wealth they acquired through trade in Brazil inevitably attracted jealousy. The value of British property in the customs house in Bahia alone was reckoned in 1822 to be around £300,000 and this, together with outstanding debts and the contents of the merchants' stores, took the total to around a million pounds, or so Commodore Hardy figured in his dispatch to the Admiralty.[20] Small wonder that in 1815 Koster found the Portuguese in Brazil critical of the commercial concessions their government had agreed to make to Britain, a country that had taken an unfair advantage of the weakness of the Portuguese monarchy. They were also critical of the fact that the British had been able to obtain grants of land conferred on them by the Anglophile regent, whereas the Portuguese in Britain were prohibited by law from owning land. Koster also had to listen to complaints about Britain's restrictions on aliens, whereas the British in Brazil could travel freely without a passport.[21]

British travellers were much impressed by the fertility of the soil and the vast tracts of land that lay uncultivated. Mawe, in his journeys through the Minas Gerais, continually refers to the possibilities it offered to European immigrants. Land could be bought in Brazil very cheaply and he was confident that Protestant immigrants would soon be granted religious toleration (as the British were in 1810). 'No territory perhaps in the world [he wrote] is so rich in natural products, and at the same time so neglected for want of an enlightened and industrious population'.[22] How many times has one heard the same sentiments echoed by many other observers throughout the countries of Latin America! Henderson's attention was drawn to the vast amount of land that was lying waste, especially near the principal towns, an amount, he wrote, that would astonish the English agriculturalist; but, he added, the land laws in Brazil did not encourage a would-be improver. To support his contention that farming immigrants with European ideas of farming would be unlikely to succeed in Brazil he cites the example of a Swiss settlement, a place with the name of Novo Friburgo, 70 miles outside Rio, that he found Brazilians disapproved of. The latter thought that the regent had been wrong to offer land to the foreigner while there were plenty of Brazilians on whom grants of land could have been bestowed. Yet, as Henderson goes on to point out, the Portuguese never worked in the fields, they left all the manual work to their slaves. Surely, he reasoned, there was ample scope for the exertions of everyone, whether Brazilian or European, in a region of nearly 2 million square miles, most of which still remained virgin soil.[23]

Mathison visited Novo Friburgo and drew a moral from what he saw. On first arrival he was struck by the neat houses laid out in squares and the pretty gardens attached to them, but he soon realized that the place was half-deserted and that of the 1200 original settlers only 300 now remained, and many of those were preparing to leave. He attributed failure to various causes. Not all the settlers had been good characters; a number of them preferred to shoot game rather than tackle the hard work of farming and anyway they soon tired of the life and moved away either to Rio or up-country where the climate was milder. Most of the settlers were Protestants but without either church or minister they suffered through lack of moral guidance. Most important of all, the departure of the king, who returned to Portugal in 1821, had meant that they were either forgotten or neglected by the regent and his government. Mathison held out this failed experiment as an awful warning to prospective settlers. As he pointed out, whatever the changes effected in the government of Brazil, there remained enormous physical difficulties of climate and of geography and the jealousy and bigotry of Brazilians who resented the competition of foreigners and any improvements or innovations.[24]

Yet not all Brazilians were so unreceptive to progressive ideas from the world outside. John Mawe, during the course of his travels in the Minas Gerais in 1809, was asked by the intendant of the province to experiment in the making of beer. Mawe thought it could well be brewed there, thus relieving the local people of the need to buy bad wine from Rio or to drink the spirits they distilled themselves. He also taught the intendant and his wife the art of making cheese and butter. On the other hand, on one estate, after showing the owner how to make butter in what he called the English fashion, he expressed grave doubts about the Brazilians ever following the instructions given, as the process involved too much time and trouble: 'They would take ten times more pains to procure fifty shillings worth of gold, at an expense of thirty shillings, than they would to obtain forty shillings worth of butter, though it were only to cost them five.' It offended his scientific mind to see such rich soil that was so well suited to the growing of grain and to dairy-farming owned and managed by those who were ignorant of the first principles of agriculture.[25] It is small wonder that Lieutenant Webster, calling at Rio in 1828, discovered that milk and butter were scarce there and remarked that no attention was paid to the conduct of scientific farming.[26]

Indolence of the native population was always the subject of criticism by Europeans and North Americans visiting Latin America. Richard Cleveland remarked disapprovingly that Brazilians he met were not interested in improving their material position: 'When a creole Portuguese possesses enough to keep him from starving, he will no longer labor, but riots in those slothful indulgences, which, from education, or rather example, and the effect of climate, he considers supreme happiness.'[27]

Impressions gained of the capital Rio depended rather on whether it was one's first sight of any city in Brazil or whether, like Maria Graham, one had spent some time in provincial towns such as Bahia and Pernambuco. Luccock commented in 1813 on the improvements that had taken place since his first arrival in that city – the construction of new streets and markets and the cleaning up of the older ones, roads widened, buildings smartened, schools and colleges instituted, botanical gardens well laid out. Insurance offices had been opened, the custom houses had been enlarged, public wharves had been constructed and the barge monopolies abolished. Three booksellers had appeared and a newspaper was published once a week, there were general increases in domestic comfort and even the streets were seen to be cleaned.

When James Henderson, Farquhar Mathison and Maria Graham visited Rio, the Portuguese court was either resident or had only recently departed and its presence over fourteen years had given the city a cosmopolitan air and public buildings it was not to lose. Even so, James Henderson thought Rio to be a primitive town which, despite the residence of the court, was centuries behind the rest of the world in the comforts and enjoyments of civilized life. He reckoned little of the public buildings which included a large public library and theatre, and considered the royal palace resembled more a factory than a kingly residence. Though Rio's cost of living was extremely high, a respect in which it resembled London, it provided none of the comforts of the latter. Henderson thought Rio an unfriendly city. He found his reception there very cold, in marked contrast to the one he received in the cities of Spanish America. He was told by an Englishman of his similar experience when in the ten years he had spent in Brazil he had never encountered any symptom of genuine hospitality, although he had shown his friendship to many. He also cited with disapproval the claims to public homage by the Queen of Portugal, whose escort, consisting of the royal cadets, forced any foreigner to dismount whenever the royal personage passed. Lord Strangford had apparently refused to comply when he met the queen on his usual ride and the royal cadets had used their swords to compel the ambassador to dismount. The only redress he was able to obtain was to see the cadets responsible forced into prison for a very brief spell. Brackenridge recounted how the US minister Thomas Sumter, when he had been threatened in a similar manner, had defended himself against the swords with his stick (leaving the queen very much offended) and thereafter always went armed when abroad. On a second occasion of his meeting the queen, who ordered her guards to force him to dismount, he drew his pistols and put spurs to his horse. On his later complaining to the king about this, he was given a written apology by the latter who offered to have the guards imprisoned.[28] When two years later Commodore Bowles was compelled to submit in the very same way, the cadets were sent to apologize, when Bowles told them they should reserve their swords for an encounter with an enemy not with a friend. On representations being made to the king by all the ministers of foreign powers, orders were eventually given for this unpopular practice to cease.[29]

Like all Englishmen arriving in Brazil, never having been in the country before, Henderson was shocked at the sight of so many black slaves. Rio's narrow streets were crowded with them, howling out their savage songs under the burdens they dragged along. There had been, apparently, humane attempts by English merchants to introduce waggons for conveying their goods from the customs sheds but this had been effectually opposed by the clerks employed in the customs house who had, through intrigue, acquired the privilege of hiring out slaves to do the carrying. He deplored the ignorance displayed by all with whom he came into contact. Books were very largely forbidden; a gazette was published twice a week on the only press (a royal one) and it told readers nothing about the country. There was only one other newspaper printed in Brazil and that was at Bahia.[30] The US citizen Henry Brackenridge, writing of his experience in 1817, thought that there was 'more printing in any one of our smallest cities, than in all Brazil' and Caldecleugh noted in September 1820 that the Rio papers (by now apparently there was more than one) were just printing news of events in Europe that had occurred in the previous March. Things changed much in the next ten years and by 1829 there were no less than fifteen national newspapers being printed and published in the capital city.[31]

Henderson had the usual complaints to make about the police force and the law: if he found a dead body washed up on the beach he was strongly advised not to go to the police or he might be accused of causing a death; of the slovenly way in which people dressed, especially women, within their own homes; about the oriental seclusion of women; about the deplorable habit of spitting and about the general apathy, so much of the day being spent in sleep. But having drawn the inevitable comparison between 'the actual condition of Brazil and that which from its pure climate, fertile soil, numerous rivers and immense extent, it is capable of attaining', he ends on an optimistic note, looking forward under the benevolent rule of the king and the future Prince Royal, to the spread of education, better land laws, the curtailing of the 'mind-degrading and extortionate influence of a numerous and slothful priesthood', and a real prospect of the hateful slave-trade being gradually if not speedily abolished. In regard to the last evil mentioned, Henderson was going to be disappointed for, though the Brazilian government, on Canning's insistence, agreed to bring an end to the slave-trade by 1830 at the latest, and in 1831 was to pass a law rendering continuance of the trade illegal, the trade continued to flourish illicitly until the middle of the nineteenth-century.[32]

Mathison in 1821 thought Rio, like other South American cities, had no pretensions to magnificence, very few towers, domes or steeples and no handsome public buildings of any sort. The streets appeared to him narrow and filthy, the churches and convents numerous but built in an undistinguished style. Inevitably the sight of negro slaves, criminals and runaways in chains, nearly naked and very noisy, aroused only 'horror, surprise and disgust'. He was very critical of the bribery and corruption that permeated official circles, impeding trade and encouraging smuggling, and outspoken on the subject of public justice which was widely replaced by private revenge, as in all undeveloped countries where trial by jury, habeas corpus and a free press were as yet unknown.[33] Seven years later Wiliam Webster found himself in agreement with much of this. The city, he wrote, failed to match the splendid scenery of the bay; the streets, though well paved, were badly lit and the shops had a slovenly appearance. There were no sewers in the town and everywhere was incredibly dirty, though the health of the citizens paradoxically was reputed to be generally good. He was intrigued rather than shocked by the sight of such a huge number of slaves dragging carts and sledges through the streets 'with apparent unconcern and a degree of hilarity' that seemed to him 'hardly credible'. The streets resounded with their uncouth singing and with the rattling of their chains. Law enforcement was, as usual, bad and the police extremely inefficient, but he noted with approval the new spirit of tolerance in religious matters and the fact that the Bible could circulate freely, the existence of an English school, several bookshops and two weekly newspapers.[34] So far as the bibles were concerned, the Reverend Hugh Silvin, the chaplain of the *Cambridge*, which called at Rio in 1826, records that at that time the local bishop was most dissatisfied with the bibles being brought in by the Bible Society, complaining of what he called 'mutilated copies'. Silvin expressed some sympathy with him, remarking that if the copies of the Scriptures were intended for use by Roman Catholics, the Bible Society should pay some attention to Catholic prejudices and opinions. A pious but unrealistic hope.[35]

Another clergyman to visit Rio two years after Silvin was Robert Walsh, the chaplain to the British embassy who, unlike the previous observers mentioned, was impressed by the capital of Brazil: its well-paved streets with flagged pavements, its massive houses built of granite and, strangest of all, its cleanliness. Not so, that other minister of religion, the Reverend Charles Stewart of USS *Vincennes*. To someone accustomed to the elegance (he wrote), the neatness and cleanliness of Boston, New York, Philadelphia and Baltimore, Rio with all its magnificent scenery, beauty of its architecture and wealth of many of its inhabitants appeared 'a most disgusting place: more so in most of its streets than even the lowest haunts of poverty and vice in New York or Philadelphia'.[36]

Walsh's reflections on Catholic observance were on the whole very favourable. Though disapproving in a puritan way of the levity, as he saw it, in certain ceremonies, such as the outlay of so many dollars (75,000) on fireworks and candles to glorify God on a festive day, and the manner in which the spectators behaved when a nun was being solemnly professed (a spectacle he found very moving): 'Those about us laughed and joked on it' and the crowd outside the church, blacks and mulattoes, shouted, laughed and hallooed all the time that the service inside was being conducted and spent time letting off squibs and crackers. He was much impressed by the way in which Sunday was observed by Brazilian families (obviously the well-to-do), the whole of the family processing to church accompanied by their household slaves. He did not approve of the continental habit of opening the shops once mass was over but, at least, he wrote, one was spared the scenes that were commonplace in England on Sundays: 'That awful display of drunkenness and blasphemy which our sabbaths present . . . squalid masses of men and women besetting gin shops.' The greatest violation of the sanctity of Sunday was committed in Rio by British sailors and those of the United States whom Walsh witnessed one Sunday afternoon – 'a desperate riot of drunken blasphemers' in the Palace Square of the capital.

Walsh was at pains to contradict the stories of the alleged immorality of the Catholic clergy in Brazil. He admitted that they often violated their church's laws on celibacy, but he praised the constancy of their attachments that 'want only legal sanction to render them even laudable'. Brazilians, he wrote, were extremely anxious to have the celibacy law repealed. (They are still waiting in the 1990s.) Walsh was also full of praise for the way that the Roman Catholic Church admitted negroes to the priesthood and contrasted the attitude of Brazilian people to the question of racial difference with that obtaining in the British West Indies. There 'a clergyman had been severely censured by his flock for presuming to administer the sacrament to a poor negro at the same table with themselves'. This had happened in Barbados and the congregation had appealed to the bishop who (rightly in the view of Walsh) summarily dismissed the complaint. 'In Brazil a black was seen [he continued] as an officiating minister' and white and black without discrimination received the sacrament from his hands. Walsh was particularly struck by the contrast between the African slave and the African once he was freed and had status: 'As a despised slave, he was far lower than other animals of burthen that surrounded him . . . advanced to the grade of a soldier he was clean and neat in his person, amenable to discipline, expert at his exercises . . . as a citizen he was remarkable for the respectability of his appearance and the decorum of his manners' and 'as a priest he seemed even more devout . . . and more correct in his manners than his white associates'.

Walsh was also impressed by attempts to spread education to the masses. In Rio there were two Lancasterian schools and primary schools of some description in every street within the city, though this sounds a pardonable exaggeration. There were military and naval academies in addition to two seminaries, open to all irrespective of status, as well as an English boarding school for those who were able to pay the fees. There were also two public libraries, one containing 60,000 volumes, as well as a fine collection of bibles, 'more extensive perhaps than in any other library in the world'. When he travelled into the interior, in the rich province of Minas Gerais, he visited the town of São João, a place of 100,000 inhabitants, that boasted a library of a thousand volumes and added 'we were surprised to find in so remote a place a number of English books. Among them were the "revolutionary" Plutarch; Smith's *Wealth of Nations*; Pinkerton's *Geography*; *Paradise Lost*; *A Sentimental Journey*; *Trials for Adultery*, with some of the periodicals; and among the newspapers we saw *The Times* and *The Chronicle*.' He discovered three people in the town who could speak English and rather more who were able to read it, so perhaps the English section of the library did not remain completely unused. But the ignorance of most Brazilians about the world outside Brazil was something that struck him forcibly; it was of course the same story in all the countries of South America and Englishmen never ceased marvelling at it. People, Walsh found, imagined the world was divided into two distinct parts, America and Portugal. They had a very vague idea about the existence of England and France but imagined that they could only be satellite states of Portugal.[37] Walsh's experience in this respect was similar to that of Luccock who recalled his astonishment at being asked by what he described as 'respectable merchants' in what part of London England was and which was largest, Britain or Madeira. He found this general ignorance extended well beyond the field of geography: 'Few of them were acquainted with more than the first principles of arithmetic; in reading, they spelled out the meaning, and to write a letter was a dreaded task.'

What Maria Graham criticized, albeit perhaps a little unfairly, was the lack of any cultural life in the society with which she mixed. In Pernambuco, she lamented, there was not a single bookshop to be found in a city of 70,000 people and only one newspaper, tolerably written. At Bahia, when she went to the theatre, she found the acting and singing atrocious, as no doubt they were by European standards, nor does this strike us today as surprising. At some stage of the proceedings there were loud calls for the national anthem, 'and not until it had been played again and again was the ballet suffered to proceed'. Clearly in the infancy of independence politics were rated more important than aesthetics, even on a supposedly cultural occasion. Rio appeared more sophisticated though scarcely more culturally advanced. Graham thought Portuguese and Brazilian ladies superior in appearance to those in Bahia: 'They look [she wrote] of higher caste; perhaps the residence of the court for so many years has polished them'; and the city seemed to her more like one in Europe than either Bahia or Pernambuco.[38]

The upper classes, according to Walsh, were not resentful of the presence of the foreigner (that is, by the end of the 1820s); it was chiefly in the countryside, where the local priest dictated opinion, that xenophobia and religious prejudice tended to die extremely hard. Walsh, while travelling in the Minas Gerais, visited the town of São

José, headquarters of the General Mining Association, and found the local people there hostile, their resentment at the presence of the foreigner being encouraged by an ancient and fanatical priest, especially since all employees of the mine, apart from black slaves, were Protestants. Most of them were Germans from the Harz mountains, recruited because they were cheaper to employ and better workers than the British. Walsh was struck by how incredibly primitive were the methods used in working the gold mines: 'I never saw a wheel in the country [he wrote] or any means of abridging labour, even a cart or a [wheel]barrow', the wretched slaves did everything.[39]

So detached from the central authority were the provinces of the interior that Walsh in his travels was compelled to carry with him quantities of copper coinage, as the bank-notes of Rio were not accepted. In consequence his purse weighed a hundredweight and his saddlebag was so heavy with coins that it raised a large tumour on his horse's shoulder.[40]

When Maria Graham first arrived in Pernambuco, it was being besieged by a rebel force opposed to the newly independent government. This revolt embraced the provinces that made up the north and north-east of Brazil, where the Portuguese still had military forces of some strength as well as a navy, and where Portuguese merchant communities were much in sympathy with the cause of Lisbon. It was in these difficult circumstances – difficult that is for the prince Dom Pedro who had just agreed to accept the title of 'Constitutional Emperor of Brazil' – that appeal was made to Admiral Cochrane, then living on his estate in Chile, to come and take charge of Brazil's navy. The account of what followed is based very largely on the *Narrative* written later by Cochrane and can scarcely therefore be considered impartial. But whatever the justice of Cochrane's complaints against the Brazilian government for the way in which he was treated by it, it is generally accepted by historians that Cochrane and his 'fleet' were largely responsible for safeguarding the independence of Brazil and preserving Brazilian unity.[41]

Cochrane, several of his officers and some of the crews who had served under him in the past two years in the Chilean navy arrived at Rio in March 1822, and the task of reorganizing and equipping a fleet capable of resisting the Portuguese was completed in the course of the next twelve months. Cochrane found that his squadron consisted of nothing more than the flagship (the *Pedro Primeiro*, with 74 guns), the *Maria de Gloria* with 32 guns, a frigate, and other smaller craft. Most of the crews were what Cochrane described as 'the worst class of Portuguese' since the higher pay given on merchant ships meant the better sailors enlisted on them. Cochrane accordingly decided to recruit as many British seamen as he could persuade to desert their ships and succeeded in getting hundreds to join him. It is reckoned that 1200 British in all were at one time serving in the navy of Brazil. Commodore Hardy told the Admiralty that great inconvenience was being caused to British merchants by Cochrane's action and the government in Rio was eventually persuaded to issue an order that no foreign seamen were to be admitted on board its warships, unless they could show a certificate that they were under no prevous engagement. But by then Cochrane had managed to find most of the men he was looking for. When on 21 March 1823 he hoisted his flag as first admiral of Brazil aboard the flagship *Pedro Primeiro*, its crew were a multi-racial mix consisting of 160 sailors from Britain and the USA, the rest of the complement being made up of what Cochrane described as 'the scum of Rio', as well as 130 blacks. The limitations under which he operated were demonstrated on the first occasion that the squadron engaged the Portuguese in what was an indecisive action. Cochrane found his orders were not always obeyed, some of his ships were sailing badly, cartridges were unfit for use, sails rotten and powder so poor that the range of shells that were fired from his guns was reduced from 2000 to 1000 yards. His marines did not understand fire exercises or how to use their firearms or swords, yet were too proud to wash down the decks or even clean out their own berths, so that seamen had to act as sweepers and scavengers instead of learning their duties on board. He also met with disloyalty among Portuguese members of the crews, who withheld powder in the magazine while their ship was engaged with the enemy; and one of his ships had to be restrained from surrendering itself to the enemy. As a result, he then transferred the best of his officers and crews to his own ship and the *Maria de Gloria*, and used these two vessels to blockade Bahia. There followed a gigantic piece of bluff. Cochrane alarmed the Portuguese vessels, bottled up in the harbour of Bahia, by sailing his flagship among them at night and threatened to send in his nonexistent fireships, and such was his formidable reputation as a reincarnation of Francis Drake, that the Portuguese garrison commander surrendered. He agreed to terms laid down by Cochrane by which the garrison of 5000, with large quantities of military stores and members of promi-nent Portuguese families, were to be embarked on seventy transports and escorted away by thirteen of their warships. The convoy headed first of all for the northern provinces of Brazil but eventually made for the Canary Islands, pursued by Cochrane in his flagship who picked off the stragglers one by one, usually in an assault by night. Every one of the Portuguese troopships was captured, the officers being forced to give parole not to serve further in the war with Brazil, while three-quarters of the entire convoy fell as prizes to Cochrane's ship, he not losing a single man. It was a triumph of daring and skill, though it said little for the morale of the Portuguese troops involved in the actions.

A similar astonishing piece of bluff persuaded the governor and the ruling junta of the port of São Luis to surrender, not only the garrison of that place but the whole province of Maranhão, being led to believe that Cochrane's flagship was only the van of a powerful expedition dispatched by the emperor from Rio. The same tactics were then adopted by one of Cochrane's officers, for Captain John Grenfell, in command of a hundred men and a captured brig, enforced the surrender of Belem and the whole of the northern province of Pará. In both these areas Cochrane set up provisional governments on behalf of the emperor.

When Cochrane eventually got back to Rio on 9 November 1823 he was welcomed personally by the emperor, created Marquis of Maranhão and given an estate in the country (a gift the assembly refused to confirm), but a bitter quarrel then ensued over the division of the various spoils. Though supported in his claims by the emperor, Cochrane had many enemies who resented his arrogance and success and the Prize Court ruled that all Portuguese property seized by Cochrane at São Luis, together with 120 vessels that Cochrane had taken possession of and valued at 2 million dollars, belonged as of right to the government. It ordered that Cochrane restore the property, sentenced him to pay exorbitant damages and enormous legal costs of the action and announced he deserved to be corporally punished for having appropriated it in the first place. A propaganda war waged in pamphlets and in newspapers against the iniquities of the British admiral, with the emperor alone taking his side and ordering that he be paid compensation for the Portuguese frigate that he had captured. Only the emperor's personal intervention ensured that the naval crews were paid and the squadron able to sail again to deal with another insurrection that had broken out in Pernambuco.

Cochrane carried on board his ships an army under General Lima which succeeded in crushing the revolt, and his squadron helped to restore to the area a sense of peace and security to which the British consul Hesketh paid tribute. Cochrane deposed the republican president and appointed a provisional government, as he had done in the northern provinces, an action that won the emperor's approval but not that of Cochrane's enemies. Cochrane then decided to take his ship into the Atlantic Ocean to give the ship's company a change of air, but on finding that it was badly damaged decided to have it repaired in England. Accordingly he set sail for Portsmouth, only to discover on arrival that he stood accused of the crime of desertion and of trying to appropriate his ship. Ordered to return at once to Rio to give an account of his commission, he considered himself to have been dismissed. In any event he was now more interested in an offer by the Greeks to take command of their newly formed fleet to fight the Turks.[42]

Cochrane used his polemical *Narrative* as a vehicle for making recriminations against the Brazilian government for the shabby way he thought he had been treated and for having had to wait thirty years before it relented and paid him something. The sum was in fact a pension for life equivalent to half the simple interest on what he reckoned was owing to him (in his view, £100,000). He died very shortly afterwards and was not to know that the government of Brazil was to grant his descendants £40,000, a not ungenerous act of restitution.[43] But whatever the rights and wrongs of the quarrel, the episode furnishes yet another example of the sour taste left when a European involved himself in Latin America in its earliest years of independence.

7 · Conclusion

If the general impression gained from accounts of those who ventured to Latin America in the early years of its independence is one of bitterness and disillusion, one is prompted to ask why this is so, whether this mood was justified by the circumstances that they encountered, how representative were these accounts and whose fault it was that they came away disappointed, angry or financially ruined.

There was clearly a lack of appreciation of the baneful consequences that flowed from the overthrow of Spanish rule – the political vacuum thus created being filled by military dictatorships, often corrupt and chronically unstable; the economic chaos that was the product of years of fighting for independence; the collapse of an organized fiscal system and destruction and neglect of farms and mines on which the local economies depended, not to mention natural disasters such as the earthquake of 1812, which almost totally destroyed Caracas. But there was also blissful ignorance of the physical geography of Latin America, the immense difficulties of transportation and communications presented there: vast distances, deserts and huge mountain ranges and a lack of roads or inland water transport. There was also ignorance of the local cultures and of the sort of civilization that obtained in a continent so long cut off artificially by its rulers from the outside world.

The difficulties encountered by British merchants, endeavouring to sell their products, arose from a lack of realization that the markets were not unlimited, that the local population was not that numerous, that the moneyed classes in the Spanish ex-colonies had either fled or had been expelled, taking with them much of their capital; that the ports at which the goods were unloaded were, at any rate in the beginning, totally ill-equipped to deal with the volume of shipping that began to arrive. Haigh and Miers discovered this in the little port of Valparaiso, Mawe and Luccock in Rio de Janeiro. There were also difficulties to be encountered by those involved in the sale of merchandise with corrupt and incompetent customs officials, of whom Consul Ricketts complained in Peru and Consul Ker Porter in Caracas. The fighting that persisted so long in Peru between the royalists and the patriots, with Lima several times changing hands, meant that merchants' property was continually at risk. Yet the merchants were fully aware of these risks, as Ricketts was at pains to point out, when they tried to get the British government to support their claim to compensation for the goods that had been either seized or destroyed, when the port of Callao was overrun. Between 1821 and 1825, as the accounts of Hall, Stevenson, Mathison and Proctor all make clear, they did extremely well in Peru. After that of course the market was glutted and there were numerous business failures.

The merchants were sometimes compelled to make loans and monetary contributions to patriot governments short of cash, and convinced that all foreigners must be rich and were draining the country of its wealth, for indeed the merchants were paid for their goods in gold and silver, till supplies were exhausted. Forced loans were levied in Buenos Aires to help pay for the war against Brazil, but also in Lima and Mexico, as Robertson and Hardy recount. There was indeed among the new regimes an ignorance of how commerce worked, as Captain Bowles did his best to point out; but standards of public conduct generally in the handling of financial affairs were still far too lax (so Beaumont thought, during his stay in Buenos Aires) for joint-stock companies to hope to flourish. Having said all this, there was never any doubt, as admitted by some of the writers quoted in various passages of this book, that many British merchants were happy to stay and were successful in setting up firms and trading with profit in more than one city in the several countries of Latin America. George Love described how in 1824 there were at least 1355 Britons making a living in Buenos Aires, a number that by 1832 had risen to 4072, according to the consular report. A fair proportion of these were merchants, not least among them the Robertson brothers who found, to use William Robertson's phrase, life in the city 'agreeable and secure'. Ricketts in 1824 wrote of twenty British firms busy doing their trade in Lima, and Andrews and Haigh described merchant colonies, neither of them large but both of them British, in Peruvian Tacna and Arequipa. Luccock's business did well in Brazil, though some Rio merchants, as Henderson notes, often encountered difficulties in recovering payment for the goods they sold. Henderson wrote of sixty British firms carrying on business there in 1819 and a further sixteen in Recife; Graham noticed eighteen in Bahia. The anonymous author of *A Sketch* described how, in 1826, there were twenty-six British business houses flourishing in Mexico City and eight in the port of Vera Cruz. By 1833 Brazil had become Great Britain's third largest foreign market[1], and in 1837 Woodbine Parish could report that the value of British goods exported into Buenos Aires was greater than the sum total of the goods that Britain exported to the whole of Europe.

Those who indulged in emigration projects, seemingly on the surface so inviting, given the climate, the unoccupied spaces, the fertile soil and the apparent willingness of patriot governments to make the way easy, had a very gloomy tale to tell. Barber Beaumont and the Robertsons in the area of the River Plate, Robert Ker Porter in Venezuela, Francis Hall in Colombia, Beaufoy in Mexico, Henderson in Brazil. Local jealousies, if not fraudulent land-grants, unfamiliarity with the kind of crops and type of farming required in the region, or the failure to realize until too late that the distances involved and the lack of roads made farming for profit, as opposed to subsistence, a very precarious if not hopeless business, as was discovered by those who invested in great tracts of land in Mexico. General O'Connor had talked optimistically in an interview with John Barclay Pentland of his scheme for 'New Erin' in Bolivia, but as Pentland commented in his report, the initial obstacle to success was getting to this remote part of the world. Beaumont had encountered rank dishonesty and the grants of land in the Plata province to which there proved to be no valid title; Robertson found that the higher wages offered to labourers in Buenos Aires inevitably drew them away from the land. Lack of security of title deprived Admiral Cochrane of an estate the government had granted him in Chile, a country in which Miers encountered a disputed title to some land on which he had built and installed machinery. It is true that there were individual British subjects who, after serving in the patriot army, settled down to farm successfully in the vicinity of Caracas, notably the two ex-army officers Colonel Stopford and Colonel Hamilton, but clearly these were exceptional cases. Yet there were plenty of immigrants who came from Britain to seek work in Buenos Aires, travelling out as individuals in response to the call for manual workers and tempted by the high wages offered. The consul-general wrote in 1832 of 1245 British artisans living and working in the city, even if the cost of living was high, the food of indifferent quality, and the housing conditions unattractive, and they were not put off by Bond Head's advice to all Britons to stay at home. At least these men were actually paid, which is more than can be said for those who took employment under the patriot governments.

Beaumont, having been encouraged by Rivadavia to bring out emigrants to Buenos Aires for settlement on farms outside the city, was unable to get his expenses paid, when the scheme for this group-emigration failed, though he pleaded personally with the head of state. Cochrane had to fight a running battle with the governments of Chile and Peru to get his sailors paid and his ships equipped. Bolívar's promise of money to Lancaster to provide for his college of education planned in Caracas could never be kept, and British merchants tried in vain to extract compensation from the Peruvian government for the loss of property they suffered in Callao. The soldiers who fought in Bolívar's army found the greatest difficulty in getting paid. James Thomson in establishing and running his schools in Buenos Aires accepted the fact that the government, though giving him every encouragement, was quite unable to pay his salary. This failure to pay for services rendered (something that caused great bitterness among those less altruistic than Thomson and who, like Cochrane, needed the money if they were to do the job they were set) was not due to dishonesty, though there was plenty of that around, but to genuine inability to find ready cash when it was required. In the period of total dislocation following the revolutionary struggle, taxes were difficult to collect, or in some cases had been abolished, and what revenue did reach the coffers of the state was spent on paying and equipping an army, provisioning it and keeping it in the field. A navy however was a novel idea and its call on the exchequer was reckoned less pressing.

It was this drain of military expenditure that caused the governments of the new states to apply to Britain and the USA for loans to keep them from going bankrupt. Bankers were sufficiently naïve, or ignorant of Latin American conditions, to lend considerable sums of money to states like Mexico and Peru, only to find after 1827 they were throwing good money after bad, when the governments defaulted on interest payments. Every bond issue in Latin America went into default within five years.[2] Military government was the order of the day, once Spanish rule had been overthrown, and money was spent in maintaining power by keeping large armies in existence. Tayloe for one, in Mexico, deplored the waste of public money maintaining armed forces for which no call existed in the shape of any external threat.

What stuck in the gullet of the North Americans and subjects of the United Kingdom was the pretence by these military despots that they were really republican liberals, believing in a democratic system and governing in accordance with a constitution. John Robertson called attention to this and ridiculed the claims of these despots. Mathison and the US diplomat Tudor contrasted the cruel and rapacious men who had taken over government in Peru with the wise, humane and enlightened viceroys who had previously ruled in the name of their king. The corruption that obtained in government circles and the indolence of public officials was something that riled men from overseas. Lieutenant Bowers and Herman Allen both fulminated against the way the rulers of Chile were behaving; Ward in Mexico deplored the government's 'lack of talent and probity', a sentiment echoed by Joel Poinsett. Henry Hill, US consul in Rio, considered that the Brazilian people were 'wholly incapable of self-government'. Political instability, though not a characteristic of Brazil, for all the diatribes of Hill, was common to all the other states of the South American continent. The removal of the rule of Spain had led to bitter quarrels between those men who wanted a centralized structure and those who wanted regional autonomy, between those with liberal and enlightened ideas and those who supported conservatism, usually coupled with religious intolerance. The US consul Brackenridge thought he would never be able to settle in the area of Buenos Aires because it was so politically unstable; Bond Head referred scathingly to the 'so-called United Provinces' of La Plata and thought, like Henry Hill in Brazil, that creoles were incapable of governing themselves. Lieutenant Hardy, in his Mexican travels, drew attention to what seemed to him the absurdities of constitutional government in the outlying province of Sinaloa.

Mining was another field in which perhaps the greatest degree of disillusion was felt and expressed. Much that went wrong was certainly due to the crooked and greedy men in London, who either issued fraudulent prospectuses or failed to provide sufficient funds, as was pointed out by Temple in Bolivia and by Henry Ward in Mexico. But there were also dishonest men in Buenos Aires, Peru and Chile, where mines were sold without proper title or were found to be exhausted or beyond repair. Head, Andrews and Robertson had experience of this in La Plata and Chile, and Ricketts in Peru drew British attention to the lack of good faith the government showed in granting the right to buy or lease mines (something that Miers found

to his cost in dealing with Chilean ministers). But there were all sorts
of other reasons why the British found that mining projects in Latin
America had little to offer. The failure to realize, when planning in
England, the enormous distances involved, the lack of any adequate
roads, the lack of water, different mining techniques, the inapplicabil-
ity of British machinery and the effects of warmer weather, wine and
women on Cornish miners. Labour costs proved to be too high, as
discovered by Stephenson in Colombia, while xenophobia played its
part, particularly in Mexico. One is left wondering whether, in the
end, British management was not the principal culprit, as indicated by
the anonymous author who had travelled widely in Mexico, for, as he
appositely pointed out, the Germans were able to make their mines
pay. Undeniably there were enormous difficulties: many mines were
difficult of access, were flooded or had had their machinery smashed.
However, not all the blame can rest entirely with local conditions. But
whatever the reasons, the fact remains that only seven of the mining
companies, floated in Latin America by Britain and by the USA,
survived after 1842.[3]

The experience of the mercenaries in Latin America was docu-
mented at considerable length, more particularly of those who went to
fight in Venezuela. The chief complaints, as has been shown earlier,
were due to the lack of regular pay, lack of food and medical attention,
and the barbarism of the creole troops. Putting into practice Bolívar's
slogan 'War to the Death' was extremely offensive to the humanitarian
principles of those accustomed to European warfare. There was also
the charge that many volunteers had been deceived by Bolívar's agents
into thinking that America offered them generous rewards in cash and
land. Furthermore there were complaints of the jealousy exhibited by
the creole officers and a certain number of their commanders, Urdaneta
and Brion especially, and the contempt shown because British officers
were for the most part ignorant of Spanish. The commanding generals
on the whole seem to have commanded British respect and only
Cochrane and Hippisley (who later retracted his accusations) were
critical of the liberator or of General San Martín. It must be admitted
that most of those who wrote their accounts and had them published
were those who had a grievance to air, however; it should be borne in
mind that there were others who were satisfied with the choice they
had made: Thomas Sutcliffe, Richard Vowell, William Miller, Captain
Guise, the last two reaching the highest rank in the army and navy
of Peru respectively. And though Cochrane found the Brazilian

government an impossible body of men to deal with and wrote sourly of his treatment by it, one has to remember that two of his lieutenants, Captain Grenfell and John Taylor, both went on to reach the rank of admiral in the newly-fledged navy of Brazil.[4] The life of mercenaries is often hard and conditions were certainly very difficult in the mountains and plains of South America, but as O'Leary, another Irishman who made a success of his mercenary calling in the service of Simón Bolívar, stated explicitly in his memoirs, most of the British and Irish volunteers endured their hardships with stoicism. What the accounts of these volunteers give to the reader most vividly is a picture of the wild, uncouth but brave army of creoles, Indians and *pardos* (mulattos) who fought for and won their country's independence.

Many of these troops were desperately poor – witness their lack of proper clothing. The poverty of the mass of the people encountered by British and US observers throughout the length and breadth of the continent is something that came as a surprise to those whose knowledge was only of western Europe or the eastern seaboard of the USA. All those Britons who crossed the pampas remarked on the destitution and squalor in which the scattered population lived. Poverty and squalor were also remarked on by those who visited Mexico, notably Beaufoy and Joel Poinsett and Madame Calderón de la Barca, who was duly appalled at the number of beggars she was forced to encounter in Mexico City. Standards of comfort and cleanliness in private houses and in wayside inns and in the streets of the capital cities were subjects that excited both shock and disgust; and amazement was expressed when poverty was sometimes seen to exist incongruously side by side with wealth and display – household utensils made of silver in a miserable dwelling with little furniture, and priceless jewellery being worn by the women while their husbands were dressed in most slatternly fashion.

Two other subjects seem to have struck the foreign observers most forcibly. One was the general lawlessness (a product of the recent revolutions) in every Latin American country and to which Brazil was no exception; the need to travel everywhere armed (not just on the pampas, where the Indian roamed); the frequency of murders in Rio de Janeiro and the indifference of the mass of the people to seeing a man struck dead in the street; the inefficiency of the police and the uncertain judicial system (though one has to remember that till 1829 no regular police force existed in London). The other subject was the lack of what a European was accustomed to find in a capital town of

western Europe, or what any North American citizen expected to find
in cities like Boston, New York, Philadelphia, Charleston or Baltimore.
Almost all of those who wrote their accounts commented unfavourably
on the indifferent architecture that graced or disgraced South America's cities (Mexico City being a notable exception). But worse was the
lack of amenities they had come to associate with a metropolis. They
deplored the quality of social life, but also the lack of education, even
of basic literacy to be found in creole society. The lack of any cultural
life, the emptyheadedness of the women who had been denied any
education, the coarse and even repulsive manners of those who moved
in 'society', smoking and spitting without restraint, no matter whether
female or male; the low state of the fine arts that Madame Calderón
remarked on in Mexico and the failure to provide, even in Brazil,
where the Portuguese royal family had resided, theatre or opera of any
quality, all jolted these western observers. They had never realized
before how completely cut off these people had been under the rule
of Spain and Portugal from the world with which they themselves
were familiar.

The experience of the educationalists was also a disappointing one.
There was clearly a great demand for schools in countries where
illiteracy was the general rule, since the Spaniards had never encouraged it, and the more enlightened patriot rulers welcomed the efforts
of a man like Thomson. But the influence of the Catholic clergy was
bound to militate against a man who brought the New Testament into
his schools, if only as a medium of instruction for reading. All
Protestants were suspect in Catholic countries in the early nineteenth
century, even more so if they came bearing gifts; and distrust of the
foreigner was widespread outside the principal urban centres; a
foreigner was in the eyes of a creole either a Jew or a heretic.
Admittedly the Bible Society, for which James Thomson acted partly
as agent, made it a policy not to proselytize, but the bibles themselves
were suspect objects. Rulers like O'Higgins and Bolívar were anxious
to support the work of Thomson, but neither of them stayed in power
for long in either Chile or Peru. Their successors were under clerical
influence and Thomson's schools got little support, if only because
the money required to keep them going was not to be found. Ricketts
reported from Peru the stiff opposition to anything that was even
tinged with Protestantism, and both Thomson and his son-in-law
Jones enjoyed little success when they worked in Mexico. The failure
of Lancaster in Caracas is another matter altogether and due entirely

to his personal defects, though once again lack of money to support his foundation was painfully evident.

Nearly all those who came to Latin America from Britain and the United States, whatever their motives, had expected to find a New World waiting to welcome them to help overthrow an oppressive rule, help to develop its undoubted wealth, open its shores to immigration and share in its new-found birth of freedom, political, economic and intellectual. Though they did discover in certain areas, notably Chile and Colombia, an enthusiasm for all things English, they also found universal strife, jealousy, hatred, rivalry and fraud, corruption in official circles, xenophobia, religious prejudice, filthiness and destitution, brutality and rudeness of manner. The overthrow of the old regime had not brought the rule of brotherhood and peace, nor therefore as yet the required conditions for foreign investment and settlement. The New World they had rediscovered was that of Caliban, not Miranda, a world that seemed to be brute not brave.

Abbreviations

CHLA   *Cambridge History of Latin America*, vol. 3: *From Indepen-*
        dence to c. 1870 edited by Leslie Bethell. Cambridge:
        Cambridge University Press, 1985
DCUS   *Diplomatic Correspondence of the United States Concerning the*
        Independence of the Latin American Nations edited by William
        R. Manning (3 vols.) New York: Oxford University Press,
        1925
DNB   *Dictionary of National Biography*, London: Smith Elder &
        Co, 1888
FO   Foreign Office records at The Public Record Office, Kew,
        Surrey
SC   Swinburne (Capheaton) manuscripts at Northumberland
        County Record Office, Newcastle upon Tyne
WO   War Office Records at The Public Record Office, Kew,
        Surrey

Notes and references

Chapter 1 The United Provinces of the River Plate

1 Popham to Admiralty 9 July 1806 cited by Henry Stanley Ferns *Britain and Argentina in the Nineteenth Century* (Oxford: Oxford University Press, 1960), p. 23.

2. *Minutes of a Court Martial of Captain Sir Home Popham* (London: Longmans & Hurst, Rees & Orme 1807), pp. 137–140.

3 *The Times* 15 September 1806 cited by R. A. Humphreys 'The Career of James Paroissien', *Liberation in South America 1806–1827* (London: University of London/Athlone Press, 1952) p. 4.

4 Whitelocke to Windham, 23 July 1807, WO 1/162 cited by H. S. Ferns. *Britain and Argentina* p. 52.

5 Major Alexander Gillespie *Gleanings and Remarks Collected During Many Months of Residence at Buenos Aires and Within the Upper Country* (Leeds: privately printed, 1818) cited by Andrew Graham-Youll *A Forgotten Colony* (London: Hutchinson & Co, 1981), p. 54.

6 Parish to Canning, No 31, 25 June 1824, FO 6/4. The English editor of the London edition of reports by two United States commissioners Caesar A. Rodney and John Graham on the state of the provinces of La Plata as they found them to be in 1818 was at pains to emphasize how the region merited better attention from Britons. The provinces contained (he wrote in 1819) an 'immense extent of fertile soil [were] blessed with a salubrious climate and fitted for the growth of every species of produce'. They therefore offered to English manufacturers the hopes of a constantly increasing market. They also offered to potential immigrants better prospects than the USA offered – the soil was more fertile, the climate more favourable and suited to growing more varieties of produce; no forests had to be cleared off the land which in any case was alloted free (in the USA it cost $2 an acre): land was available near the port of debarkation, clothing was cheap and food abundant (Caesar Augustus Rodney and John Graham *The Reports of the Present State of the United Provinces of South America* . . . laid before Congress (London: Baldwin, Craddock and Joy, 1819).

7 Ponsonby to Canning, 20 October 1826, FO 6/13 cited by Ferns *Britain and Argentina*, p. 185.

8 John Lynch, 'The River Plate Republics from Independence to the

Paraguayan War *CHLA* (8 vols.) (Cambridge: Cambridge University Press, 1985) vol. 3, pp. 626–628, 632, 634.

9 An Englishman, *A Five Years' Residence in Buenos Aires During the Years 1820–1825* (London: G. Hobert, 1825) pp. 35–43, 50, 97–9.

10 Hon. Nina L. Kay Shuttleworth, *A Life of Sir Woodbine Parish* (London: Smith, Elder & Co, 1910) p. 292.

11 An Englishman, *Five Years* p. 42.

12 Gerald S. Graham and R. A. Humphreys (ed.), *The Navy and South America 1807–1823* (London: Navy Records Society, 1923) xxvii, pp. 244–8.

13 Henry Marie Brackenridge, *A Voyage to South America Prepared by Order of the American Government in the Years 1817 and 1818 in the Frigate 'Congress'* (2 vols.) (London: John Miller, 1820) vol. 1, pp. 289–290, vol. 2, pp. 205, 220. Brackenridge noted favourably the lack of a military caste in Buenos Aires, in marked contrast to Brazil, though, since the country was at war, the military were much in evidence, with 'drums continually beating, trumpets braying and troops everywhere in motion . . . the regulars are but the soldiers of the republic and are carefully refrained from insulting the citizens'. There also were no guards patrolling the streets in daytime (a feature of life in Rio de Janeiro) 'insolently jostling the passengers from the pavements' (ibid. vol. 2, p. 109). Brackenridge formerly had been a judge in the state of Louisiana and had a good knowledge of the Spanish language.

14 Francis Bond Head, *Rough Notes taken during some Rapid Journeys Across the Pampas and Among the Andes* C. Harvey Gardiner (ed.), (Carbondale and Edwardsville: South Illinois University Press, 1967. First pub. London: John Murray, 1826) pp. 9–10, 159–160.

15 John Parish Robertson and William Parish Robertson, *Letters on Paraguay Comprising the Account of a Five Years' Residence in that Republic under the Government of the Dictator Francia* (3 vols.) (London: John Murray, 1838) vol. 1, pp. 65–8, 81.

16 J. A. Barber Beaumont, *Travels in Buenos Aires and the Adjacent Provinces of the Rio de la Plata* (London: James Ridgway, 1828) pp. 239–240, 249.

17 Robertsons, *Letters on Paraguay* vol. 1, pp. 284, 301–2.

18 Ibid 3, pp. 227–9.

19 Ibid 3, pp. 20–21.

20 Ibid 2, pp. 281–5, 3 pp. 101–103, 111–195.

21 R. A. Humphreys, 'British Merchants and South American Independence' *Tradition and Revolt in South America* (London: Weidenfeld & Nicholson, 1963) p. 115. John P. Robertson and William P. Robertson *Letters on South America* (3 vols.) (London: John Murray, 1843) vol. 1 pp. 60–64, 177–83, 206.

22 Robertson, *Letters on Paraguay* vol. 3, pp. 227–54. Robertsons, *Letters on South America* vol. 1, pp. 59, vol. 3, p. 101.

23 Robertson, *Letters on Paraguay* vol. 3, pp. 257–61.

24 Sir Woodbine Parish, *Buenos Aires and the Provinces of the Rio de la Plata* (London: John Murray, 1852 2nd ed.) p. 338.

25 Robertson, *Letters on South America* vol. 2 pp. 61.

26 Tom B. Jones, *South America Rediscovered* (Minneapolis: University of Minnesota Press, 1949) pp. 32–3.

27 Samuel Haigh, *Sketches of Buenos Aires, Chile and Peru* (London: Effingham Wilson, 1831) pp. vii, 42–52. Joel R. Poinsett, US consul-general for Buenos Aires, Chile and Peru, made the same journey across the pampas in November 1811 – it took him a month to reach Santiago, sleeping in his carriage or on the ground to avoid the vermin in the filthy posthouses. In his opinion 'the miserable state of the interior of this country' was due to the great abundance of livestock. 'It is not uncommon to see [he wrote] a proprietor of a league square of land owning several thousand head of cattle, and sheep, and horses, living in a miserable hut, and having the bare necessities of life. His home is covered with hides; his furniture is made of the same materials. His yard is enclosed by a few stakes, bound together with thongs; and he may be seen, with his herdsmen, seated by a fire, cutting off slices of beef from a spit . . . and eating it without bread or salt' (J. Fred Rippy, *Joel R. Poinsett Versatile American* (Durham NC: Duke University Press, 1935) pp. 39–41 citing *DCUS* vol. 1, p. 462).

28 Head, *Rough Notes* pp. 30–1, 141.

29 Robert Proctor, *Narrative of a Journey Across the Cordillera of the Andes and of a Residence in Lima and Other Parts of Peru* (Edinburgh: Archibald Constable. London: Hurst Robinson, 1825) pp. 4, 10, 17.

30 Alexander Caldcleugh, *Travels in South America During the Years 1819–21* (2 vols.) (London: John Murray, 1825) vol. 1, pp. 239, 262–4.

31 Head, *Rough Notes* p. 31.

32 Proctor, *Narrative* pp. 32, 45.

33 John Miers, *Travels in Chile and La Plata* (2 vols.) (New York: Arus Press, 1970, reprinted from 1826 edn) vol. 1, p. 14. As well as being a mineralogist and chemist, Miers became an expert botanist. Parish, *Buenos Aires* pp. 325–6.

34 Robertson, *Letters on Paraguay* vol. 2, pp. 211, 228, 258–62.

35 Head, *Rough Notes* pp. 11–15.

36 Caldcleugh, *Travels* vol. 1, p. 182.

37 Edward Temple, *Travels in Various Parts of Peru Including a Year's Residence at Potosí* (2 vols.) (London: Henry Colburn and Richard Bentley, 1830) vol. 1, pp. 75–6. Theodorick Bland, special commissioner of the USA to South America, wrote of the gauchos in 1818: 'The bedding and clothing of the family, and the whole household furniture, exhibit a scene of laziness and dirt, yet mingled with apparent cheerfulness, great kindness, much natural intelligence, and an evident independence of character.' He added that 'they may be considered as the most formidable guerilla or partisan soldiery that ever existed'. (Bland to John Quincy Adams 2 November 1818, *DCUS* vol. 1, pp. 416–17).

38 Miers, *Travels* p. 49.

39 Charles Darwin, *The Voyage of the Beagle* (New York: Bantam Books, 1972, first pub. 1845) pp. 35–6.

40 Parish, *Buenos Aires* pp. 99–107. An Englishman, *Five Years' Residence* p. 4. Miers, *Travels* pp. 3–4.

41 Haigh, *Sketches* pp. 8–21. These first impressions of Buenos Aires were

shared by H. M. Brackenridge: 'Its domes and steeples, and heavy masses of buildings give it an imposing but somewhat gloomy aspect. Immense piles of dingy, brown-coloured brick, with little variety, heavy and dull ... Compared to Philadelphia or New York, it is a vast mass of bricks piled up without taste, elegance or variety.' He was also, as was Haigh, very much impressed by the beauty of the women of the city (Brackenridge, vol. 1, pp. 242, 260).

42 Head, *Rough Notes* pp. 19–20.

43 Beaumont, *Travels* pp. 82–6.

44 An Englishman, *Five Years' Residence* pp. 6–10. When Temple stayed at Faunch's hotel in November 1825, he found it fairly primitive, with nothing about it to induce a traveller to fancy himself in an English hotel. His bedroom was little larger than the berth of the ship he had travelled out on and its door opened into the yard. But by the time that he published his book (1829) the hotel had moved into a large, well-appointed house, the property of an English merchant (Temple, *Travels* vol. 1, pp. 60–3).

45 Shuttleworth, *A Life* pp. 295–9.

46 Ibid., pp. 325–32.

47 Robertson, *Letters on South America* vol. 3, pp. 102, 114.

48 Graham and Humphreys, *The Navy* pp. 282–8. W. G. D. Worthington, special agent of the USA to Buenos Aires, Chile and Peru, dined with Captain Bowles at his beautiful *quinta* in the suburbs of Buenos Aires. 'The English seem very fond of this place', he wrote to Adams in 1819, 'they seem to be locating themselves in South America pretty permanently' (Worthington to John Quincy Adams 7 March 1819 *DCUS* vol. 1, p. 522).

49 James Thomson, *Letters on the Moral and Religious State of South America* (London: James Nisbet, 1827) pp. 1–5, 265–76. Caesar Rodney, a US commissioner, reported in November 1818 that in Buenos Aires there were open eight public schools and five schools for the poor under the charge of monasteries; in the countryside there were parish schools (Brackenridge, *Voyage* vol. 1, Appendix p. 25).

50 Brackenridge, *A Voyage* vol. 2, pp. 141–2.

51 Ferns, *Britain and Argentina* pp. 135–6.

52 Head, *Rough Notes* pp. xvi, xviii, 159–160, 173–4. *Reports Relating to the Failure of the River Plata Mining Association* (London: John Murray, 1827) passim.

53 Ferns, *Britain and Argentina*, pp. 135–6.

54 Captain Joseph Andrews, *A Journey from Buenos Aires Through the Provinces of Cordova, Tucumán and Salta to Potosí, Thence by the Deserts of Caranja, in the Years 1825–26* (2 vols.) (London: John Murray, 1827) vol. 1, pp. vi, ix–xix.

55 Gillespie, *Gleanings* pp. 76–8, 120.

56 Temple, *Travels*, vol. 1, pp. 229–30.

57 Beaumont, *Travels* pp. 112–24, 127, 153–8, 161–202.

58 Ferns, *Britain and Argentina* pp. 138–40.

59 Ibid., pp. 137–42.

60 Head, *Rough Notes* p. 172.

61 Ferns, *Britain and Argentina* pp. 138–40. Brackenridge vol. 2, p. 255.

62 Head, *Rough Notes* pp. 169–72.
63 Beaumont, *Travels* p. 223.
64 Colonel Anthony King, *Twenty-Four Years Service in the Argentine Republic*
    (London: Longman, Brown, Green, Longmans, 1846) pp. 12–13.

Chapter 2 Chile

1 Professor David Bushnell, 'The Independence of Spanish South America'
   CHLA vol. 3, p. 106.
2 Ibid., pp. 128–31. Simon Collier, 'Chile from Independence to the War
   of the Pacific' *CHLA* vol. 3, pp. 584–6.
3 Captain Basil Hall, *Extracts from a Journal Written on the Coasts of Chili,
   Peru and Mexico in the Years 1820, 1821, 1822* (2 vols.) (Edinburgh:
   Archibald Constable & Co, 1824) Vol. 2, pp. 89–90. Hall was a man of
   wide interests who became a Fellow of the Royal Society.
4 Haigh, *Sketches* pp. vii, 178–85.
5 Peter Schmidtmeyer, *Travels in Chile over the Andes in the Years 1820 and
   1821* (London: Longmans and others, 1824) pp. 199, 318.
6 Miers, *Travels* vol. 2, pp. 337–8. The United States agent W. G. D.
   Worthington complained bitterly in 1818 of the customs arrangements at
   Valparaiso. The customs house was at Santiago, almost a hundred miles
   away, and the whole cargo had to be sent there before any packages could
   be opened or sold, save for a few heavy articles like iron. The importer
   had therefore to meet the expense of hiring assistants and pack mules and
   feeing or bribing the officials and consulate if his business was to flourish
   at all. He cited the example of one US ship whose cargo was valued at
   $197,000 having to pay charges of this kind amounting to $1195 (Worthington to John Quincy Adams, 4 July 1818, *DCUS* vol. 2, pp. 974–5).
7 Robert A. Humphreys, (ed.) *British Consular Reports on the Trade and
   Politics of Latin America 1824–1826* Camden Series vol. LXIII (London:
   Royal Historical Society, 1940) p. 94 n. 1 citing Nugent to Canning
   28 May 1826 FO 16/5.
8 Captain Frederick William Beechey RN, *Narrative of a Voyage to the Pacific
   and Bering's Strait* (2 vols.) (London: Henry Colburn and Richard Bentley,
   1831) vol. 1, pp. 19–20.
9 Lieutenant William Bowers RN, *Naval Adventures During Thirty-Five
   Years' Service* (2 vols.) (London: Richard Bentley, 1833) vol. 2, pp. 98,
   100.
10 Miers, *Travels* vol. 1, pp. 426–49. William Bennet Stevenson, *A Historical
    and Descriptive Narrative of Twenty Years' Residence in South America* (3
    vols.) (London: Hurst Robinson & Co, 1825) vol. 3, p. 162.
11 Farquhar Mathison, *Narrative of a Visit to Brazil, Chile and the Sandwich
    Islands During the years 1821 and 1822* (London: Charles Knight, 1825)
    p. 176.
12 Maria Graham (later, Lady Callcott), *Journal of a Residence in Chile During
    the Year 1822* (London: Longman and Green, 1824) pp. 131, 156, 179.
    Maria Graham's first husband, Captain Graham RN, died in 1822 as his

ship was rounding Cape Horn. She is best known as the author of the best-seller *Little Arthur's England.*

13 Stevenson, *Narrative* vol. 3, pp. 162–5.

14 Charles Samuel Stewart, *A Visit to the South Seas in the US Ship 'Vincennes' During the Years 1829 and 1830* (2 vols.) (New York: John P. Haven, 1831)

15 Haigh, *Sketches* pp. 130, 136, 143, 253–6, 270–1.

16 Reverend H[ugh] S[ilvin], Chaplain, *Journal Written on Board HMS 'Cambridge' from January 1824 to May 1827* (Newcastle: privately printed, 1829).

17 *Campaigns and Cruises in Venezuela and New Granada and in the Pacific Ocean from 1817 to 1830* (3 vols.) (London: Longmans & Co, 1831) vol. 3, pp. 398–9.

18 Miers, *Travels* vol. 1, pp. 426–31.

19 Hall, *Extracts* p. 33.

20 Haigh, *Sketches* p. 130. Schmidtmeyer, *Travels* pp. 236, 241.

21 Head, *Rough Notes* pp. 101, 106, 109–10.

22 Mathison, *Narrative* pp. 199–200.

23 Isaac Foster Coffin, *Diario de un joven Norte-Americano detentido en Chile durante el periodo revolucionario de 1817–1819 (traducido del Ingles por JTM* (Santiago: Imprenta Elzeviviana, 1898) pp. 124, 131, 149.

24 Schmidtmeyer, *Travels* pp. 323–4.

25 Miers, *Travels* vol. 2, pp. 241–55. Edgar Vaughan, *Joseph Lancaster in Caracas 1824–1827 and His Relations With the Libertador Simón Bolívar* (2 vols.) (Caracas: Ediciones del Ministerio de Educación, 1987) vol. 1, p. 165.

26 Thomson, *Letters* pp. 11–23, 276.

27 Schmidtmeyer, *Travels* p. 324.

28 Graham, *Residence in Chile* pp. 157, 281. Thomson, *Letters* pp. 15–16. Vaughan, *Joseph Lancaster* vol. 1, p. 167. In 1824 Pope Leo XII was to denounce Bible societies in his encyclical 'Ubi Primum' for disseminating versions of the Scriptures not authorized by the Catholic Church and enjoined bishops to warn their people against indiscriminate reading of the Bible. Herman Allen, the United States minister who arrived in Chile in April 1824, wrote that 'a most wicked and abandoned clergy still directs the destinies of the state'. Only when this malign influence was removed did he think Chile would shave off its lethargy 'and rise to the elevation of a civilized people' (Allen to Henry Clay, 1 September 1825, *DCUS* vol. 2, pp. 1103–4).

29 Miers, *Travels* vol. 1, p. 480. Beechey, *Narrative* vol. 1, pp. 15–17.

30 Bowers, *Naval Adventures* vol. 2, p. 100.

31 Miers, *Travels* vol. 2, pp. 223–4, 241–7. Allen to J. Q. Adams, 9 February 1825, *DCUS* vol. 2, p. 1102.

32 Darwin, *Voyage* p. 222.

33 Stevenson, *Narrative* pp. 57, 64.

34 Mathison, *Narrative* p. 204. Stevenson, *Narrative* vol. 3, pp. 275–7. Proctor, *Narrative* pp. 107–8. Thomas Earl of Dundonald, *Narrative of Services in the Liberation of Chili, Peru and Brazil from Spanish and Portuguese Domination* (2 vols.) (London: James Ridgway, 1859) vol. 1, pp. 70–71.

Richard, J. Cleveland, *A Narrative of Voyages and Commercial Enterprises* (2 vols.) (Cambridge Mass: John Owen, 1842) vol. 2, p. 141.

35 Graham and Humphreys, *The Navy* pp. 224–9. Graham, *Residence in Chile* pp. 164, 170, 282–4. D. A. G. Worthington, the United States agent, who had met San Martín in Buenos Aires and again when he went to Chile, was enormously impressed by the patriot general: 'I think him the greatest man I have seen in South America – and had he have been born with us, wou'd have been a distinguished republican' (Worthington to J. Q. Adams, 7 March 1819, *DCUS* vol. 1, p. 533).

36 Dundonald, *Narrative* vol. 1, pp. 71–72.

37 Bowers, *Naval Adventures* vol. 2, pp. 100–1.

38 Miers, *Travels*, vol. 2, pp. 168, 171, 175–6, 205.

39 Dundonald, *Narrative* vol. 1, pp. 247–8. Allen to J. Q. Adams, 9 February 1825, *DCUS* vol. 2, p. 1102.

40 Miers, *Travels* vol. 1, pp. 1–2, 276–85.

41 Ibid., vol. 2, pp. 287–93.

42 Ibid., vol. 2, pp. 329–31, 335–6.

43 Hall, *Extracts* vol. 2, pp. 12–13, 17, 20–21, 29, 32, 33.

44 Head, *Rough Notes* pp. 120–8.

45 Andrews, *A Journey* vol. 2, pp. 202–27.

46 Miers, *Travels* vol. 2, pp. 417–27. After a stay in Buenos Aires, Miers went to Rio de Janeiro where he also built a mint. One traveller wrote of Chile's mines, after visiting the country in 1805, 'the riches of this country consist in what is produced from the land, not from what is dug out of it' (Amasa Delano, *A Narrative of Voyages and Travels in the Northern and Southern Hemispheres* (Boston: privately printed, 1817) p. 233.

47 *DNB* vol. XI (London: Smith and Elder, 1887) pp. 165–75. F. A. Kirkpatrick, 'Establishment of Independence in Spanish America' *Cambridge Modern History* vol. X, p. 292. Donald E. Worcester, *Sea Power and Chilean Independence* (Gainesville: University of Florida Press, 1962) pp. 26, 31, 32.

48 Dundonald, *Narrative* vol. 1, pp. 1–5. Worthington, the United States agent, witnessed Cochrane's arrival at Santiago. 'His first appearance [he wrote] is not prepossessing. He is about 40 years old, very tall and not corpulent, rather of a stripling appearance; not courtly in his address, but very plain and bold in his remarks and opinions; yet not authoritative or pompous' (Worthington to J. Q. Adams, 26 January 1819, *DCUS* vol. 2, p. 1026). Worthington remarked on the way in which the government of Chile had scraped the barrel to pay for the purchase of its ships of war: 'It is a fact that a large part of the *Lautaro* and the *San Martín* and I suspect the others, were paid for in piles and chests of old plate, candlesticks, maté cups, dishes, etc etc' (ibid., 1029). The United States consul Judge Prevost, a warm supporter of the Chilean government, tried to persuade the latter against developing a navy and a merchant marine, and rely instead on hiring the former, whenever necessity demanded, and employ foreign vessels for the carriage of goods; a course of action that Maria Graham considered to be against Chile's best interests (Graham, *Journal of a Residence in Chile* pp. 183–4).

49 Graham, *Residence in Chile* p. 156.

50 Graham and Humphreys, *The Navy* pp. 263–5, 332. One naval captain who served under Cochrane was the United States citizen Charles Witney Wooster who sailed the *Columbus* (renamed *Araucano*) from North America to Valparaiso. He resigned in June 1819 after a dispute he had with Cochrane, but was later, in March 1822, appointed commander of the Chilean navy, after Cochrane had resigned his post. He led the attack against Chiloé and finally resigned in 1829. (John J. Johnson, 'Relations of the United States with Chile', *Pacific Historical Review XIII* (Berkeley and Los Angeles: University of California Press 1944).

51 Mathison, *Narrative* p. 202.

52 Dundonald, *Narrative* vol. 1, pp. 41–7, 50–4. Stevenson, *Narrative* vol. 3, p. 226.

53 Dundonald, *Narrative* vol. 1, pp. xi, xii, xvi, 233–6, 238–41, 256, 258–9.

54 Ibid., vol. 1, pp. 274–6.

55 Ibid., vol. 1, pp. xvi.

56 Thomas Sutcliffe, *Sixteen Years in Chile and Peru from 1822–1839* (London: Fisher Son & Co, 1841) pp. 6–15, 20, 72, 86–8, 96–100, 108, 125, 127, 132, 134, 138, 171, 188, 197, 237–9, 246, 288.

57 *Campaigns and Cruises* pp. 248, 278, 354, 386–7, 397–458.

58 John Miller, *Memoirs of General Miller in the Service of the Republic of Peru* (2 vols.) (Longman and others, 1829) vol. 1, pp. 177–218, 245–66.

59 Simon Collier, *Ideas and Politics of Chilean Independence 1808–1833* (Cambridge: Cambridge University Press, 1967) pp. 202–3. Rev. H. S., *Journal* p. 133. Graham, *Residence in Chile* p. 165.

Chapter 3 Peru and Bolivia

1 David Bushnell, 'The Independence of Spanish South America' *CHLA* vol. 3, pp. 134–6, 145–6.

2 Heraclio Bonilla, 'Peru and Bolivia from Independence to the War of the Pacific' *CHLA* vol. 3, p. 548.

3 Hall, *Extracts* vol. 1, pp. 90–100, 118–127.

4 Ibid., vol. 1, pp. 212–30, 241–60.

5 Ibid., vol. 2, pp. 64–5.

6 Mathison, *Narrative* pp. 264–5, 287–90, 352–7.

7 William Tudor to J. Q. Adams, 3 May 1824, *DCUS* vol. 3, pp. 1749–52.

8 Proctor, *Narrative* pp. 112, 131–51, 191, 196–9, 340–73.

9 Darwin, *Voyage* pp. 348, 352. Tudor told Henry Clay, the US secretary of state, in August 1826, that though a predilection for republican governments was natural to all Americans, he had to admit that Peru was singularly destitute of the requisite character for sustaining an elective republic' (Tudor to Clay, 24 August 1826, *DCUS* vol. 3, pp. 1805–11).

10 Andrews, *Journeys* vol. 2, p. 175.

11 Haigh, *Sketches* p. 377.

12 Humphreys, *Consular Reports* pp. 107–8 citing Ricketts to Canning no. 26, 27 December 1826, FO 61/8.

13 Bowers, *Naval Adventures* vol. 2, pp. 196, 222–3.
14 Graham and Humphreys, *The Navy* pp. 248–50, 268–72.
15 Ibid. pp. 277, 309–13, 328–30, 333–4, 338–41, 349. Cleveland, *A Narrative* vol. 2, pp. 163–5, 171, 181, 189, 196. Hogan to J. Q. Adams, 9 October 1821, *DCUS* vol. 2, pp. 1056–8 (punctuation amended).
16 Hall, *Extracts* vol. 1, pp. 41–5.
17 Graham and Humphreys, *The Navy* pp. 365–6. Proctor, *Narrative* p. 153.
18 Proctor, *Narrative* p. 217.
19 Bowers, *Naval Adventures* vol. 2, pp. 281–3.
20 Ricketts to Canning no. 17, 10 June 1827, FO 61/11 pp. 329–34. Kelly to Bidwell, 25 February 1829, FO 61/14 pp. 223–9.
21 Hall, *Extracts* vol. 1, pp. 267–8.
22 Mathison, *Narrative* p. 224.
23 Stevenson, *Narrative*, vol. 1, pp. 349–50.
24 Proctor, *Narrative* p. 290. Bonilla, 'Peru' p. 541.
25 Haigh, *Sketches* pp. 380–2.
26 Humphreys, *Consular Reports* p. 116.
27 Bonilla, 'Peru' p. 545.
28 Humphreys, *Consular Reports* p. 156.
29 Ricketts to Dudley, 15 December 1827, FO 61/12 pp. 15–31.
30 Ricketts to Canning no. 14, 11 May 1827, FO 61/11 pp. 261–76.
31 Robertsons, *Letters on Paraguay* pp. 71–3.
32 Ricketts to Canning no. 14, 11 May 1827, FO 61/11 pp. 261–76.
33 Dundonald, *Narrative* vol. 1, pp. 16–17.
34 Dundonald, *Narrative* vol. 1, pp. 20–31, 76–82, 103–8, 124, 127–35, 150–8, 160–3, 169, 187–9, 227. Stevenson, *Narrative* vol. 3, 298. Bowers, *Naval Adventures* vol. 2, pp. 136–9.

There were other points of difference between Cochrane and San Martín over strategy and tactics in the war in Peru. Cochrane was highly critical of San Martín's failure to attack the royalist force of Canterac when the latter succeeded in relieving Callao on 9 September 1821, inaction that General Miller defended. Miller wrote that the patriot forces were mostly only raw recruits while Canterac's men were hardened veterans.

Again Cochrane censured San Martín for not pursuing Canterac after the latter withdrew his forces and Callao surrendered to the patriot army. San Martín's inaction found a defender in the British naval officer Basil Hall, who pointed out that if Callao was held, the patriots could not be driven from Peru, whereas if they were once defeated, the tide would turn against them and they would be expelled (Worcester, *Sea Power* pp. 69–70 citing Miller, *Memoirs* vol. 1, p. 335 and Hall, *Extracts* vol. 2, pp. 69–70).

35 Salvador Madariaga, *Bolívar* (London: Hollis & Carter, 1952) p. 404.
36 Miller, *Memoirs* vol. 1, p. 277 n; vol. 2, pp. 10–26, 46–9, 72, 89, 103, 105, 136–7, 146–7, 199, 229. After the war of independence, Miller was appointed governor of Potosí and made a Grand Marshal of Peru. In 1826 he retired to London and was allowed to draw $20,000 for his services to Peru. In 1834 he went back to Peru and was appointed commander-in-

chief (Alfred Hasbrouck, *Foreign Legionaries in the Liberation of Spanish South America* (New York: Columbia University Press, 1928) pp. 323–4).

37 Ricketts to Dudley, 15 December 1827, FO 61/12 pp. 15–31.

38 Reverend H. S., *Journal* p. 41. Thomson, *Letters* pp. 33–5, 52–3, 61–3, 67–70, 78, 81, 110, 162–3, 285. C. S. Stewart, *A Visit to the South Seas in the US Ship 'Vincennes' During the Years 1829 and 1830* (New York: John P. Haven, 1831) vol. 1, pp. 199–200.

39 Proctor, *Narrative* pp. 238–41.

40 Reverend H. S., *Journal* p. 94.

41 Proctor, *Narrative* pp. 241–3. Haigh, *Sketches* p. 375.

42 Cleveland, *A Narrative* vol. 2, pp. 179, 197.

43 Proctor, *Narrative* pp. 112–25, 212–13. Cleveland, *A Narrative* vol. 2, pp. 201–2.

44 Proctor, *Narrative* pp. 235–58.

45 Ricketts to Planta, 23 January 1826, private and confidential FO 61/7 p. 47; 16 September 1826, FO 61/8 pp. 127–30.

46 Ricketts to Canning no. 19, 16 September 1826, FO 61/8 pp. 99–123; no. 15, 14 May 1827, FO 61/11 pp. 285–90.

47 Henry Winram Dickinson and Arthur Titley, *Richard Trevithick* (Cambridge: Cambridge University Press, 1934) pp. 159–87. Francis Trevithick, *Life of Richard Trevithick* (2 vols.) (London: 1872) vol. 2, pp. 254, 279. Miers, *Travels* vol. 2, pp. 436–43.

48 Temple, *Travels* vol. 1, pp. 290–422; vol. 2, pp. 35–8, 98, 200–64. *A Brief Account of the Proceedings of the Potosí, La Paz and Peruvian Mining Association* (London: J. Ridgway, 1829) passim. The accounts of the failure of this company by John B. Pentland in his report to Consul-General Ricketts and by Ricketts in his dispatch to Dudley of 15 December 1827 enclosing the report of Pentland (FO 16/12) differ from that given by Temple. Pentland makes out that the association bought two mines for £10,000 on the assurances of Garcia and Paroissien, only to find on arrival in Bolivia that they no longer had any title to them. Ricketts states that the association lost $80,000 without even possessing a single mine.

49 Andrews, *Journeys* vol. 2, pp. 55–6, 89–90, 104–6, 129.

50 Miller, *Memoirs* vol. 2, pp. 291–4.

51 Ricketts to Dudley, 15 December 1827, FO 61/12 pp. 15–31.

52 Temple, *Travels* pp. 353, 390.

53 John Barclay Pentland, 'Report on Bolivia' J. Valerie Fifer (ed.) *Camden Miscellany vol. XXV* (London: The Royal Historical Society, University College, London, 1974) pp. 175 n; 226.

54 J. Valerie Fifer, *Bolivia: Land, Location and Politics Since 1825* (Cambridge: Cambridge University Press, 1972) p. 30, citing Masterman to Bidwell, 8 January 1843, FO 126/11.

Chapter 4 La Gran Colombia

1 Bushnell, 'The Independence of Spanish South America' *CHLA* vol. 3, pp. 115–42. Angostura is today called Ciudad Bolívar.

2 Robert F. McNerney jun. (ed. and trans.), *Bolívar and the War of Independence. Memórias del General Daniel Florencio O'Leary. Narración* Abridged version (Austin: University of Texas Press, 1970) pp. 4–5. O'Leary, a native of Cork in Ireland, arrived in Venezuela in 1818 as a volunteer officer in a cavalry regiment. Soon assigned to Bolívar's guard of honour, he became the liberator's principal aide.

3 Hasbrouck, *Foreign Legionaries* pp. 37–8. Eric Lambert, *Voluntarios Ingleses y Irlandeses en la Gesta Bolivariana* (Caracas: Edición de la Corporación Venezolana de Guyana, Julio de 1981) vol. 1, p. 142. George Laval Chesterton, *Peace, War and Adventure* (2 vols.) (London: Longmans and others, 1853) vol. 2, p. 29.

4 Lambert, *Voluntarios* vol. 1, pp. 45, 48.

5 Hasbrouck, *Foreign Legionaries* p. 40. Gustavus Hippisley, *A Narrative of the Expedition to the Rivers Orinoco and Apuré in South America* (London: John Murray, 1819) p. 24.

6 Lambert, *Voluntarios* vol. 1, pp. 40–2, 74–5, 84–5. Royal Proclamation, 27 November 1817, FO 83/29.

7 Hansard vol. 40, *Parliamentary Debates 1819* pp. 858–9, 887–9. The effect of the Foreign Enlistment Act was probably a deterrent, as there were few prosecutions for its infringement. George Dawson Flinter, acting for the Spanish ambassador in London, claimed to have prevented the sailing of an organized expedition from Ireland. But what really ended the further enlistment of British subjects was Bolívar's decree of September 1820, ordering the cessation of foreign recruitment (D. A. G. Waddell, 'Anglo-Spanish Relations and the "Pacification of America" during the "Constitutional Triennium" 1820–1823' *Annuario de Estudios Americanos* tomo XLVI (Sevilla: Escuela de Estudios Hispano-Americanos, 1989) pp. 458–9. 'British Neutrality and Spanish-American Independence. The Problem of Foreign Enlistment' *Journal of Latin American Studies* 19 (London: 1987) p. 16.

8 Hasbrouck, *Foreign Legionaries* pp. 58, 75–8, 82–3. Lambert, *Voluntarios* pp. 44, 63, 105–8, 272–5.

9 Ibid., pp. 99, 217.

10 An officer of the Colombian Navy, *Recollections of a Service of Three Years During the War of Extermination in the Republics of Venezuela and Colombia* (2 vols.) (London: Hunt & Clarke, 1828) vol. 1, pp. 169–73. John S. Crone, *Concise Dictionary of Irish Biography* (London: Longmans Green & Co, 1928) p. 52. According to Colonel Stopford, adjutant-general at one time to Bolívar, Devereux had arrived in England a bankrupt merchant at a time when troops were being raised to fight in South America. He then visited Ireland, put out he was in Bolívar's service and authorized to raise troops. He sold commissions according to rank at from £100 to £800 and with these funds shipped off nearly 1500 'of the most restless and riotous characters that were ever got together' under officers who knew nothing of military discipline. Bolívar, who was then at Cuenca, was delighted to learn of the troops' arrival and forwarded a diploma of general of division to Devereux. Stopford was entrusted with conveying the diploma and was amazed to find on landing at Margarita that Devereux had not accom-

panied his force (Walter Dupouy, *Sir Robert Ker Porter's Caracas Diary 1825–1842* (Caracas: Instituto Otto y Magdalena Blum, 1967) p. 33.

11 Hasbrouck, *Foreign Legionaries* pp. 140–54.

12 Ibid. Alexander Alexander, *His Life* John Howell (ed.) (2 vols.) (Edinburgh: William Blackwood, 1830) vol. 2, p. 162. On the great monument erected at Caracas in 1950 to honour the heroes of the War of Independence, M'Gregor's name appears as a general of division.

13 Hasbrouck, *Foreign Legionaries* p. 371. Madariaga, *Bolívar* pp. 316–7.

14 Hippisley, *Narrative* p. 442. Alexander, *Life* vol. 2, pp. 27–9. *Campaigns* vol. 1, p. 113. Lambert, *Voluntarios* p. 212.

15 *Recollections* vol. 1, pp. 68, 124. Chesterton, *Peace, War* pp. 59, 114.

16 *Recollections* vol. 1, pp. 169–73. Dupouy, *Porter's Diary*, pp. 33–4.

17 Captain William J. Adam, *Journal of Voyages to Margueritta, Trinidad and Maturín in the Years 1819 and 1820* (Dublin: M. R. Tims, 1824) pp. 153–60.

18 Alexander, *Life* vol. 2, pp. 144, 173.

19 *Recollections* vol. 2, pp. 77–82.

20 Ibid., vol. 2, pp. 82–3, 160–1, 166, 167.

21 Eric T. D. Lambert (ed.), *Carabobo 1821. Some Accounts Written in English* (Caracas: Fundación John Boulton, 1974) pp. 22–3.

22 Charles K. Webster (ed.), *Britain and the Independence of Latin America 1812–1830 Select Documents from the Foreign Office Archives* (2 vols.) (London, New York, Toronto: Oxford University Press, 1938) vol. 1, p. 77. Lambert, *Voluntarios* pp. 128, 335–6.

23 Madariaga, *Bolívar* p. 312. Lambert, *Carabobo* pp. 18, 24. Hasbrouck, *Foreign Legionaries* pp. 389, 391.

24 *Recollections* vol. 1, pp. 10–11. I am indebted to Mrs Marian Harding, assistant archivist at the National Army Museum, London, for helping me to identify George Woodberry as possibly the author of *Recollections*.

25 *Campaigns* vol. 1, p. 1. Lambert, *Voluntarios* p. 91.

26 Alexander, *Life* vol. 1, pp. 271–323; vol. 2, pp. 23–5, 133–4. Lambert, *Voluntarios* p. 214.

27 Chesterton, *Peace, War* vol. 2, pp. 29–30, 45. Hasbrouck, *Foreign Legionaries* p. 100. Bernard Naylor, *Accounts of Nineteenth-Century South America. An Annotated Checklist of Works by British and United States Observers* (London: University of London, The Athlone Press, 1969) p. 22.

28 Lambert, *Voluntarios* pp. 44, 48. Hasbrouck, *Foreign Legionaries* pp. 75, 100, 371. Madariaga, *Bolívar* pp. 316, 317.

29 Adam, *Journal* pp. 9–12.

30 James H. Robinson, *Journal of an Expedition 1400 Miles up the Orinoco and 300 up the Arauca* (London: Black, Young & Young, 1822) pp. 1–2.

31 James Hackett, *Narrative of an Expedition which Sailed from England in 1817 to Join the South American Patriots* (London: John Murray, 1818) pp. iv–vi.

32 Charles Brown, *Narrative of the Expedition to South America which Sailed from England at the Close of 1817* (London: John Booth, 1818) pp. 1–2, 189–91.

33 George Flinter, *The History of the Revolution of Caracas* (London: W. Glindon, 1819) pp. viii–ix, 195–8, 203–5.

34 *New Annual Register for 1817* British and Foreign History section, p. 333.
35 Lambert, *Voluntarios* pp. 253–5, 302–3. McNerney, *O'Leary* p. 303.
36 Hippisley, *Narrative* p. 395 cited by Madariaga in *Bolívar* p. 313.
37 *Recollections* vol. 1, pp. 173–83.
38 Ibid., pp. 182–3. Alexander, *Life* vol. 2, pp. 127–9, 133, 280–1.
39 Adam, *Journal* pp. 157–9.
40 Brown, *Narrative* pp. 114–15. Chesterton, *Peace, War* pp. 48–53, 59. *Recollections* vol. 1, p. 126.
41 *Recollections* vol. 1, pp. 134–58. Adam, *Journal* p. 82.
42 *Campaigns* pp. 163–5.
43 Alexander, *Life* vol. 2, pp. 38–9.
44 Hippisley, *Narrative* pp. 299–306, 320.
45 *Recollections* vol. 2, pp. 45–7.
46 Ibid., pp. 77–86.
47 Hippisley, *Narrative* p. 398.
48 Chesterton, *Peace, War* pp. 111–12, 136–40. There is a report in *The Times* newpaper of 3 July 1819 from a British naval officer on board the *Lee* that while his ship lay at Margarita, a Major Bates escaped to it, after serving with the patriot army, having been placed under arrest for transmitting a memorial from his regiment demanding their seven months' arrears of pay. Several sailors from Brion's squadron also deserted to the *Lee*, 'disgusted with the cold-blooded assassinations going on'. The report continues that if the *Lee* had sent boats for all those who wished to desert, 'Admiral Brion would not have had many British subjects to remain with him'.
49 *Campaigns* p. 68.
50 *Recollections* vol. 1, pp. 243–51; vol. 2, p. 193.
51 Chesterton, *Peace, War* pp. 135, 153. Miller, *Memoirs* vol. 2, p. 359. Colonel Edward Stopford had retired from the British Army as a lieutenant in the Life Guards in 1818. He then joined the volunteers in South America and served under Bolívar as his adjutant-general. After the war he stayed on in Venezuela, became a landowner, money-lender and speculator, as well as editor of the bilingual newpaper *El Colombiano*, owned by the British firm of Powles & Co (Vaughan, *Joseph Lancaster* vol. 1, p. 211).
52 Hippisley, *Narrative* pp. 299–306, 320, 382, 431–40, 461–2. *New Annual Register for 1819* Literary Retrospect and Selection section pp. 70–1. *Recollections* vol. 2, pp. 45–7, 217–18.
53 Madariaga, *Bolívar* p. 223. William Tudor, US consul in Lima, told Henry Clay in 1826: 'General Bolívar's model is now Napoleon and his ambition is equally boundless.' When the electoral college at Lima elected Bolívar president for life, Tudor was reminded of the scenes he had witnessed years before in Paris when Napoleon overthrew the Directory and got himself elected as France's First Consul. 'He is the model and Bolívar imitates him as nearly as circumstances permit . . . Military glory is his predominant passion, conquest and extensive empire his aim.' He would end up, Tudor believed, being accursed as a brilliant military usurper, 'and add another to the list of military madmen' (Tudor to Clay, 5 July, 24 August 1826, *DCUS* vol. 3, pp. 1799–1800, 1805–11). D. F. O'Leary,

Correspondencia de Extranjeros Notables con el Libertador (2 vols.) (Madrid: 1920) vol. 1, pp. 87–90. I am indebted to Professor D. A. G. Waddell for this reference.

54 Dupouy, *Porter's Diary* pp. 196–203, 282. Porter was an author, painter and traveller, had seen twenty-three years' service as a surgeon in the British army and in 1804 had been appointed historical painter to the Czar of Russia. He accompanied General Moore to the Peninsula, was present at the latter's death before Coruña and later returned to St Petersburg, after which he travelled in the Middle East. He was knighted in 1813 and married the daughter of a Russian prince (*DNB* vol. 46, pp. 190–2).

55 An officer late in the Colombian service, *The Present State of Colombia* (London: John Murray, 1827) pp. 57–8, 115.

56 *Recollections* vol. 2, pp. 173–6.

57 Robinson, *Journey* p. 198. Hippisley, *Narrative* pp. 417–20.

58 Madariaga, *Bolívar* pp. 304–5, citing O'Leary, *Memórias* vol. 1, p. 507. Alexander, *Life* vol. 2, pp. 78–9.

59 Chesterton, *Peace, War* p. 66. Alexander, *Life* vol. 2, p. 265. *Recollections* vol. 1, pp. 66–7, 167.

60 Chesterton, *Peace, War* p. 115. Hippisley, *Narrative* p. 467.

61 *Recollections* vol. 1, p. 32. Hippisley, *Narrative* p. 467.

62 Ibid., pp. 248–9, 266.

63 Ibid., pp. 233–4, cited by Madariaga, *Bolívar* p. 267. *Recollections* vol. 1, pp. 41–2, 52–7, 102.

64 Hippisley, *Narrative* pp. 12–13, 190. *Narrative of a Voyage to the Spanish Main in the ship 'Two Friends'* (London: John Miller, 1819) p. 186.

65 *Campaigns* pp. 66–8.

66 Robinson, *Journey* pp. 193–5.

67 Ibid., pp. 163–5.

68 Ibid., pp. 166, 178–9.

69 Brown, *Narrative* p. 140.

70 Hippisley, *Narrative* pp. 414–15, 463.

71 Hasbrouck, *Foreign Legionaries* p. 85. Hippisley, *Narrative* p. 447.

72 Alexander, *Life* vol. 2, pp. 35–7, 61–2, 83, 113.

73 Hippisley, *Narrative* p. 420. *Recollections* vol. 1, pp. 3–5, 29, 44, 70–1; vol. 2, pp. 221–2. Lambert, *Voluntários* p. 198 citing O'Leary, *Detached Recollections* p. 21.

74 Alexander, *Life* vol. 2, p. 34. Robinson, *Journey* p. 94. *Campaigns* pp. 23–4, 47. Chesterton, *Peace, War* p. 89.

75 Charles Stuart Cochrane, *Journal of a Residence and Travels in Colombia During the Years 1823 and 1824* (2 vols.) (London: Henry Colburn, 1825) vol. 2, pp. 108–9, 140, 144–5, 186, 283, 381. Francis Hall had at one time been an officer in the Irish Legion.

76 *Notes on Colombia Taken in the Years 1822–23 with an Itinerary of the Route from Caracas to Bogotá* by an officer of the United States Army (Philadelphia: H. C. Carey and I. Lea, 1827) p. 95. Beaufort T. Watts, United States minister to Bogotá, wrote in January 1826 that 'English enterprise, English wealth and intelligence ... [had] penetrated the passes of the

Andes, as well as the Indies . . . where mercantile influence . . . [could] be
required' (E. Taylor Parks, *Colombia and the United States 1765–1934*,
(Durham N. C.: Duke University Press, 1935) p. 115 citing Watts to Clay,
5 January 1826).

77 Cochrane, *Journal* pp. 5–6, 481, 488.

78 John Hankshaw, *Letters Written from Colombia During a Journey from
    Caracas to Bogotá and Thence to Santa Martha in 1823* (London: G. Cowie
    & Co 1824) pp. 77, 82.

79 Colonel John Potter Hamilton, *Travels Through the Interior Provinces of
    Colombia* (2 vols.) (London: John Murray, 1827) vol. 1, pp. 155, 189,
    244–5; vol. 2, pp. 153–6, 250–9.

80 Colonel Francis Hall, *Colombia in its Present State* (London: Baldwin
    Craddock & Co, 1824) pp. 15, 36–7, 48–50, 65–8, 74–89, 114–15, 129.
    Richard Bache thought that the amount of land in Colombia under
    cultivation compared to what was waste was 'as a speck in the ocean'.
    'The face of the country [he continued] suggests the image of a youth
    prematurely seamed with the wrinkles of age' (*Notes on Colombia* p. 156).

81 *Present State* pp. 177–8.

82 Dupouy, *Porter's Diary* pp. 24–7.

83 John C. Jeaffreson, *The Life of Robert Stephenson* (2 vols.) (London:
    Longman, Green and others, 1864) vol. 1, pp. 67–101.

84 *Present State* pp. 178–81.

85 Dupouy, *Porter's Diary* pp. 24, 45, 51, 60, 147.

86 The immigrants were mostly ex-soldiers from the Inverness area or
    weavers from Aberdeen. The superintendent, the Rev. John Ross, was an
    alcoholic and had to be dismissed and a number of the heads of families
    were also addicted to drink. On hearing of the misconduct of these
    settlers, the association instructed its agent to cease issuing them with
    rations, though by contract they were entitled to receive them for eight
    months from the time of their arrival (Vaughan, *Joseph Lancaster* Vaughan,
    'The Guayrians at Guelph in Upper Canada' *Historic Guelph XVIII*.
    (Guelph, Ontario: Guelph Historical Society, 1979) Part II. Hans P.
    Rheinheimer, *Topo: the Story of a Scottish Colony near Caracas 1825–27*
    (Edinburgh: Scottish Academic Press, 1938).

87 Dupouy, *Porter's Diary* p. 170. Vaughan, *Joseph Lancaster* vol. 2, pp. 65–8.

88 Dupouy, *Porter's Diary* pp. 213–14. Vaughan, *Joseph Lancaster* vol. 2,
    pp. 133–4.

89 Dupouy, *Porter's Diary* pp. 235–6, 270. Vaughan, *Joseph Lancaster* vol. 2,
    pp. 133–4.

90 Dupouy, *Porter's Diary* pp. 158, 434. Richard Bache took 84 days to travel
    from Caracas to Bogotá, by 52 stages of, on an average, 20 miles each: no
    small distance, he commented, in view of the difficulties of the road, the
    dilatoriness of the muleteers, the procrastination of the village *alcaldes* and
    delays occasioned by adjusting baggage. At one stage the road was so bad,
    'some of the leaps which the mules were obliged to make were three feet
    in perpendicular height, and were performed with difficulty, even without
    the rider' (*Notes on Colombia* pp. 149, 220). Francis Hall summed up the
    matter of the difficulties of communication when he wrote, 'throughout

the whole of the Republic there is not a road passable for wheel-carriages, nor even one which can be travelled without risk of life or limb' (Hall, *Colombia* p. 45).

91 Dupouy, *Porter's Diary* p. 51.

92 Colonel John Potter Hamilton, *Travels Through the Interior Provinces of Colombia* (2 vols.) (London: John Murray, 1827) vol. 1, pp. 253–4. Colonel William Duane, a US citizen, who travelled in New Granada in 1822 and 1823 also described how he found twenty-nine Lancasterian schools established in the department of Boyacá (Vaughan, *Joseph Lancaster* vol. 1, p. 81 citing William Duane, *A Visit to Colombia in the Years 1822 and 1823* (Philadelphia: privately printed, 1826))

93 Vaughan, *Joseph Lancaster* vol. 1, pp. 122–3, 132, 135, 170–2. David Bushnell, 'Education in Colombia' *History of Latin American Civilization* (London: Methuen, 1969) vol. 2, pp. 26–36.

94 Vaughan, *Joseph Lancaster* vol. 2, pp. 92–105, 111–20.

95 Ibid., vol. 2, p. 223. Thomson, *Letters* pp. 241–3, 256, 259. Hamilton, *Travels* vol. 2, pp. 254–5.

96 John Hankshaw, *Letters from Colombia During a Journey from Caracas to Bogotá and Thence to Santa Martha in 1823* (London: G. Cowie & Co, 1824) pp. 52, 70, 101.

97 Gaspard Théodore Mollien, *Travels in the Republic of Colombia in the Years 1822 and 1823* trans. from the French (London: C. Knight, 1824) p. 354.

98 Jeaffreson, *Life* vol. 1, pp. 103–4.

99 Moore to van Buren, 27 March 1830, *DCUS* vol. 2, p. 1357.

100 Dupouy *Porter's Diary* pp. 46–7, 79, 108, 345–6, 362.

101 Ibid., pp. 45, 148, 379.

102 Ibid., pp. 28, 32–3.

Chapter 5 Mexico

1 Timothy Anna, 'The Independence of Mexico and Central America'; Jan Bazant, 'Mexico from Independence to 1867' *CHLA* vol. 3, pp. 93–4, 429, 431, 438.

2 Tulio Halperin Donghi, 'Economy and Society in Post-Independence South America' *CHLA* vol. 3, p. 305. *Britain and the Independence of Latin America 1812–1830* select documents from the Foreign Office archives ed. Charles K. Webster (2 vols.) (London, New York and Toronto: Oxford University Press, 1938) vol. 1, pp. 21, 24.

3 Madame Calderón de la Barca, *Life in Mexico* with introduction by Sir Nicholas Cheetham (Boston: 1842; London etc: Century, 1987) pp. xix–xxi.

4 Henry George Ward, *Mexico in 1827* (2 vols.) (London: Henry Colburn, 1828) vol. 1, pp. vi–vii.

5 Ibid., vol. 1, pp. 16–17, 19; vol. 2, p. 178.

6 William Bullock, *Six Months' Residence and Travels in Mexico* (2 vols.) (London: John Murray, 1825) vol. 1, p. 30.

7 Lt Robert William Hardy RN, *Travels in the Interior of Mexico in 1825,*

1826, 1827, 1828 (London: Henry Colburn and Richard Bentley, 1829) pp. 57, 224.

8 Bullock, *Six Months* vol. 1, pp. 33–4.

9 Hardy *Travels* pp. 5–9.

10 Mark Beaufoy, *Mexican Illustrations* (London: Carpenter & Son, 1828) pp. 236–7, 239–40.

11 Joel R. Poinsett, *Notes on Mexico Made in the Autumn of 1822* (London: John Miller, 1825) pp. 254, 265–6.

12 *A Sketch of the Customs and Society of Mexico in a Series of Familiar Letters and a Journal of Travels in the Interior During the Years 1824, 1825 and 1826* (London: Longmans & Co, 1828) p. 89.

13 SC ZSW 536/44.

14 Ward, *Mexico* vol. 2, p. 236.

15 Poinsett, *Notes* pp. 66–7.

16 Ward, *Mexico* vol. 1, pp. 34–5; vol. 2, p. 236.

17 Hardy, *Travels* p. 38. C. Harvey Gardiner (ed.), *Mexico 1825–1828. The Journal and Correspondence of Edward Thornton Tayloe* (Chapel Hill: University of North Carolina Press, 1959) pp. 50–1.

18 Poinsett to Clay, 10 March 1829, *DCUS* vol. 3, pp. 1675–6. In 1822 Poinsett had noted the Mexican addiction of all classes to the sport of cock-fighting – one common to every country throughout the length of Latin America and to which various British observers had drawn attention with disapproval. At San Luis de Potosí Poinsett remarked on a priest who was betting on a likely fighting cockerel and 'miserable wretches half-naked ... put five and some as much as twenty dollars, into the broker's hands, to stake on their favourite bird. Some *Señoras*, not the most lady like, but very finely dressed, were smoking cigars and betting' (Poinsett, *Notes* p. 245).

19 Captain George Francis Lyon RN, *Journal of a Residence and Tour of Mexico in the Year 1826* (2 vols.) (London: John Murray, 1828) vol. 2, p. 126. Bullock, *Six Months* vol. 1, pp. 123, 159, 160. Beaufoy, *Mexican Illustrations* pp. 74–80.

20 Calderón, *Life in Mexico* pp. 127–8. Bullock, *Six Months* vol. 1, pp. 179–81.

21 Calderón, *Life in Mexico* pp. 127–8.

22 Hardy, *Travels* pp. 193, 455. Lyon, *Journal* vol. 1, pp. 248–9.

23 Lyon, *Journal* vol. 1, p. 151.

24 Bullock, *Six Months* pp. 52–3.

25 Calderón, *Life in Mexico* pp. 221, 225.

26 Vaughan, *Joseph Lancaster* p. 336. Thomson, *Letters* pp. 294–5.

27 Ward, *Mexico* vol. 1, pp. 350–1, 354. SC ZSW 536/43.

28 Lyon, *Journal* vol. 1, pp. 267–8.

29 Hardy, *Travels* pp. 270, 274.

30 Beaufoy, *Mexican Illustrations* pp. 136–9, 147.

31 *A Sketch* pp. 153, 173–5.

32 Ward, *Mexico* vol. 2, pp. 459–60.

33 Beaufoy, *Mexican Illustrations* pp. 137–9.

34 Calderón, *Life in Mexico* pp. 264–6. Poinsett in 1822 had been much

struck by the religious devotion of the Mexican people he encountered. Remarking on the passage of a priest who was carrying the sacred Host to the dying, he wrote that 'In an instant all was still [in what was a very busy street]. Shopkeepers and their customers, *léperos* and noisy children, all doffed their hats and knelt on the pavement, where they remained until the host was out of sight'. And when the *Angelus* sounded at midday, 'everyone stopped, pulled off his hat and prayed a short prayer or was supposed to do so. The solemn stillness that succeeded the bustle of a crowded street at this moment is very striking ... this is the first place where I have seen the people generally pray at noon' (Poinsett, *Notes* pp. 95–6).

35 Beaufoy, *Mexican Illustrations* pp. 110–11.
36 Hardy, *Travels* pp. 524–6. Lyon, *Journal* vol. 1, p. 280; vol. 2, pp. 40–1. Beaufoy, *Mexican Illustrations* pp. 234–9. Calderón, *Life in Mexico* p. 342. William Parish Robertson, *A Visit to Mexico* (2 vols.) (London: Simpkins Marshall & Co, 1853) vol. 2, pp. 20–1.
37 Hardy, *Travels* p. 517.
38 SC ZSW 536/44, Ward had been attached to the British embassy in Madrid from 1819 to 1823.
39 Calderón, *Life in Mexico* p. 235.
40 Poinsett to Clay, 28 October 1828, *DCUS* vol. 3, pp. 1669–70. Rippy, *Poinsett* p. 128.
41 Hardy, *Travels* pp. 435–6.
42 Gardiner, *Tayloe* pp. 72–3.
43 Beaufoy, *Mexican Illustrations* p. 112.
44 Ward, *Mexico* vol. 1, pp. 429–31.
45 Ibid., vol. 1, p. 449. Bullock, *Six Months* vol. 1, pp. 12, 23.
46 *A Sketch* pp. 68, 71, 183–5.
47 Bullock, *Six Months* vol. 1, pp. 220–5.
48 Humphreys, *Consular Reports* p. 303 n2.
49 Ibid., pp. 331, 333, 339, 342.
50 Beaufoy, *Mexican Illustrations* pp. 171–2, 256.
51 Ward, *Mexico* vol. 2, pp. 64–7. Robertson, *A Visit* vol. 2, p. 186.
52 Ward, *Mexico* vol. 2, pp. 57–92, 143–6, 161–2, 309, 323–4, 337, 352, 377, 402–3, 432, 459–60, 627–37, 688–9.

The anonymous author of a journal described his experiences on first arriving at Real del Monte in 1824. It was a 'solemn and triumphal entry' into a once-existent town which now had 'the air of a village sacked by a horde of Cossacks, or of something yet more desolate'. Roofs were falling in, walls crumbling, the whole village was 'a mass of ruins'. The villagers were thrilled at the arrival of those who were going to reactivate the place and rang bells, and said prayers in the church. A company official, at the same time, described the deplorable state of the mines: most of the shafts had fallen in, 'leaving their former site only to be detected by the immense craters, overgrown with brushwood at their mouths' (Robert W. Randall, *Real del Monte. A British Mining Venture in Mexico* (Austin & London: University of Texas Press, 1972) pp. 46–7, 61.

Vetch recorded the difficulties in getting the first machinery ashore in

June 1824 at the open roadstead of Mocambo – it was too dangerous to land at Vera Cruz while the Spaniards still held San Juan d'Ulloa and the Mexican authorities refused permission to land the cargoes at the nearby good harbour of Anton Lizardo. There was a shortage of draft and pack mules and further delays were imposed by the customs, 'all the more galling [commented Vetch] as instead of finding our operations facilitated on account of the value of the objects in benefiting this country, we are treated with a harshness that is never extended to sale goods' (ibid., pp. 56–7).

The hazards of travel in the rainy season across the mountains to Real del Monte proved to be very considerable. On one occasion a sudden rainfall caused twenty-one mules to be swept to their deaths, and on another a waggon containing 36 hundredweight of iron was washed away in the heavy rain, nine mules being drowned, and several men very narrowly escaping the same fate suffered by the mules (Lyon, *Journal* vol. 2. pp. 161, 166 cited by Randall, *Real del Monte* p. 60).

53 Lyon, *Journal* vol. 2, pp. 156, 258–61.
54 Calderón, *Life in Mexico* pp. 172–4.
55 Robertson, *A Visit* vol. 2, pp. 240–2.

When after investing at a loss for twenty-five years the company transferred its mining rights to local entrepreneurs, the latter soon started to make a profit (*CHLA* vol. 3, pp. 310–11 citing Randall, *Real del Monte* pp. 81, 100–8, 54–6.

Randall analyses the reasons for the failure of the British company to balance its books: the decision to build initially a large and expensive surface plant that exhausted the capital available and necessitated extensive borrowing; the decision to drain at great cost the lowest levels of a mine that proved in the end a disappointment, so far as the value of the ore it contained; and the difficulties caused by dual control in London and in Mexico, when it took three months to get a reply to any dispatch from either end. There were also labour troubles with the Mexicans over the way in which they were paid, and troops had to be sent to the area in 1827 and 1828 in order to prevent the miners from resorting to violence to obtain their demands. Though a settlement was eventually reached over pay, labour troubles recurred in 1833 and again in 1840–41 (Randall, *Real del Monte* pp. 71, 100–2, 134–44, 213–5).

The anonymous author of a pamphlet entitled *Notes and Reflexions on Mexico, its Mines, Policy etc.*, published in 1827, is firm in his opinion that the reasons for failure of the British mining companies to prosper lay with the British and not the Mexicans. 'It must [he wrote] be granted by all that the companies have met with the greatest liberality and fairness; that the feelings of the people have been most decidedly favourable, more especially those of the leading men and of the priesthood, and that the government has afforded them every protection that they could demand.' The chief faults of the companies concerned were, he believed, their extravagance and the poor quality of their management. They were always demanding more capital while never able to show a profit; yet the one German company in the country that had started with limited capital at a relatively late stage in the game, when the British had chosen all the mines they wanted, had always fulfilled its contractual obligations and was now paying a dividend (*A Traveller in Mexico and other countries of South America, Notes and Reflexions on Mexico, its Mines, Policy* etc. (London: J. M. Richardson, 1827) pp. 33–4, 40n).

56 Hardy, *Travels* pp. 12, 20, 227–8, 238–9, 250–1, 312–13, 448–9. Ward, *Mexico* vol. 2, pp. 593–4.

Chapter 6 Brazil

1 John Mawe, *Travels in the Interior of Brazil* (London: Longmans and others, 1823) pp. 1–2.

2 John Luccock, *Notes on Rio de Janeiro and the Southern Parts of Brazil During a Ten Years' Residence in that Country from 1808 to 1818* (London: Samuel Leigh, 1820) p. 31. Herbert Heaton, 'A Merchant Adventurer in Brazil' *The Journal of Economic History* VI no. 1 May 1946 (New York: New York University Press, 1946) pp. 1–23.

3 Henry Koster, *Travels in Brazil* (2 vols.) (London: Longmans and others, 1817) vol. 1, pp. 2, 293. Koster returned to England in 1811 for a few months but then returned to Pernambuco later that year.

4 James Henderson, *A History of Brazil* (London: Longmans and others, 1821) pp. 11, 447.

5 Maria Graham (Calcott), *Journal of a Voyage to Brazil and Residence There During Part of the Years 1821, 1822 and 1823* (London: Longmans and others, John Murray, 1824) passim.

6 Reverend Robert Walsh, *Notices of Brazil in 1828 and 1829* (2 vols.) (Boston: Richardson, Lord, Holbrook and others, 1831) vol. 1, pp. 199–211.

7 Dundonald, *Narrative* vol. 2, passim. William Henry B. Webster, *Narrative of a Voyage to the South Atlantic Ocean in the Years 1828, 1829 and 1830 Performed in the Sloop 'Chanticleer'* (2 vols.) (London: Richard Bentley, 1834) vol. 1, pp. 36–48; vol. 2, pp. 30–82.

8 Mawe, *Travels* pp. 455–66. Heaton, 'A Merchant Adventurer' pp. 6–8.

9 Ibid., pp. 8–9.

10 Ibid., p. 16.

11 Henderson, *A History* pp. 90–3, 390–2.

12 Graham, *Voyage to Brazil* p. 146.

13 Caldecleugh, *Travels* pp. 53–4.

14 Graham, *Voyage to Brazil* p. 189. Walsh, *Notices* vol. 1, p. 86. Luccock also bore witness to the general abundance of English wares: 'I have never dined in a Brazilian house, where part of the furniture of the table was not English, particularly the earthenware and glass' (Luccock, *Notes on Rio* p. 130).

15 Alan K. Manchester, *British Preeminence in Brazil. Its Rise and Decline* (New York: Octagon Books, 1964) pp. 75–99.

16 Graham, *Voyage to Brazil* p. 221.

17 Walsh, *Notices* vol. 1, p. 261.

18 Graham, *Voyage to Brazil* pp. 148, 166.

19 Walsh, *Notices* vol. 1, pp. 181–4, 258. Henderson, *A History* p. 96.

20 Graham and Humphreys, *The Navy* pp. 360–1 citing Hardy to Croker, 29 October 1822.

21 Koster, *Travels* vol. 2, pp. 314–5, 322. Brackenridge remarked on arriving off Rio, the little sandy bays in its vicinity occupied by elegant country houses, some built by English merchants who had grown very rich (Brackenridge, *A Voyage* vol. 1, p. 94).

22 Mawe, *Travels* p. 390.

23 Henderson, *A History* pp. 5–6, 88.

24 Mathison, *Narrative* pp. 35, 37, 46–52. 'Of the 10,000 or so Europeans [mostly Swiss and Germans] who arrived in Brazil between 1823 and 1830 more than 6000 ended up in the southern frontier province of Rio Grande do Sul' (Leslie Bethell and Joé Murilo de Carvalho 'Brazil from Independence to the Middle of the Nineteenth Century' *CHLA* vol. 3, p. 687).

25 Mawe, *Travels* pp. 255, 262, 269, 333–6, 348, 390.

26 Webster, *Narrative* p. 87.

27 Cleveland, *A Narrative* vol. 2, pp. 12–13.

28 Henderson, *A History* pp. 50–1, 70. Brackenridge, *A Voyage* vol. 1, pp. 106–7.

29 Henderson, *A History* pp. 57, 70, 71, 74, 76.

30 Brackenridge, *A Voyage* vol. 1, p. 127.

31 Caldecleugh, *Travels* vol. 1, p. 170. Jones, *South America* p. 192.

32 Henderson, *A History* pp. 79–80, 386, 498–500. Leslie Bethell and José Murillo de Carvalho, Brazil from Independence to the Middle of the Nineteenth Century' *CHLA* vol. 3, p. 741.

Luccock commented on the lawlessness he found prevalent in the streets of Rio. 'When a body dropped in the street, though in broad daylight, the murderer walked on, and the people beheld him as if he had done nothing amiss, and even made way for his escape' (Luccock, *Notes on Rio* p. 134).

Henry Hill, the US consul in Rio between 1818 and 1821, 'a forthright man who spoke his mind', had the lowest possible opinion both of Brazilians and of their government. Perhaps his intemperate diatribes in his dispatches to the secretary of state (John Quincy Adams) in 1821 were responsible for his recall. 'What a ridiculous people these Brazilians are [he wrote] ... wholly incapable of self-government.' The political and religious institutions of the country appeared to him arbitrary and corrupt. The government had lost all moral principle and degenerated into a weak despotism, 'supported by an imbecile and rapacious Hierarchy and dispirited Nobility'. The laws were 'multi-farious and contradictory' and administered with partiality; 'the magistracy is venal and the people immoral, ignorant and superstitious. It is impossible to convey any just idea of the difficulties, delays and expenses that were opposed to getting any business through the public offices.' The administration of the revenues was 'iniquitous and uncontrolled by authority, honour or honesty', but 'public justice was still more aggravated, heinous and offensive to good Government, reason and morality' (Hill to J. Q. Adams, May 1821, *DCUS* vol. 2, pp. 713–21).

33 Mathison, *Narrative* pp. 7–8, 11–13, 134, 138–9.
34 Webster, *Narrative* vol. 1, pp. 36–48.
35 Rev. H. S., *Journal* p. 195.
36 Walsh, *Notices* vol. 1, p. 99. Stewart, *A Visit* p. 98.
37 Walsh, *Notices* vol. 1, pp. 204–8, 211, 217, 241, 380; vol. 2, p. 84. Luccock, *Notes on Rio* p. 105.
38 Graham, *Voyage to Brazil* pp. 98, 104–5, 111–12, 139–40, 166, 169.
39 Walsh, *Notices* vol. 2, pp. 57, 60.
40 Ibid., vol. 2, p. 12.
41 Leslie Bethell, 'The Independence of Brazil' *CHLA* vol. 3, p. 190 n.12.
42 Dundonald, *Narrative* vol. 1, pp. xiii–xvi; vol. 2, passim. Condy Raguet to J. Q. Adams, 2 August 1824, *DCUS* vol. 2, p. 800.
43 Bethell, 'Independence' p. 190 n.12. Dundonald, *Narrative* vol. 1, pp. xii–xiv, xvi.

Chapter 7 Conclusion

1 Bethell, 'The Independence of Brazil' *CHLA* vol. 3, p. 191.
2 J. Fred Rippy, 'Latin America and the British Investment "Boom" of the 1820s' *The Journal of Modern History* June 1947 (Chicago: University of Chicago Press) pp. 122–9.
3 Ibid.
4 Bethell 'The Independence of Brazil' *CHLA* vol. 3, p. 190 n.12.

Bibliography

Original Sources

Manuscript

Public Record Office, Kew, London
 FO 6/4, 6/13 (Buenos Aires)
 FO 61/7–15 (Peru)
 WO 1/162
Northumberland County Record Office, Newcastle upon Tyne ZSW 536 (Swinburne (Capheaton) *archive*) mss

Printed

British Library, London
Adam, Captain William J., *Journal of Voyages to Margueritta, Trinidad and Maturín in the Years 1819 and 1820* Dublin: M. R. Tims, 1824.

Alexander, Alexander, *His Life* edited by John Howell. (2 vols.) Edinburgh: William Blackwood, 1830.

Andrews, Captain Joseph, *A Journey from Buenos Aires Through the Provinces of Cordova, Tucumán and Salta to Potosí, Thence by the Deserts of Caranja in the Years 1825–26* (2 vols.) London: John Murray, 1827.

An Englishman [George Love], *A Five Years' Residence in Buenos Aires During the Years 1820–1825* London: G. Hobert, 1825.

An Officer late in the Colombian service, *The Present State of Colombia* London: John Murray, 1827.

An Officer of the Colombian Navy, *Recollections of a Service of Three Years During the War of Extermination in the Republics of Venezuela and Colombia* (2 vols.) London: Hunt and Clarke, 1828.

An Officer of the United States Army [Richard Bache], *Notes on Colombia Taken in the Years 1822–23 with an Itinerary of the Route from Caracas to Bogotá* Philadelphia: H. C. Carey and I. Lea, 1827.

A Sketch of the Customs and Society of Mexico in a Series of Familiar Letters and a

Journal of Travel in the Interior During the Years 1824, 1825 and 1826 London: Longmans & Co, 1828.

A Traveller in Mexico and other countries of South America, *Notes and Reflexions on Mexico, its Mines, Policy etc.* London: J. M. Richardson, 1827.

Beaufoy, Mark, *Mexican Illustrations* London: Carpenter & Son, 1828.

Beaumont, J. Barber, *Travels in Buenos Aires and the Adjacent Provinces of the Rio de la Plata* London: James Ridgway, 1828.

Beechey, Captain Frederick William RN, *Narrative of a Voyage to the Pacific and Bering's Strait* (2 vols.) London: Henry Colburn & Richard Bentley, 1831.

Bowers, Lt William RN, *Naval Adventures During Thirty-Five Years' Service* (2 vols.) London: Richard Bentley, 1833.

Brackenridge, Henry Marie, *A Voyage to South America Prepared by Order of the American Government in the Years 1817 and 1818 in the Frigate 'Congress'.* (2 vols.) London: John Miller, 1820.

Brand, Lt Charles RN, *Journal of a Voyage to Peru* London: Henry Colburn, 1828.

Brown, Charles, *Narrative of the Expedition to South America Which Sailed from England at the Close of 1817* London: John Booth, 1818.

Bullock, William, *Six Months' Residence and Travels in Mexico* (2 vols.) London: John Murray, 1825.

Caldecleugh, Alexander *Travels in South America During the Years 1819–20–21* (2 vols.) London: John Murray, 1825.

Calderón de la Barca, Madame, *Life in Mexico* Boston: 1842. London: Century, 1987.

Callcott, Lady Maria (also and better known as Maria Graham), *Journal of a Residence in Chile During the Year 1822* London: Longman & Green, 1824.

Journal of a Voyage to Brazil and Residence There during Part of the Years 1821, 1822 and 1823 London: Longmans and others, 1824.

Chesterton, George Laval, *Peace, War and Adventure* (2 vols.) London: Longmans and others, 1853.

Campaigns and Cruises in Venezuela and New Granada and in the Pacific Ocean from 1817 and 1830 [probably by Richard Longueville Vowell] (3 vols.) London: Longmans & Co, 1831.

Cleveland, Richard J, *A Narrative of Voyages and Commercial Enterprises* Cambridge, Mass: John Owen, 1842.

Cochrane, Charles Stuart, *Journal of a Residence and Travels in Colombia During the Years 1823 and 1824* (2 vols.) London: Henry Colburn, 1825.

Darwin, Charles, *The Voyage of the 'Beagle'* London: 1845. New York: Bantam Books, 1972.

De Bonelli, L. Hugh, *Travels in Bolivia with a Tour across the Pampas* (2 vols.) London: Hurst and Blackett, 1854.

Delano, Amassa, *A Narrative of Voyages and Travels in the Northern and Southern Hemispheres* Boston: privately printed, 1817.

Diplomatic Correspondence of the United States Concerning the Independence of the Latin American Nations edited by William R. Manning (3 vols.) New York: Oxford University Press, 1925.

Duane, Colonel William, *A Visit to Colombia in the Years 1822 and 1823* Philadelphia: privately printed, 1826.

Dundonald, Thomas Cochrane, Earl of, *Narrative of Services in the Liberation of Chili, Peru and Brazil from Spanish and Portuguese Domination*, (2 vols.) London: James Ridgway, 1859.

Dupouy, Walter (ed.), *Sir Robert Ker Porter's Caracas Diary 1825–1842* Caracas: Instituto Otto y Magdalena Blum, 1967.

Flinter, George, *The History of the Revolution of Caracas* London: W. Glindon, 1819.

Gardiner, C. Harvey (ed.), *Mexico 1825–1828. The Journal and Correspondence of Edward Thornton Tayloe* Chapel Hill: University of North Carolina Press, 1959.

Gillespie, Major Alexander, *Gleanings and Remarks Collected During Many Months of Residence at Buenos Aires and Within the Upper Country* Leeds: privately printed, 1818.

Graham, Gerald S. and Humphreys, Robert A. (eds.), *The Navy and South America 1807–1823* London: Navy Records Society, 1923.

Hackett, James, *Journal of an Expedition which Sailed from England in 1817 to Join the South American Patriots* London: John Murray, 1818.

Haigh, Samuel, *Sketches of Buenos Aires, Chile and Peru* London: Effingham Wilson, 1831.

Hall, Captain Basil, *Extracts from a Journal Written on the Coasts of Chili, Peru and Mexico in the Years 1820, 1821 and 1822* (2 vols.) Edinburgh: Archibald Constable & Co, 1824.

Hamilton, Colonel John Potter, *Travels Through the Interior Provinces of Colombia* (2 vols.) London: John Murray, 1827.

Hankshaw, John, *Letters from Colombia During a Journey from Caracas to Bogotá and Thence to Santa Martha in 1823* London: G. Cowie & Co, 1824.

Hardy, Lt Robert William RN, *Travels in the Interior of Mexico in 1825, 1826, 1827 and 1828* London: Henry Colburn and Richard Bentley, 1829.

Hansard vol. 40, *Parliamentary Debates 1819* London: Hansard 1819.

Head, Francis Bond, *Rough Notes Taken During Some Rapid Journeys Across the Pampas and Across the Andes* (ed. C. Harvey Gardiner) London: John Murray, 1826. Carbondale and Edwardsville: South Illinois University press, 1967.

Reports Relating to the Failure of the River Plata Mining Association London: John Murray, 1827.

Henderson, James *A History of Brazil* London: Longmans and others, 1821.

Hippisley, Gustavus, *A Narrative of the Expedition to the Rivers Orinoco and Apuré in South America* London: John Murray, 1819.

Humphreys, Robert A. (ed.), *British Consular Reports on the Trade and Politics of Latin America 1824–1826* Camden Series vol. LXIII. London: Royal Historical Society, 1940.

King, Colonel Anthony, *Twenty-Four Years' Service in the Argentine Republic* Longmans and others, 1846.

Koster, Henry, *Travels in Brazil* (2 vols.) London: Longmans and others, 1817.

Lambert, Eric, (ed.), *Carabobo 1821. Some Accounts Written in English* Caracas: Fundación John Boulton, 1974.

Luccock, John, *Notes on Rio de Janeiro and the Southern Parts of Brazil During a Ten Years' Residence in that Country from 1808 to 1818* London: Samuel Leigh, 1820.

Lyon, Captain George Francis RN, *Journal of a Residence and Tour of Mexico in the Year 1826* (2 vols.) London: John Murray, 1828.

Mathison, Farquhar, *Narrative of a Visit to Brazil, Chile and the Sandwich Islands During the Years 1821 and 1822* London: Charles Knight, 1825.

Mawe, John, *Travels in the Interior of Brazil* London: Longmans and others, 1823.

Mayer, Brantz, *Mexico As It Was and Is* New York: J. Winchester, New World Press. London, Paris: Wiley & Paterson, 1844.

Miers, John, *Travels in Chile and La Plata* (2 vols.) London: 1846. New York: Arus Press, 1970, reprinted from the 1826 edn.

Miller, John, *Memoirs of General Miller in the Service of the republic of Peru* London: Longmans and others, 1829.

Minutes of a Court-Martial of Captain Sir Home Popham, London: Longmans & Hurst, Rees & Orme, 1807.

Mollien, Gaspard Theodore, *Travels in the Republic of Colombia in the Years 1822 and 1823* (trans. from the French), London: C. Knight, 1824.

Narrative of a Voyage to the Spanish Main in the Ship 'Two Friends' London: John Miller, 1819.

Parish, Sir Woodbine, *Buenos Aires and the Provinces of the Rio de la Plata* London: John Murray, 1852, 2nd edn.

Pentland, John Barclay, *Report on Bolivia* (ed.) J. Valerie Fifer *Camden Miscellany* vol. XXV, London: The Royal Historical Society, 1974.

Poinsett, Joel Roberts, *Notes on Mexico Made in the Autumn of 1822* London: John Miller, 1825.

Porter, Captain David USN, *Journal of a Cruise Made to the Pacific Ocean in the United States Frigate 'Essex' in the Years 1812, 1813 and 1814* (2 vols.) New York: Wiley and Halstead, 1822.

Proctor, Robert *Narrative of a Journey Across the Cordillera of the Andes and of a*

Residence in Lima and Other Parts of Peru Edinburgh: Archibald Constable. London: Hurst Robinson, 1825.

Reverend H. S. [Hugh Silvin], *Journal Written on Board HMS 'Cambridge' from January 1824 to May 1827.* Newcastle: privately printed, 1829.

Robertson, William Parish, *A Visit to Mexico* (2 vols.) London: Simpkins, Marshall & Co, 1853.

Robertson, John Parish and William Parish, *Letters on Paraguay Comprising the Account of a Five Years' Residence in that Republic under the Government of the Dictator Francia* (3 vols.) London: John Murray, 1838.

Letters on South America (3 vols.) London: John Murray, 1843.

Robinson, James H., *Journal of an Expedition 1400 Miles up the Orinoco and 300 up the Arauca* London: Black, Young and Young, 1822.

Rodney, Caesar Augustus and Graham, John *The Reports of the Present State of the United Provinces of South America ... Laid before Congress* London: Baldwin, Craddock & Joy, 1819.

Schmidtmeyer, Peter, *Travels in Chile over the Andes in the Years 1820 and 1821* London: Longmans and others, 1824.

Semple, Robert, *A Sketch of the Present State of Caracas* London: Robert Baldwin, 1812.

Stevenson, William Bennet, *A Historical and Descriptive Narrative of Twenty Years' Residence in South America* (3 vols.) London: Hurst Robinson & Co, 1825.

Stewart, Charles Samuel, *A Visit to the South Seas in the US Ship 'Vincennes' during the Years 1829 and 1830* New York: John P. Haven, 1831.

Sutcliffe, Thomas, *Sixteen Years in Chile and Peru from 1822 to 1839* London: Fisher Son & Co, 1841.

Temple, Edward, *Travels in Various Parts of Peru Including a Year's Residence at Potosí* (2 vols.) London: Henry Colburn & Richard Bentley, 1830.

A Brief Account of the Proceedings of the Potosí, La Paz and Peruvian Mining Association London: Ridgway, 1829.

Thompson, G. A., *Narrative of an Official Visit to Guatemala from Mexico* London: John Murray, 1829.

Thomson, James, *Letters on the Moral and Religious State of South America* London; James Nisbet, 1827.

Walsh, Reverend Robert, *Notices of Brazil in 1828 and 1829* (2 vols.) Boston: Richardson, Lord, Holbrook and others, 1831.

Ward, Henry George, *Mexico in 1827* (2 vols.) London: Henry Colburn, 1828.

Webster, Charles K. (ed.), *Britain and the Independence of Latin America 1812–1830. Select Documents from the Foreign Office Archives* London, New York and Toronto: Oxford University Press, 1938.

Webster, William Henry B, *Narrative of a Voyage to the South Atlantic Ocean in the Years 1828, 1829 and 1830 Performed in the Sloop 'Chanticleer'* (2 vols.) London: Richard Bentley, 1834.

Secondary Sources

Books and Pamphlets

An Inquiry into the Plans, Progress and Policy of the American Mining Companies, London: John Murray, 1825.

Cambridge History of Latin America (vol. 3) (ed. Leslie Bethell) Cambridge: Cambridge University Press, 1985.

Collier, Simon, *Ideas and Politics of Chilean Independence 1808–1833* Cambridge: Cambridge University Press, 1967.

Dickinson, Henry Winran and Titley, Arthur, *Richard Trevithick* Cambridge: Cambridge University Press, 1934.

English, Henry, *A General Guide to the Companies Formed for Working Foreign Mines* London: Boosey & Sons, 1825.

Fifer, J. Valerie, *Bolivia: Land, Location and Politics since 1825* Cambridge: Cambridge University Press, 1972.

Ferns, Henry Stanley, *Britain and Argentina in the Nineteenth Century* Oxford: Oxford University Press, 1960.

Graham-Youll, Andrew, *A Forgotten Colony* London: Hutchinson & Co (Publishers) Ltd, 1981.

Hasbrouck, Alfred, *Foreign Legionaries in the Liberation of Spanish South America* New York: Columbia University, 1928.

Hanke, Lewis (ed.), *History of Latin American Civilization* (2 vols.) vol. 2 'The Modern Age' USA: Little Brown and Co Inc, 1967. London: Methuen, 1969.

Humphreys, Robert A., *Liberation in South America 1806–1827. The Career of James Paroissien* London: University of London, The Athlone Press, 1952.

Jeaffreson, John Cory, *The Life of Robert Stephenson* (2 vols.) London: Longman, Green and others, 1864.

Jones, Tom B., *South America Rediscovered* Minneapolis: University of Minnesota Press, 1949.

Lambert, Eric, *Voluntários ingleses y irlandeses en la Gesta Bolivariana* (tomo 1). Caracas: Edición de la Corporación venezolana de Guyana, Julio de 1981.

Madariaga, Salvador, *Bolívar* London: Hollis and Carter, 1952.

Manchester, Alan K., *British Preeminence in Brazil. Its Rise and Decline* New York: Octagon Books, 1964.

Mulhall, Michael G., *The English in South America* Buenos Aires, London, Stanford: 1878.

Naylor, Bernard, *Accounts of Nineteenth Century South America. An Annotated Checklist of Works by British and United States Observers* London: University of London, The Athlone Press, 1969.

New Annual Register for 1817 (British and Foreign History), 1819 (Literary Retrospect and Selection), 1823 (History of Europe), 1824 (State Papers), 1825 (Public Documents) London: William Stockdale 1818–25.

Parks, E. Taylor, *Colombia and the United States 1765–1934* Durham NC: Duke University Press, 1935.

Quirk, Robert E., *Mexico* New Jersey: Prentice Hall Inc, 1971.

Randall, Robert W., *Real del Monte. A British Mining Venture in Mexico* Austin: University of Texas Press, 1972.

Rippy, J. Fred, *Rivalry of the United States and Great Britain over Latin America* New York: Octagon Books Inc, 1964.

Joel R. Poinsett Versatile American Durham NC: Duke University Press, 1935.

Robertson, William Spence, *The Rise of the Spanish American Republics as Told in the Lives of their Liberators* New York: The Free Press. London: Collins and Macmillan, 1918.

Salmon, David, *Joseph Lancaster* London, New York, Bombay: Longmans, Green & Co, 1904.

Shuttleworth, Hon. Nina Kay, *A Life of Sir Woodbine Parish* London: Smith Elder & Co, 1910.

Street, John, *Artigas and the Emancipation of Uruguay* Cambridge: Cambridge University Press, 1959.

Taggart, Edward, *A Memoir of the Late Captain Peter Heywood RN* London: Effingham Wilson, 1832.

Trevithick, Francis, *Life of Richard Trevithick* (2 vols.) London: 1872.

Vaughan, Edgar, *Joseph Lancaster in Caracas (1824–1827)* (2 tomos) Caracas: Ediciones del Ministério de Educación, 1987 and 1989.

Waddell, D. A. G., *Gran Bretagna y la Independencia de Venezuela y Colombia* Caracas: Imprenta del Ministério de Educación, 1983.

Worcester, Donald E., *Sea Power and Chilean Independence* Gainesville: University of Florida Press, 1962.

Articles

Ferns, Henry Stanley, 'The Beginnings of British Investment in Argentina' *The Economic History Review* 1953. Kendal, Cumbria: printed for the Economic History Society pp. 341–352.

Fisher, John, 'Silver Production in the Viceroyalty of Peru 1776–1824' *Hispanic American Historical Review* vol. 55, 1975, Durham NC: Duke University Press pp. 25–43.

Heaton, Herbert, 'A Merchant Adventurer in Brazil' *The Journal of Economic History* VI no. 1, May 1946. New York: New York University Press, 1946, pp. 1–23.

Humphreys, Robert A., 'British Merchants and South American Independence' *Tradition and Revolt in South America* London: Weidenfeld and
Nicholson, 1963, pp. 106–29.

Johnson, John J., 'Relations of the United States with Chile' *Pacific Historical
Review* XIII 1944. Berkeley and Los Angeles: University of California
Press.

Metford, John Callan James, 'The Recognition by Great Britain of the United
Provinces of Rio de la Plata' *Bulletin of Hispanic Studies.* Liverpool
Institute of Hispanic Studies October-December, 1952, pp. 201–24.

Rippy, J. Fred, 'Latin America and the British Investment "Boom" of the
1820s' *The Journal of Modern History* 19, June 1947. Chicago: University
of Chicago Press, pp. 122–9.

Waddell, D. A. G., 'Anglo-Spanish Relations and the "Pacification of
America" during the "Constitutional Triennium" 1820–1823' *Annuario
de Estudios Americanos* tomo XLVI. Sevilla: Escuela de Estudios Hispano-
Americanos, 1989, pp. 455–86.

'British Neutrality and Spanish-American Independence. The Problem of
Foreign Enlistment' *Journal of Latin-American Studies* 19. London: 1987
pp. 1–18.

Williams, Judith Blow, 'The Establishment of British Commerce in Argentina'
Hispanic American Historical Review vol. 15, 1935. Durham NC: Duke
University Press pp. 43–64.

Williams, John Hoyt, 'Paraguayan Isolation under Dr Francia. A Re-Evalua-
tion'. *The Hispanic American Historical Review* vol. 52/1, 1972. Durham
NC: Duke University Press pp. 102–22.

Index

Allen, Herman (US minister to Chile): criticises clergy in Chile, 192 (n. 28); despairs of Chilean government, 43,179

Andrews, Captain Joseph: describes Tacna as resembling British colony, 64, 176; encounters dishonesty over mining concessions, 25, 48, 179–80; reports on mining prospects in Bolivia, 85; in Chile, 48; in La Plata provinces, 25–6

Anglophilism: among Chileños, 55–6; Colombians, 119, 120–21

Angostura: Bolívar establishes base at, 90; congress of in 1819, ix; garrison commanded by Bermudez, 113; taken by Bolívar, 89

Arismendi, General Juan Bautista: Anglophile, 112; commands Margarita garrison, 112; gives banquet in honour of Devereux, 96; impressions of, 112–13; tells British volunteers they are not needed, 93

Artigas, José: leader of anti-federalists, 12, 29; Robertson's impression of, 12–13

Banda Oriental: struggle for control of, 7, 8, 29

Banks: loans to Latin America, 2; to Mexico, 133, 178; to Peru, 63. *See also* Financial difficulties of governments

Beaufoy, Mark: anti-Catholic prejudice, 143; compliments Mexican army, 143–4; criticises Mexicans' appearance, 136–7, 181; Mexican navy, 146; would-be British farmers in Mexico, 148, 177; travels in Mexico, 134

Beaumont, J. A. Barber: impression of Buenos Aires, 20; pessimism about prospects of joint-stock companies, 11, 176; tries to organise immigration to La Plata provinces, 10, 26–8, 177, 178; views on disunion of and public standards in La Plata provinces, 10, 11

Beechey, Captain Frederick William, RN: comments on English trade in Chile, 33; on Talcahuana and Concepción, 40

Bermudez, General José Francisco: commander at Angostura, 113; retakes Guyana la Vieja, 118

Bible Society: its bibles criticised by bishop, 167; Lancaster acts as agent for, 128; opposed by clergy in Caracas, 128–9; sends agents to Latin America, 3; supported by civil authorities in Caracas, 128

Bolívar, General Simón (the 'Liberator'): allows Chesterton to return home sick, 107; anxious to supply wants of British troops, 107, 110; becomes dictator of Peru, 59; campaigns of 1813–22, 89–90, 97–9; dislikes Hippisley, 94; dispute with Lancaster, 127–8; emulates Napoleon, 199 (n. 53); friendship with Ker Porter, 131; gets Trevithick to design carbine, 81–2; gives money to Scottish immigrants, 125; hopes British companies will buy Bolivian mines, 85; impressed by Elsom; impressions of by British officers, 107–8, 110; by Ker Porter, 109–10; interest in education, 77, 128, 182; lack of preparation for arrival of volunteers excused, 103; leaves Peru, 60; loses popular support, 129; makes partial payment to British contingent, 105; name given to Bolivia, 60; orders cessation of foreign recruitment, 197 (n. 7); proclaims 'War to the Death', 117–18; promises to volunteers, 92; quarrel with Hippisley, 105, 108–9; regulates rations of British Legion, 104; simply dressed, 115; tells British he wants large, organised contingents, 93; witness at marriage of Lancaster, 128;

Bonaparte, Joseph: revolt of Spain against his rule, x

Bonaparte, Napoleon: incorporates Spain into his empire, x; initiates Continental blockade, 1; Portuguese court escapes his clutches, xi

Bowers, Lt. William, RN: criticises government corruption in Chile, 42–3, 179; describes Valparaiso, 33; depreciates contribution of Guise to Chilean navy, 73; likes Chileños, 40; praises British naval officers' handling of disputes, 68; trades with both sides in civil war, 65

Bowles, Captain William, RN: comments on Anglophilism in Buenos Aires, 21–2; ignorance of commerce of Buenos Aires government, 9, 176; impressed by San Martín, 42; intervenes on behalf of British merchants, 8–9; refusal to dismount for Queen of Portugal, 165; suspicious of Cochrane's motives, 51; unwilling to break blockade of Callao, 65

Brackenridge, Henry M.: 164; career, 188; comments on political instability of La Plata government, 9, 179; compares salaries in Buenos Aires and USA, 28; describes experiences in Brazil, 156; impressions of Buenos Aires, 9, 22, 188 (n.13), 189–90 (n. 43); notes lack of press in Brazil, 165

Brazilians: appearance of women, 169; character of, 163; habits of, 165; racial attitudes approved, 168

Brion, Captain-General (Admiral) Luis: advances money to pay British volunteers, 105; commands patriot fleet, 102; described, 113; desertions from his squadron, 199 (n. 48); failure to destroy Spanish squadron, 114; jealousy of British officers, 113–14; obsession with uniforms and rank, 114

British Legion; 95, 98, 102, 103, 104–5, 118. See also Volunteers; Hippisley, Gustavus

British manufactures: losses in Brazil, 157–8; in Chile 33; market for in Brazil, 157–8; in Buenos Aires, 5, 8, 14; in Chile, 35, 66; in Colombia, 119–20; in Mexico, 147; 159, 160; in Peru, 69. See also British merchants

British merchants: arrive in Brazil, 155; berated for selling shoddy goods, 11–12; compelled to make forced contributions and loans, 8–9, 67, 146, 176; character and attitude of in Brazil described, 161; complain of blockade at Callao, 65; to consul-general, 68; difficulties encountered generally, 175–6; in Brazil,

159; in Mexico, 146, 147, 148; in Peru, 70; disappointment and frustration of, 29; dominate trade in Chile, 33; 147, 148; in Peru, 70; disappointment and frustration of, 29; dominate trade in Chile, 33; face ruin in Peru in 1826, 69–70; fail to prosper on Pacific coast of Mexico, 148; find profitable market in Brazil, 159, 160; firms established in Mexico City and Vera Cruz, 148; forced to provide transports for Peruvian troops, 71; hampered by import duties in Peru, 70; hopes of market in Venezuela, 92; in Buenos Aires, 7; influence of, 200–201 (n. 76); interests looked after by naval officers, 8; leave Lima for Callao, 63; life-style in Lima described, 78; losses in Chilean market, 33; mistakes in estimating size and nature of market in Brazil, 157; pay contribution to government of Peru, 71; petition for protection of British warship at Valparaiso, 33; poor prospects in Buenos Aires for joint-stock companies, 11, 176; prospects for in Colombia, 120; provide arms for Indian troops, 100; provide money for Bible Society, 128; refusal to pay forced levy in Angostura, 105; refused compensation for losses in Lima and Callao, 68, 178; resident in Santiago, 37; safety of in Lima, 62, 176; sign petition against Foreign Enlistment Act, 92; suffer from inadequacy of Rio's port facilities, 158; from lack of market research, 147, 175; trade in Peru, 64, 65, 69, 176; in Rio de la Plata provinces, 22; try to leave Callao, 63; wealth of in Brazil, 161; willingness to trade with both royalists and patriots, 65, 68

British naval officers: Captain Martin rescues ships' papers at Callao, 68; Captain Prescott protects merchants in Lima, 67, 71; fulfil role of consuls, 3, 8, 67; intervention with Artigas, 12; with Canterac, 67; social life of in Chile, 35; take service in Chilean navy, 50–51, 73. See also Bowles, Captain William; Cochrane, Thomas; Hardy, Commodore Sir Thomas

Buenos Aires: admiration of inhabitants for USA, 22; Anglophilism of inhabitants, 21–2; anti-clericalism in, 10; attitude of government to immigration, 26–9; commercial treaty with Britain, 8; description of, 7, 18–19, 20, 21, 188 (n. 13), 189–90 (n. 43); English attracted to, 190 (n. 48); Faunch's hotel at, 190 (n.

44); high cost of living in, 28–9;
immigrants prosper in, 29; mining
speculation in, 24, 25; roads in and
around, 14; schools in started by
Thomson, 22; target for jealousy of
adjoining provinces, 10–11, 23–4; viceroyalty of becomes United Provinces of
La Plata, 6; views on of Englishmen, 5–6,
18–21; of Brackenridge, 9

Caldecleugh, Alexander: comments on
Brazilian newspapers, 165; describes
Brazilian imports from Britain, 159;
impressions of Brazil, 156; journey across
pampas, 16; indulgent towards gauchos,
17
Callao: 64, 74, 75, 81; archives destroyed in,
69; blockade of by Cochrane, 51, 60, 65;
by Prescott, 71; description of, 63; failure
of Cochrane to capture, 72; flourishes as
port, 61; frigate *Esmeralda* cut out at, 73;
levy on property of merchants in, 67;
mutiny of patriot forces in, 59, 63, 68;
royalists surrender, 60
Calderón de la Barca, Madame Frances
Erskine: admires Real del Monte mine,
153; described, 135; comments on lack of
education of women, 141, 182; on Mexico
City and its inhabitants, 139–40, 182;
impressed by religious devotion of
Mexicans, 143; refers to incidence of
robbery, 144
Canning, George (British Foreign Secretary
1822–7): attempts to end Brazilian slave
trade, 166; complained to by British
merchants in Lima, 68; favours
recognition of Spanish colonies, x, xi;
prevents French intervention in Spanish
America, xi; respected by Chileños, 56;
sends consuls to Chile, 32; to Mexico,
133; missions to Colombia and Mexico,
133; signs treaty with Mexico, 124
Canterac, General: demands contribution
from British merchants, 67; occupies
Lima, 76, 78; relieves Callao then
withdraws from, 195 (n. 34)
Chilean government: denies Cochrane
reward for capture of Valdívia, 52; eager
to encourage foreign investment, 31;
ignores Hardy's protests about seizure of
ships by Cochrane, 66; navy of, 50–51;
obstructiveness and corruption of, 42–6;
opens ports to foreign trade, 31, 32; pays
Cochrane compensation, 53; unable to
pay mercenaries, 52. *See also* O'Higgins,
Bernardo; Zenteno

Chileños: commented on by Cochrane, 43;
criticised by Allen and Miers, 40; liked by
British, 40; Anglophilism, 56; lack of
discipline of troops, 72
Chiloé: captured by royalists, 31
Cleveland, Richard: deplores Brazilian lack
of enterprise, 163; lack of intellectual life
in Lima, 79; describes experiences in
Brazil, 157; ignores Cochrane's blockade
of Callao, 66; impressed by piety of
Peruvians, 78
Cochrane, Thomas (later 10th Earl of
Dundonald): 194 (n. 50); accepts
compensation from Chilean government,
53; account of experiences commanding
Brazilian navy, 156, 170–73; accused of
fraud, 53, 74; amicable relations with
Basil Hall, 21; bitterness about treatment
by Chile, 54; blockades Callao, 60, 65;
captures Valdívia, 51–2; comments on
Chileños, 43; created admiral of Chilean
navy, 49, 50; description of, 193 (n. 48);
detains British and US merchant ships,
65–6; difficulty in getting sailors paid, 52,
53, 73–4, 178; enforcement of discipline
on crews, 72; enmity with Zenteno, 42,
53; estate in Chile confiscated, 53, 177;
failure to capture Callao, 72; love of gold,
75; not prosecuted under Foreign
Enlistment Act, 53–4; offers resignation,
52; purchases estate at Quintero, 45;
quarrels with Brazilian government,
172–3, 180–81; with San Martín, 53,
73–4, 180, 195 (n. 34); with Zenteno and
Chilean ministers, 52; refuses Freire's
offer of renewed command, 53; relations
with Bowles, 51; reorganises Chilean
fleet, 50; replies to protests of Hardy, 66;
resigns and accepts offer from Brazil, 53,
54; views of mercenaries about, 51;
Vowell serves under, 54; welcomed in
Chile, 50, 55
Coffin, Isaac: comments on Chileans'
cultural deficiencies, 37–8
Concepción: described, 40; ravaged by civil
war, 40
Cornish miners: accompany Bond Head to
La Plata provinces, 23; dislike living in
Buenos Aires, 28–9; disorderly conduct
of, 123, 149–50, 152; experience of little
relevance in Latin America, 23;
intractability, 26, 123
Corruption, deceit and obstruction by
government: 179; in Ancón, 68; in Chile,
42–3, 44–6, 176, 191 (n. 6); in
Colombian and Venezuelan ports, 120,

130, 176; in Lima, 61–2, 63, 69; in Peru generally, 70–72, 81; in Mexico, 144–6, 204–5 (n. 52); in Rio de Janeiro, 158–9, 166

Crime: frequency generally, 181; incidence of in Mexico, 144, 152; in Rio de Janeiro, 165, 181

Crimes against Humanity: committed by *llaneros*, 111; executing prisoners of war, 52, 100, 117–18; expulsion of Spaniards from Peru, 62; murder of English officers in Chile, 54; shock Europeans, 117–18, 180

Cultural scene: adverse comments on in Brazil, 165, 169, 182; in Caracas, 130; in Chile, 37–8; generally, 181–2; in Lima, 79; architecture criticised, 182; libraries in Brazil, 168–9

Darwin, Charles: contrasts gauchos and *guasos*, 41; describes gaucho, 18; experiences in Peru, 64

Devereux, John (General in army of Bolívar): admired by Venezuelans, 96; career, 197–8 (n. 10); character, 95; criticised, 99; deception of recruits by, 95, 103; incompetence, 95; loquacity, 95–6

Dictators in Latin America: views on by J. P. Robertson, 10

Dundas, Henry, 1st Viscount Melville: views on importance of Rio de la Plata, 5

Education: Bolívar's interest in, 77, 128; English boarding-school in Rio, 166, 168; ignorance encountered, 116, 141, 165, 169; illiteracy in Venezuela, 130; lack of among Mexicans, 139, 140; numerous schools in Rio, 168; opposition of clergy to Protestant-run schools, 39, 141–2, 182; schools started in Buenos Aires, 22; in Chile, 38–9; in Colombia, 126–7, 202 (n. 92); in Mexico, 141–2; in Peru, 76; in Venezuela, 127–8; women's education neglected, 141. *See also* Lancaster, Joseph; Thomson, James

Financial difficulties of governments: 175, 178, 182: of Bolívar in Venezuela and Colombia, 91, 104–5, 108, 110, 178, 180; of Brazil, 172–3; of Buenos Aires, 22, 178; of Caracas town council, 127–8, 178, 183; of Chile, 52–3, 178, 193 (n. 48); of Mexico, 146; of Mexico City, 140; of Peru, 60, 69, 70, 128, 178

Foreign Enlistment Act: Cochrane not prosecuted under, 53–4; effects of, 197

(n. 7); passed, x, 92; petition against, 91–2

Francia, Doctor José Gaspar Rodriguez de: dictator of Paraguay, 10; methods of rule, 11; refusal to grant more trading licences, 13; relations with Robertson brothers, 12, 13; releases British subjects, 14; seeks diplomatic relations with Britain, 12, 14

Freire, Ramón: 54; allows governmental corruption, 43; brings back clerical censorship, 39; offers Cochrane command of Chilean navy, 43; rule of, 31–2; threatens to displace O'Higgins, 52; tries to induce Cochrane to return to Chile, 53

Gillespie, Major Alexander: enlarges on economic prospects of La Plata provinces, 26; eulogises Buenos Aires, 5–6, 7

Graham, Maria (Lady Maria Calcott): 39, 191–2 (n. 12); adverse opinion of cultural life in Brazil, 169; comments on Anglophilism of Chileños, 56; British officers in navy of Chile, 50–51; English character of Valparaiso, 34; insularity and coarseness of British merchant families in Brazil, 161; considers Chile needs navy, 193 (n. 48); critical of San Martín, 42; experience in Brazil, 156; finds Pernambuco under siege, 170; remarks on numbers of British merchants in Brazil, 159, 177; of English ships in Rio harbour, 160; of drunken and destitute British and US sailors in Rio, 160; shocked at Catholic observances in South America, 39

Great Britain: annexes Buenos Aires, 5; commercial relations with Latin America, x, xi; neutrality in Spain's colonial struggle, x, 92; passes Foreign Enlistment Act, x, 92; relations with Portuguese court, xi; with Spanish government, x, 92; signs treaties with Brazil, 1, 159; with Buenos Aires, 8; with Mexico, 124; suffers from Continental blockade, 1. *See also* Canning, George

Gauchos: compared to *guasos*, 41; definition of, 7; manners and way of life described, 17–18, 189 (n. 37); purchase British manufactures, 14; travel at gallop, 15

Guasos: compared to gauchos, 41

Haigh, Samuel: comments on British merchants in Arequipa, 64, 176; trade in Valparaiso, 32; complains of noise of church bells, 78; describes journey across pampas, 14–15, 16; impressions of

Buenos Aires, 19; of Santiago and
Valparaiso, 35; witnesses ruin of British
merchants in Peru, 69
Hall, Captain Basil, RN: 191 (n. 3); defends
tactics of San Martín, 195 (n. 34);
describes Santiago, 37; Valparaiso port,
32; experiences in Callao and Lima, 60,
61; inspecting mines in Chile, 46; notes
popularity of British products in Peru, 69,
176; praises work of British naval officers
acting as consuls, 67
Hall, Colonel Francis (hydrographer): 119,
200 (n. 75); comments on roads in
Colombia, 201–2 (n. 90); extends warning
to prospective immigrants, 121–2, 177;
views on prospects for immigrants in
Gran Colombia, 121
Hamilton, Colonel John: appointed British
commissioner in Colombia, 120; buys
farm in Colombia, 120, 177; criticises
Catholic clergy, 120, 121; encounters
Anglophilism on travels, 120–21;
optimism regarding European
immigration prospects, 120; supports
Bible Society in Caracas, 128
Hankshaw, John: author of 'Letters written
from Colombia', 117; favours distribution
of bibles among Indians, 129; impressed
by character of Indians, 129; optimistic
about prospects for immigrants, 120
Hardy, Lt. Robert William, RN: describes
hardships of travel in Mexico, 136;
obtains concession to fish for pearls, 134;
reports corruption in government in
Mexico, 145–6, 179
Hardy, Commodore (Vice-Admiral from
1825) Sir Thomas: commands squadron
in South American waters, 65; complains
to Cochrane over detention of British
ships, 65, 66; over encouraging desertions
from ships in Brazil, 177; evaluates
British property in Brazil, 161; intervenes
on behalf of cargo of Lt. Bowers, 68, 176
Head, Francis Bond: admires gaucho way of
life, 17; advises British poor against
emigration to Buenos Aires, 28–9, 178;
describes journey across pampas, 14–15,
16; employed by mining company, 23, 25;
experiences of inspecting mines in Chile,
24, 47–8, 179–80; impressions of Buenos
Aires, 19; of Santiago, 37; religious
prejudice of, 37; reports on mining
prospects in La Plata provinces, 23–5,
179–80; on United Provinces of Rio de la
Plata, 9–10, 179
Henderson, James: complains of lawlessness

and manners of Brazilians, 165–6;
dislikes Rio de Janeiro, 164; goes to
Brazil, 155–6; reports on British
mercantile success in Brazil, 159, 176–7;
on difficulty of recovering debts in Brazil,
159, 176; shocked at sight of slaves, 165,
166; thinks immigration in Brazil
impeded by land laws, 162, 177
Hill, Henry (US consul in Rio de Janeiro):
low opinion of Brazilians and their
government, 179, 207
Hippisley, Gustavus (Lt.-Colonel in army of
Bolívar): accuses Lopez of deception, 91,
109; admires Páez, 111; Mariño, 112;
career of, 98–9; character of, 94;
describes Arismendi, 113; Brion, 113;
dress of his regiment, 114; indiscipline of
a British regiment, 101; patriot cavalry,
116–7; disillusion with service under
Bolívar, 99; dislikes Bolívar, 94; has
Lopez arrested for debt, 99; his *Narrative*,
98–9; impression of Bolívar, 108–9, 180;
leaves England, 93; quarrels with Bolívar,
108; raises and equips regiments, 92;
resigns commission, 109
Hogan, Michael: complains of detention of
US ships, 66
Humboldt, Alexander: 82–3, 98; blamed for
misleading posterity, 148; report on
Potosí mines, 83; writings on Latin
America, 1, 149

Immigration: agencies for, 2; British farmers
fail to prosper in Mexico, 148;
encouraged by Latin American states, 2;
failure of Beaumont to organise, 26–8,
177; by Robertsons, 28, 177; by Scots in
Venezuela and Colombia, 124–6, 177,
201, (n. 86); by Swiss in Brazil, 162–3;
Head advises British poor against, 28–9;
favourable prospects for in Brazil, 162,
177; in Colombia, 120, 121, 177; in La
Plata provinces, 186 (n. 6); immigrants
prosper in Buenos Aires, 29; need for in
Venezuela, 126, 201 (n. 80); O'Connor
projects Irish colony, 86, 177;
unfavourable prospects for in Bolivia, 86
Indians: Araucanian tribe in Chile, 41;
attack travellers on pampas, 16; character
described, 75–6, 129; conscripted into
Mexican navy, 146; employed in mining,
26–7, 151; good relations with General
Miller, 75; in Mexico City, 138, 139; lack
of education, 139; *monteneros* feared in
Lima, 61

Irish Legion: 95, 102; *See also* Devereux, John; Volunteers (soldiers and sailors)

King, Anthony: experience of military service in La Plata provinces, 29

Lancaster, Joseph: character, 127, 182–3; experience of running school in Caracas, 127; goes to Venezuela, 3; leaves Venezuela after quarrel with Bolívar, 127, 178; quarrels with Ker Porter, 125; sponsors Scots immigrants in Venezuela, 124–5

Lima: described by Proctor, 78–9; extent of British property in, 65; fear of slave revolt in, 61; foreigners distrusted in, 60; inhabitants described, 79; parlous state of, 61–3; patriot forces enter, 59, 60 retaken by royalists, 59, 63; sacked by Canterac's troops, 78; San Martín takes possession of, 61; social life in, 79; spared assault by San Martín, 59; views of Ricketts on, 79–80

Loans by European banks: 60, 63, 178

Looting: by British Legion at Barcelona, 105–6; by Chileño troops/sailors, 72; licensed by Páez, 106; punished by Cochrane, 72

López Méndez, Luis: accused of deception, 91; arrested for debt, 99; fails to advance money to Hippisley, 108; recruiting agent in London for Bolívar, 91; threatened with deportation, 91

Love, George: describes Buenos Aires and its inhabitants, 7–8, 18, 20, 176

Luccock, John: arrives Brazil, 155, describes limitations of Rio port, 158, notes improvements in Rio, 164; surprised at ignorance of Brazilian merchants, 169; writes account of impressions of interior of Brazil, 155

Lyon, Captain George Francis, RN: comments on ignorance of Mexicans, 140, 141; describes hazards of travel in Mexico, 205 (n. 52); uses medical skills on Mexicans, 140–41

Mariño, General Santiago: popularity with British, 112

Mawe, John: allowed to travel freely in Brazil 1808–9, 155; author of *Travels*, 155; critical of Brazilians' lack of farming enterprise, 163; describes glut of British goods in Rio, 157–8; improvement in Brazilian market after 1810, 159

Mathison, Farquhar: contrasts patriot rule

unfavourably with royalist, 62, 179; impressions of Brazil, 156; Lima, 61–2; Santiago, 37; Valparaiso, 34; meets mercenaries in Chile, 41; notes number of British vessels in Callao port, 69, 176

Melville, Viscount *see* Dundas, Henry

Mexico City: beggars and dirt in, 138; crime in 144; growing prosperity, 138; impressions of, 139–40, 182

Mexico's inhabitants: character, habits and living conditions, 139–40, 181; religious devotion, 203–4 (n. 34)

Miers, John: advises against buying land in Chile, 45, 177; builds mint at Buenos Aires, 193 (n. 46); comments on Chileños' character, 40; cultural deficiencies of Chileños, 38, 39; exiguity of Chilean market, 33; religious intolerance in Chile, 39; criticises British optimism about mining in Chile, 48; Chilean licensing of ports, 45–6; deplores government corruption in Chile, 43, 179–80; describes Concepción, 40; Santiago, 36–7; travel across pampas, 18; Valparaiso, 33–4; experiences dealing with Chilean officials, 43–4, 46; leaves Chile, 44

Miller, William (General in army of Peru): admired by Indians, 75; career, 195–6 (n. 36); defends tactics of San Martín, 195 (n. 34); description of, 75; experiences as mercenary in South America, 55; in service of Peruvian government, 75; impression of Bolívar, 108; verdict on British mining companies, 85

Mines and Mining: destruction of mines in Colombia, 123; in Peru, 80–82; in Potosí, 83; in Mexico, 149, 204 (n. 52); difficulties generally in exploiting, 180; hopes of exploiting successfully, 2; inspection of by Andrews, Hall and Miers, 25–6, 46–8, 85; Miers's experience of refining copper in Chile, 43–4; Pentland's optimism about prospects in Bolivia, 85; primitive methods used in Brazil, 170; unfavourable prospects in Chile, 48–9, 193 (n. 46); unsuccessful attempts to exploit in Colombia and Venezuela, 119, 122, 123–4; in Mexico, 148–53; Ricketts reports on in Peru, 80–81. *See also* Mining companies

Mining Companies: 179–80; criticised, 83–5; difficulties encountered by in Chile, 31, 47–9; in La Plata provinces,

23–5; employment of Head to supervise, 23; encounter religious prejudice in Mexico, 143; failures of, 80, 81, 82–5, 149–51, 196 (n. 48), 205 (n. 55); formation in London, 2, 22; fortunes of Real del Monte company, 135, 149–50, 152–3, 205 (n. 55); General Mining Association in Brazil, 170; lack of success of Colombian Mining Association, 122–4; mistakes made by, 80, 81, 82–5, 179–80

Morillo, General Pablo: crushes rebel resistance in Venezuela, 89; orders reprisals against rebels, 118; releases British officer from captivity, 98

O'Connor, General Francis Burdett: project for Irish colony in Bolivia, 86

O'Higgins, Bernardo: attempts religious toleration, 39; described, 41–2; dictatorship of, 31; encourages Thomson to set up schools, 38–9, 182; gives Sutcliffe commission, 54; issues Miers with permits, 46; orders retrial of Miers's case, 44; pleased at Cochrane's capture of Valdívia, 52; persuades Cochrane not to resign, 52; threatened with displacement by Freire, 52; welcomes Cochrane, 50; Miers, 44

O'Leary, General Daniel Florencio: Bolívar's chief aide, 197 (n. 2); describes Gran Colombia, 90; praises volunteer soldiers, 101, 181

Páez, General José Antonio: allows looting, 106, 112; Anglophile, 110; anxious to supply wants of British troops, 107; cavalry of, 102, 110; friendship with Ker Porter, 131; his guard of honour, 115; impressions of, 110–12 ; popularity with his men, 111

Pampas: population of, 7, 15; travel across described, 14–17, 189 (n. 27)

Parish, Sir Woodbine (British consul-general in Buenos Aires): describes journey across pampas 16–17; scenes at signing of commercial treaty, 8; dislike of Buenos Aires, 20–21; estimate of value of British exports to Buenos Aires, 14, 177; eulogises Buenos Aires, 6, 7; first impression of Buenos Aires, 18–19; persuades Francia to release British subjects, 14; reports number of British in Buenos Aires, 7–8, 177

Paroissien, James: employed by Mining

Association to mine in Potosí, 82–4; general in Peruvian army, 82

Patriot armed forces in Chile: quality and discipline, 35–6

Patriot armed forces in Gran Colombia: arms of 100, 115, 116–17; character, 100, 101, 117, 181; contempt for non-Spanish-speakers, 117; dress, 115, 116–17, 181; habits, 116; ignorance and lack of sophistication, 100, 115, 116; mock British foppery, 117

Patriot armed forces in Mexico: approved by Beaufoy, 143–4; conscripts in navy perish, 146

Pearl fisheries: concession in Colombia, 119, 122; hopes of exploiting, 2; failure to find pearls in Gulf of California, 153

Pentland, John Barclay: account of failure of Potosí Mining Company, 196 (n. 48); describes difficulties of travel in Bolivia, 86, 177; reports on prospects of trade in Bolivia, 70, 85

Poinsett, Joel Roberts (US minister to Mexico): appointed minister to Mexico, 135; comments on beggars in Mexico City, 138; deplores public corruption, 145, 179; described, 134; dissatisfied with level of education in Mexico, 141; horrified by Mexican poverty, 137, 181; observations on cock-fighting, 203 (n. 18); recounts journey across pampas, 189 (n. 27); verdict on Mexican people, 137–9

Political instability: 67; in Bolivia, 86; in Brazil, 170–73; in Chile, 31–2, 54–5; in Gran Colombia, 120, 129–30; in Mexico, 133; in Peru, 60, 64, 176, 194 (n. 9); in United Provinces of La Plata, 9–10, 23–4

Ponsonby, Viscount John: considers Beaumont's immigration schemes foolish, 28; detests Buenos Aires, 21; eulogises Buenos Aires, 6, 7

Popham, Captain (later Rear-Admiral) Sir Home Riggs, RN: eulogises Buenos Aires, 5, 7; overestimates population of River Plate area, 5, 7

Porter, Sir Robert Ker (British consul-general in Caracas): attacks free press in Colombia and Venezuela, 130; believes British public deceived over economic prospects in Venezuela, 126; career, 200 (n. 54); dealings with Scottish immigrants 124–26; 177; deplores lack of civilised society in Caracas, 130; describes arrival of Bolívar in Caracas, 109–10; experience on first arrival in Venezuela, 131; friendship with Bolívar and Páez, 131;

quarrels with Lancaster, 125; thinks
dictatorship needed in Gran Colombia,
130

Portugal: court goes to Brazil, xi, 1; king of
returns from Brazil, xi, 163; recognises
Brazilian independence, xi; signs
commercial treaty with Britain over Brazil
trade, 1, 159

Proctor, Robert: deplores dances of
mulattos in Lima, 79; describes
experiences in Peru, 63–4; travel across
pampas 15–16; William Miller, 75; Lima,
78–9; treatment of slaves in Peru, 79; has
poor opinion of Peruvians, 79; views on
Catholic clergy in Peru, 77; religious
observances in Peru, 77–8

Pueyrredón, Juan Martin de: supreme
director of La Plata provinces, 6,
unwilling to treat with British naval
officers, 9

Religious Evangelists: attracted to Latin
America, 2–3; distribution of bibles
favoured by Hankshaw, 129; Lancaster
acts as agent for Bible Society. See also
Bible society

Religious Prejudice: active in Brazil,
169–70; in Caracas, 130; in Chile, 192
(n. 28); in Colombia, 120–22; in Mexico,
134, 142, 152; in Peru, 71, 75–6, 77;
attempts to overcome in Chile, 39; bishop
of Rio allows building of Protestant
church, 161; criticises bibles of Bible
Society, 167; Haigh comments on
disappearance of in Chile, 35; lack of in
Rio de Janeiro, 166; in Gran Colombia,
128; met by English travellers and mining
companies in Mexico, 142–3; priests
oppose Bible Society in Caracas, 128–9;
waning slowly in Mexico, 142. See also
Roman Catholic Church

Ricketts, Charles Milner (British consul-
general in Lima): approves Lima and
Limeños, 79; comments on Peruvian
government's lack of good faith, 81, 179;
criticises influence of priests, 75–6, 182;
dislikes Lima and Peru, 80; lacks
sympathy for complaints of British
merchants, 68, 176; low opinion of
character of Peruvian Indians, 75–6;
plays down optimism over trade prospects
in Bolivia, 70, 85–6; reports on condition
of Peruvian mines, 80–81; difficulties for
traders, 90, 176; failure of Potosí Mining
Company, 196 (n. 48); failure to establish
schools in Peru, 77; lack of specie in

Peru, 70; success of British traders, 70,
176

Rio de Janeiro: comment on by Graham,
155; described, 164, 166, 167;
inadequacy of its port, 158, 175;
Portuguese court arrives at, 155

Rivadavia, Bernadino: encourages foreign
investment in La Plata provinces, 6,
22–3; setting up of schools by Thomson,
22; forced to resign as president of La
Plata provinces, 6, 29; liberal regime of
inspires foreign confidence, 9;
uncooperative over immigration schemes,
24; over mining concessions, 24

River navigation: unsuccessful attempts to
navigate Magdalena river, 122; run
steamboats on River Orinoco, 122

Roads: bad condition or lack of in Bolivia,
86; in and around Buenos Aires, 14; in
Colombia and Venezuela, 120, 123, 126,
201–2 (n. 52); generally in Latin America,
175, 177, 180; in La Plata provinces, 23,
83; in Mexico, 135–6, 146, 148, 205 (n.
52); built by Rio del Monte Mining
Company, 153

Robertson, John Parish: commercial agent
for Peruvian government, 71; criticises
state of roads, 14; describes Paraguay, 11,
17; failure of immigration scheme, 28,
177; interviews Artigas, 12; likes Buenos
Aires, 21; mining speculations of, 25,
179; prefers trading in Buenos Aires, 13;
relations with Francia, 12–13; reports
levies on British merchants in Peru, 71,
176; views on South American dictators,
10, 179. See also Robertson, William
Parish

Robertson, William Parish: appreciates
Buenos Aires, 21, 176; comments on
robbery in Mexico, 144; contrasts
Mexico's resources with its poverty, 146;
describes Paraguay, 11; joins brother
John, 12; relations with Francia, 13. See
also Robertson, John Parish

Roman Catholic Church: attitude in
Colombia criticised by Hamilton, 120;
bishops oppose schools run by
Protestants, 142; clergy in Brazil praised,
168; clerical censorship in Chile, 39;
observances in Latin America criticised
by Graham, 39; approved by Walsh in
Brazil, 167; opposition to Bible Society,
129, 167, 192 (n. 28); power reduced by
government in Chile, 37; Protestants
granted toleration in Brazil, 161–2;
supports introduction of mining

companies and mining machinery, 151, 152, 205 (n. 55); views of Proctor on clergy and religious practice in Peru, 77–8. *See also* Religious prejudice

San Martín, General José de: 60, assumes title of 'Protector of Peru', 73; compared to Zenteno, 42; impressions of by Bowles and Graham, 42, 61; by Hall, 61; by Worthington, 193 (n. 35); lands at Pisco, 59; leaves Peru, 59, 76; liberates Chile, 31–2; promises freedom for slaves in Peru, 61; quarrel with Cochrane, 53, 73–4; rule unpopular with wealthy and clergy in Lima, 59; tactics defended, 195 (n. 34); takes possession of Lima, 61; welcomes Miers, 44; Thomson's attempt to start schools in Peru, 76

Santiago: description of, 35–7; schools in 38–9

Schmidtmeyer, Peter: comments on limited market in Valparaiso, 32–3; schools in Santiago, 39; describes Santiago, 37

Silvin, Reverend Hugh: comments on indiscipline of Chilean troops, 36; contacts with Peruvian clergy, 77

Slaves: carry out all manual work in Brazil, 162, 170; contempt shown for in Brazil, 168; effects of sight of on British, 165, 166; promised freedom in Peru, 61; proportion of population in Brazil, 157; trade in detested by Europeans, 166; made illegal in Brazil, 166; treatment of in Brazil contrasted with that in Peru, 79

Spain: closure of colonies to foreigners, 1; constitutional regime in, x, xi; French intervention in, xi; recognises Mexico, 133; relations with Britain, x, 92; sends Morillo to suppress colonial revolt, 89

Stephenson, Robert: comments on political turmoil in Colombia, 129; describes experiences as agent for mining company in Colombia, 2, 123–4, 180

Stevenson, William Bennet: describes Araucanian Indians, 41; impressed by prosperity of Valparaiso, 34–5; notes popularity of British products in Peru, 69, 176; secretary to Cochrane, 52

Stewart, Reverend Charles: describes Valparaiso, 35; dislikes Rio, 167; writes of experiences of Rio de Janeiro, 157

Stopford, Colonel Edward: career, 197 (n. 10), 199 (n. 51); offers employment to Scots immigrants, 124; settles in Venezuela, 124, 177

Sucre, General Antonio José de: comments on British mining speculation, 83–4; leaves Bolivia, 86; liberates Ecuador, 90

Sutcliffe, Thomas: experiences as mercenary in Chile and Peru, 54

Tayloe, Edward Thornton: shocked by poverty and dirt in Mexico City, 138; wasteful extravagance of Mexican government, 146, 178; stays in Mexico, 135

Temple, Edward: describes attempts to buy mines in Bolivia, 82–4; gaucho way of life, 17–18; hotel in Buenos Aires, 190 (n. 44); critical of conduct of mining company, 84, 179; enlarges on prospects for agricultural development in La Plata provinces, 26; reaction to O'Connor's project for Irish colony in Bolivia, 86

Thomson, James: acknowledges Bible Society in Caracas has failed, 129; attempts to start schools in Mexico, 141; fate of his schools in Lima, 77; leaves Chile for Peru, 39; missionary work in Quito, Bogotá and Caracas, 128; optimistic report to British and Foreign Schools Society, 77; salary unpaid in Buenos Aires, 22, 178; starts schools in Buenos Aires, 22; in Chile, 38–9; in Peru, 76; welcomed by O'Higgins, 38; Rivadavia, 22; San Martín, 76

Travellers: attracted to Latin America, 2; dangers encountered by, 16; hardships of 15–17, 136

Trevithick, Richard: experience of mining in Peru, 81–2; goes to Peru, 2

Tudor, William (US consul in Lima): despairs of democracy in Peru, 194 (n. 9); reports disillusion of Limeños with 'liberation', 62, 179

United States of America: commercial interest in Latin America, 1; diplomatic missions to Latin America, 3; recognises Latin American states, 1; trade with Mexico, 147. *See also* Allen, Herman; Brackenridge, Henry; Hill, Henry; Hogan, Michael; Poinsett, Joel Roberts

Urdaneta, General Rafael: impressions of, 112; rejects plea to spare prisoners, 118; unwilling to accept British officers' resignations, 106–7

Valdivia: capture from royalists by Cochrane and Chilean fleet, 31, 41, 51–2

Valparaiso: 44, 46, 51, 52, 60; attempted royalist blockade of, 55; becomes almost

British colony, 31, 34; customs arrangements at, 191 (n. 6); description of, 32–5; estimated population, 33–4; growth as port, 32; market at glutted, 32, 33, 175; prosperity of, 34–5; volume of trade passing through, 33

Volunteer soldiers and sailors: accounts of experiences in Gran Colombia, 97–103; composition of contingents going to Venezuela, 93; death from drink, 122; desertions among, 106, 199 (n. 48); despised by patriot troops, 117; discontent with pay and conditions, 104–5, 180; disillusion of those serving in Chilean navy, 51, 52; in army of Bolívar in Venezuela, 91, 99, 100, 101; dislike experiences in La Plata provinces, 29; extravagant dress of, 114–15, 117; form Bolívar's guard of honour, 103; fortitude of, 101, 181; go to fight under Bolívar, x, 90, high casualty rate, 97; incompetence of officers, 99, 101–2; indiscipline of, 101–2; inducements to enlist, 91; looting by, 105–6; officers criticised, 117; try to resign, 106–7; quality of commanders, 94–5; revulsion at having to execute prisoners, 118; sufferings in Margarita, 103; on mainland, 103–4; wants seen to by Bolívar, 107, 110

Vowell, Richard Longueville: describes dress of Bolívar and his officers, 115; experiences as mercenary, 54–5, 97; hardships of march to Bogotá, 104; reception by Bolívar, 107; scene of massacre of prisoners, 118; recounts indiscipline in Chilean navy, 36

Walsh, Reverend, Robert (chaplain to British Embassy in Rio de Janeiro): comments on Catholic clergy in Brazil, 168; Catholic observances in Brazil, 167; general ignorance of Brazilians about Europe, 169; methods of mining in Brazil, 170; money in Brazil, 170; religious prejudice in Brazil, 169–70; Rio de Janeiro, 167; spread of education in Brazil, 168; treatment of blacks in Brazil, 168

Ward, Sir Henry G. (British Chargé d'affaires in Mexico): 133, 204 (n. 38); analyses mining enterprises in Mexico, 148–52; author of *Mexico in 1827*, 134; comments on bribery and corruption of officials, 145, 179; criticises Cornish miners, 152; mining companies 149–50, 179; pearl-fishery enterprise, 153; use of only one Mexican port by British, 146; emphasises difficulty of travel in Mexico, 135; notes difference between English and Mexican life-styles, 138; diminution of religious prejudice, 142, 143; strikes balance between optimism and pessimism over Mexico's future, 135

Whitelocke, General John: views on Buenos Aires, 5

Xenophobia: 180; jealousy of Brion, 113–14; lack of in Bolivia, 85; manifested in Brazil, 160–63, 169–70; in Chile, 54; in Colombia, 120; in Mexico, 142, 148, 150, 152, 153; in Peru, 64, 68, 70–71, 76, 80; in Venezuela, 100, 112; shown by creole officers in Venezuela, 112, 117

Zenteno (Governor of Valparaiso, Minister for War in Chile): criticised by Cochrane, 42; quarrel with Cochrane, 52, 53